How to Be
a Perfect Stranger
——— VOL. 2 ———

How to Be
a Perfect Stranger
——————— VOL. 2 ———————
A Guide to Etiquette in
Other People's Religious Ceremonies

Edited by Stuart M. Matlins
& Arthur J. Magida

Walking Together, Finding the Way
SKYLIGHT PATHS Publishing
WOODSTOCK, VERMONT

How to Be a Perfect Stranger, Vol. 2: A Guide to Etiquette in Other People's Religious Ceremonies

© 1999 by SkyLight Paths Publishing

Library of Congress Cataloging-in-Publication Data

The Library of Congress cataloged the Jewish Lights Publishing edition as follows:

Matlins, Stuart M.
Magida, Arthur J.
   How to be a perfect stranger, vol. 2: a guide to etiquette in other
   people's religious ceremonies / edited by Stuart M. Matlins and
   Arthur J. Magida.
       p.   cm.
   ISBN 1-879045-63-X (HC)
   1. Religious etiquette—United States. 2. United States—Religion—20th century. I. Title.
   BJ2010.M34 1995   95-37474
   291.3'8—dc20   CIP

1999 First Quality Paperback Edition, updated & expanded

10 9 8 7 6 5 4 3 2 1

ISBN 1-893361-02-0 (pb)

Manufactured in the United States of America
Cover art by Camille Kress
Book and jacket design by Chelsea Dippel

The symbols on the jacket represent (clockwise, from top right) the Unitarian Universalist, Sikh, Baha'i, and Orthodox faiths.

Walking Together, Finding the Way
Published by SkyLight Paths Publishing
A Division of LongHill Partners, Inc.
Sunset Farm Offices, Rte. 4 / P.O. Box 237
Woodstock, Vermont 05091
Tel: (802) 457-4000   Fax: (802) 457-4004
www.skylightpaths.com

Contents

Acknowledgments

A book such as this is the product of many contributions by many people. It could be no other way given the broad tapestry of religions in North America. If nothing else, the willingness of those approached for their wisdom and their knowledge about their specific denominations indicates that American religious leaders are eager to be properly understood—and to properly understand others.

Instrumental in the evolution of *How to Be a Perfect Stranger* were Richard A. Siegel and William Shanken, who developed the original concept and helped get the first volume into gear. Stuart M. Matlins, publisher of SkyLight Paths, developed the methodology for obtaining the information, and with Arthur J. Magida, editorial director of SkyLight Paths, oversaw the research and writing and provided the impetus for the project. Sandra Korinchak, editor, shepherded the project from start to finish with the help of Jennifer Goneau, editorial assistant. Rev. Dr. Joan Brown Campbell, the General Secretary of the National Council of Churches, generously agreed to write the foreword to this volume. Research assistant Susan Parks helped ensure that certain denominations responded promptly to our requests. And Jordan D. Wood generously assumed an initiative that delighted us all. Michael Schwartzentruber, series editor of Northstone Publishing, compiled the Canadian data and information included in the revised and updated edition.

The essay on Native American/First Nations faiths was written by

Dan Wildcat, a member of the Wyuchi Tribe of Oklahoma and a sociology professor at the Haskell Indian Nations University in Lawrence, Kansas.

All other chapters were based on information obtained from an extensive questionnaire filled out by clergy and other religious experts coast-to-coast. Without the help of the following, this volume would never have become a reality:

Timothy Addington, Executive Director of
Ministry Advancement, The Evangelical Free Church of North
America, Minneapolis, Minnesota

Rev. E. Wayne Antworth, Director of Stewardship and Communications, The Reformed Church in America, New York, New York

Leroy Beachy, Beachy Amish Mennonite, Millersburg, Ohio

Ronald R. Brannon, General Secretary, The Wesleyan Church,
Indianapolis, Indiana

Ellen K. Campbell, Executive Director,
Canadian Unitarian Council, Toronto, Ontario

Sharon Glidden Cole, Administrative Assistant,
Executive Offices, The Christian and Missionary Alliance,
Colorado Springs, Colorado

Archpriest George Corey, Vicar,
Antiochian Orthodox Archdiocese, New York, New York

Alf Dumont (member, First Nations), St. John's United Church,
Alliston, Ontario

Rev. Ora W. Eads, General Superintendent,
The Christian Congregation, Inc., LaFollette, Tennessee

Lois Hammond, Evangelical Free Church of Canada,
Langley, British Columbia

Father Gregory Havrilak, Director of Communications,
Orthodox Church in North America, New York, New York

Marvin Hein, General Secretary, The General Conference of
Mennonite Brethren, Fresno, California

Rev. Donald E. Hodgins, Central Canada District, The Wesleyan
Church of Canada, Belleville, Ontario

John Hurley, Archivist and Public Relations Officer,
Unitarian Universalist Association of Congregations,
Boston, Massachusetts

Rev. B. Edgar Johnson, Former General Secretary,
The Church of the Nazarene, Kansas City, Missouri

Wesley Johnson, Executive Assistant, The Evangelical Free
Church of North America, Minneapolis, Minnesota

Hari Dharam Kaur Khalsa, The Mukhia Sardarni Sahiba,
Sikh Dharma of New Mexico, Española, New Mexico

Rev. Dr. Ralph Lebold, Past President Conrad Grebel College,
University of Waterloo, Waterloo, Ontario

David A. Linscheid, Communications Director,
General Conference Mennonite Church, Newton, Kansas

Dr. Gordon MacDonald, Pentecostal Holiness Church of Canada,
Surrey, British Columbia

The Very Reverend Protopresbyter Frank P. Miloro,
The American Carpatho-Russian Orthodox Greek Catholic
Diocese of the U.S.A., Johnstown, Pennsylvania

Mr. Ronald R. Minor, General Secretary,
The Pentecostal Church of God, Joplin, Missouri

Rev. Dr. David Ocea, The Romanian Orthodox
Episcopate of North America, Grass Lake, Minnesota

Wardell Payne, Research Consultant on African American
Religions, Washington, D.C.

Pal S. Purewal, former president, Sikh Society of Alberta,
Edmonton, Alberta

Rev. Frank Reid, Senior Pastor, Bethel African Methodist Episcopal
Church, Baltimore, Maryland

Howard E. Royer, Director of Interpretation,
The Church of the Brethren, Elgin, Indiana

Trish Swanson, Former Director, Office of Public Information,
Baha'is of the United States, New York, New York

Lois Volstad, Executive Secretary, Executive Offices, The Christian
and Missionary Alliance, Colorado Springs, Colorado

Deborah Weiner, Director, Public Relations, Unitarian Universalist
Association of Congregations, Boston, Massachusetts

Ronald D. Williams, Communications Officer, International
Church of the Foursquare Gospel, Los Angeles, California

Pamela Zivari, Director, Office of Public Information,
Baha'is of the United States, New York, New York

Introduction

When the first volume of *How to Be a Perfect Stranger* received the Benjamin Franklin Award for the "Best Reference Book of the Year," we were pleased and proud. From our research, we had known that many people were looking forward to this practical, helpful book. What we did not expect was that so many people would tell us in letters and in person that they not only *referred* to this intriguing volume, they were *reading* it from cover to cover—and they wanted, and needed, more. Therefore, we compiled this second volume of *How to Be a Perfect Stranger*. People are hungry for information about their neighbors' faiths, and need it at a most practical level.

The 20 denominations in Volume 1 were typically among the largest in North America, with membership, in many cases, running into the millions. Volume 2 is devoted to denominations with fewer members, but most still over 50,000—or to those that are less frequently encountered, such as Native American religions, and the Amish, Mennonite, Baha'i and Sikh faiths.

One of the special features of this volume is a chapter on Native faiths. As you will see, it differs in presentation and content from the other chapters in either volume of *How to Be a Perfect Stranger*. Because there is not a single Native American/First Nations faith, we found the standard question-and-answer format used in these volumes inadequate to properly explain the practices and spirituality of indigenous North American peoples. At the same time, their faith differs so basically from those religions in the Judeo-Christian and Islamic traditions or from Hinduism or Buddhism (which are in Volume 1) that adhering to the standard format would have been more of a disservice than a virtue. For example, ceremonies and their content vary greatly among tribal groups, and even native religions' basic concept of a Creator bears little relation to concepts of a Creator in most western and Asian religions.

This chapter was written by a Native American, Dan Wildcat, a member of the Wyuchi Tribe of Oklahoma and a sociology professor at the Haskell Indian Nations University in Lawrence, Kansas.

The enthusiastic reception from readers and reviewers to Volume 1 suggests that, while each denomination in North America worships in its own unique and idiosyncratic way, we fervently want to know what is going on in the churches and mosques and synagogues and meeting halls that sustain our spiritual life. But perhaps even more fervent is the urge to be personally comfortable and inwardly and outwardly respectful of other beliefs and traditions, customs and rituals when dealing with a faith not our own. While we may not subscribe to another's religious beliefs, we just as surely wish to understand the basis of that faith and the purposes and manner of its rituals and ceremonies.

This impulse is certainly rooted in the fact that we North Americans live in a remarkably fluid society. There is movement between class and race; between the many cultures that form the patchwork known as "American culture"; and between religions, that most personal—and often most deeply embedded—of the institutions that shape us, inform us, inspirit us, enlighten us.

As North Americans, we often celebrate the diverse ways we worship God. This pluralism and cross-fertilization, we say, is part of what makes North America special, and it often occurs at the most personal of levels. It is not uncommon, for instance, to be invited to a wedding, a funeral or a religious celebration in the home of a relative or friend of a different faith from one's own. Such exposure to the religious ways of others can give us a deep appreciation for the extraordinary diversity of faith and the variety of ways it surfaces.

Also, as the insightful Catholic writer, Father Andrew M. Greeley, has observed, religion is "a collection of...'pictures'" that we use to give order and meaning to our lives and everything around them. Viewing others' "religious 'pictures'" and noting the contrast between what we see and what we've experienced in our own religious traditions can also deepen and solidify our own faith by making us consider how our tradition speaks to us, comforts us and challenges us.

Yet, we may be uncomfortable or uncertain when we meet "the other" on his or her own turf: What does one do? Or wear? Or say? What should one *avoid* doing, wearing, saying? What will happen during the ceremony? How long will it last? What does each ritual mean? What are the basic beliefs of this particular religion?

Will there be a reception? Will there be food? Will there be grace before we eat? Are gifts expected? When can I leave?

These are just some of the practical questions that arise because of the fundamental foreignness of the experience. *How to Be a Perfect Stranger* addresses these concerns in a straightforward and non-judgmental manner. Its goal is to make a well-meaning guest feel comfortable, participate to the fullest extent feasible, and avoid violating anyone's religious principles. It is not intended to be a comprehensive primer on theology. It's a guidebook to a land where we may be strangers, but where, on the whole, those on whose celebratory turf we soon will be treading want us to be as comfortable, relaxed and unperturbed as possible.

After all, as the philosopher George Santayana said, "Religion in its humility restores man to his only dignity, the courage to live by grace." And there is nothing more mutually grace-full than to welcome "the stranger"—and for "the stranger" to do his or her homework before entering an unfamiliar house of worship or religious ceremony.

We've all been strangers at one time or another or in one place or another. If this book helps turn the "strange" into the less "exotic" and into the less confusing (but not into the ordinary), then it will have satisfied its goal of minimizing our anxiety and our confusion when face-to-face with another faith—while, at the same time, deepening our appreciation and our understanding of that faith. While we pray and worship in thousands of churches, synagogues, mosques and temples around the country, these denominational fences are not insurmountable. Indeed, these fences come complete with gates. It is often up to us find the key to those gates. We hope that this book helps in the search for that key.

A few notes on the way in which *How to Be a Perfect Stranger* was compiled and structured:

Each chapter is devoted to a particular religion or denomination; each is organized around that religion's life cycle events, religious calendar and home celebrations.

Basic research was conducted through an extensive questionnaire that was completed in almost all cases by the national office of each religion and denomination. For those denominations whose national office did not respond to the questionnaire, we obtained responses from clergy of that particular faith. To minimize error in nuance, drafts of each chapter were forwarded for comments to those who had filled out the questionnaire.

How to Be a Perfect Stranger is not intended as a substitute for the social common sense that should prevail at social or religious events. For example, if a chapter advises readers that "casual dress" is acceptable at a religious service, this is not to suggest that it is appropriate to show up in Bermuda shorts. Or if a certain denomination allows visitors to use a flash or a video camera, the equipment should not be used in such a way that it disrupts the religious ceremony or disturbs worshippers or other visitors.

The guidelines in this book are just that. They should not be mistaken for firm and unbendable rules. Religious customs, traditions and rituals are strongly influenced by where people live and the part of the world from which their ancestors came to North America. As a result, there may be a variety of practices within a single denomination. This book is a general guide to religious practice, and it's important to remember that *particulars* may sometimes vary broadly within individual denominations.

Terms within each chapter are those used by that religion. For example, the terms "New Testament" and "Old Testament" appear in almost every chapter about various Christian denominations. Some Jewish people may find this disconcerting since they recognize only one testament. The purpose is not to offend, but to portray these religions as they portray themselves. The goal of this book, one must remember, is to be "a perfect stranger." And "perfection" might well begin with recognizing that when we join others in celebrating events in their religion's vernacular, we are obliged, as guests, to know the customs, rituals and language of the event.

For future editions of *How to Be a Perfect Stranger*, we encourage readers to write to us and suggest ways in which this book could be made more useful to them and to others. Are there additional subjects that future editions should cover? Have important subtleties been missed? We see this book—and the evolution of our unique North American society—as an ongoing work-in-progress, and we welcome your comments. Please write to:

Editors, *How to Be a Perfect Stranger*
SkyLight Paths Publishing
Sunset Farm Offices, Rte. 4
P.O. Box 237
Woodstock, Vermont 05091

Foreword

The religious landscape of North American people has been in flux to one degree or another since the arrival of the first Europeans to these shores. Despite this, the cultural consciousness of North American people was largely Protestant Christian until fairly recently. However, from about the middle of this century, the *rate* of change and diversification of religious affiliation within the United States and Canada has increased appreciably. Today, any residual sense of the North American population as a religious monolith has been dispelled even in small towns and throughout the countryside.

In the United States, for example, about 96 percent of our citizens profess a belief in God and the nation continues to reflect one of the highest rates of religious affiliation among industrialized countries. The confluence of recent immigration patterns and a growing awareness among North Americans of world religions has helped produce in our country today a more open and vital attitude toward all religions.

In an earlier era, those who practiced a faith other than the Protestant or Roman Catholic traditions of Christianity often did so in relative obscurity. Today, the vigorous religious rites and customs of a host of faiths take place in full public view. This reality, which is the manifestation of the venerable North American right to free exercise of religions, is a national treasure of great worth.

The great North American experiment in a pluralistic republic democracy is well served by the growing religious pluralism and the diversity of our people. It is freshly infused in each generation as new people bring their religious and cultural legacy to the workplace, the public square and to their newly founded houses of worship, reinvigorating our land and our sense of the holy.

How to Be a Perfect Stranger provides all North Americans with an inviting point of entry into the world of religious pluralism. As we become more comfortable with the ways in which others pray, marry, bury and celebrate, we can move more effectively toward a sense of our single, yet diverse peoplehood. Although we are diverse racially, religiously and culturally, we are united by principles and ideals that celebrate our very differences.

How to Be a Perfect Stranger equips each of us to enter into the religious realm of our neighbors. By providing us with practical information concerning what to bring, where to sit or stand, when to participate and when to refrain from participating, this volume serves as a great encouragement for all of us to know the faith traditions of each other, and to help erode the walls of ignorance that too often separate or confuse us. By bringing us out of our respective religious communities, each of which has a tendency to be more insular than we might like, *How to Be a Perfect Stranger* can help us appreciate and know the vast variety of our religious voices. Together, these voices create an extraordinary choir of ritual and celebration, piety and devotion, faith and resilience that is truly part of the bedrock of our nation.

Schools, businesses, public libraries and libraries in churches, synagogues and mosques will want to have a copy of *How to Be a Perfect Stranger* on hand, a volume that can reap big dividends during celebrations of our quintessential North American right of religious liberties.

Rev. Dr. Joan Brown Campbell

General Secretary
National Council of Churches

Chapter 1 Contents

1
African American Methodist Churches

(known as the African Methodist Episcopal Church; the African Methodist Episcopal Zion Church; the Christian Methodist Episcopal Church; the Union American Methodist Episcopal Church, Inc.; and the African Union First Colored Methodist Protestant Church)

I · HISTORY AND BELIEFS

The African American Methodist churches began in the late 18th century and throughout the 19th century as a reaction to racial discrimination. The broader Methodist Church had originated in the early 18th century in England under the preaching of John Wesley, an Anglican priest who was a prodigious evangelical preacher, writer and organizer. While a student at Oxford University, he and his brother had led the Holy Club of devout students, whom scoffers called the "Methodists."

Wesley's teachings affirmed the freedom of human will as promoted by grace. He saw each person's depth of sin matched by the height of sanctification to which the Holy Spirit, the empowering spirit of God, can lead persons of faith.

Although Wesley remained an Anglican and disavowed attempts to form a new church, Methodism eventually became another church body. During a conference in Baltimore, Maryland, in 1784, the Methodist Church was founded as an ecclesiastical organization and the first Methodist bishop in the United States was elected.

Blacks had originally been attracted to the Methodist Church because its original evangelism made no distinctions between the races and John Wesley, the founder of Methodism, had strongly denounced slavery and the African slave trade on the grounds that they were contrary to the will of God. Initially, many Methodists—clergy and laity—opposed slavery, called upon church members to desist from trafficking in slaves, and urged them to free any slaves they did own. But as Methodists became more numerous in the South, the Church gradually muted its opposition to slavery.

In 1787, black members of Philadelphia's St. George's Methodist Episcopal Church withdrew from the church after experiencing discrimination, and the African Methodist Episcopal Church was officially established as a denomination on April 16, 1816.

The African Methodist Episcopal Zion Church was founded in 1796 after blacks were denied the sacraments and full participation in the John Street Methodist Church in New York City, located in a state with the largest slave population outside of the South.

And the Christian Methodist Episcopal Church was founded in 1870, four years after African American members of the Methodist Episcopal Church, South (M.E.C.S.) petitioned the Church to be allowed to create a separate Church that would be governed by the M.E.C.S. In 1870, the General Conference of the M.E.C.S. voted to let black members be constituted as an independent church, not as a subordinate body. This reflected the post-Civil War period's imperatives calling for independence for African Americans and the reconstruction of American society.

Two smaller African American Methodist churches are the Union American Methodist Episcopal Church, Inc., with 15,000 members in 55 congregations, and the African Union First Colored Methodist Protestant Church, with 5,000 members in 33 congregations. Both of these were founded in 1865.

Local African American Methodist churches are called "charges." Their ministers are appointed by the bishop at an annual conference, and each church elects its own administrative board, which initiates planning and sets local goals and policies.

Number of U.S. churches:

African Methodist Episcopal: 8,000
African Methodist Episcopal Zion: 3,100
African Union First Colored Methodist Protestant Church: 33
Christian Methodist Episcopal Church: 2,300
Union American Methodist Episcopal Church, Inc.: 55

Number of U. S. members:

African Methodist Episcopal: 3.5 million
African Methodist Episcopal Zion: 1.2 million
African Union First Colored Methodist Protestant Church: 5,000
Christian Methodist Episcopal Church: 718,900
Union American Methodist Episcopal Church, Inc.: 15,000

(data from the Directory of American Religious Bodies and the
1998 Yearbook of American and Canadian Churches)

For more information, contact:

African Methodist Episcopal Church
1134 11th Street, N.W.
Washington, DC 20001
(202) 371-8700

African Methodist Episcopal Zion Church
Office of the General Secretary
P.O. Box 32843
Charlotte, NC 28232
(704) 332-3851

African Union Methodist Protestant Church
602 Spruce Street
Wilmington, DE 19801
(302) 994-3410

Christian Methodist Episcopal Church
4466 Elvis Presley Boulevard
Memphis, TN 38116
(901) 947-3135

II · THE BASIC SERVICE

To the African American Methodist denominations, worship is a congregation's encounter and communion with God and with one another in God's name. It includes praise and prayer, scripture readings, a sermon and sometimes Holy Communion.

Most African American Methodist services last about one hour.

APPROPRIATE ATTIRE

Men: A jacket and tie. No head covering is required.

Women: A dress. The arms do not necessarily have to be covered nor do hems have to be below the knees. Open-toed shoes and modest jewelry are permissible. No head covering is required.

There are no rules regarding colors of clothing.

THE SANCTUARY

What are the major sections of the church?

- *The platform or chancel,* a raised section at the front of the church. This is where the leaders and the choir function.
- *The nave,* where congregants sit on pews.

THE SERVICE

When should guests arrive and where should they sit?

Arrive at the time for which the service has been called. An usher will indicate where to sit. There are usually no restrictions on where to sit.

If arriving late, are there times when a guest should *not* enter the service?

Yes. Ushers will seat you when appropriate.

Are there times when a guest should *not* leave the service?

No.

Who are the major officiants, leaders or participants and what do they do?

- *The pastor,* who presides, preaches and celebrates communion.
- *The associate pastor or the assisting layperson,* who aids the senior pastor in leading the service.
- *The choir or soloists,* who sing hymns and psalms.

What are the major ritual objects of the service?

- *Bread,* which is eaten during Holy Communion and which signifies the body of Jesus Christ.
- *Grape juice,* which the pastor presents to congregants to drink during Holy Communion and signifies the blood of Jesus Christ.

What books are used?

Books vary from congregation to congregation within each of the African American Methodist denominations, but the Bibles usually used are the King James Version, the New Revised Standard or the New International Version. Also, most African Methodist Episcopal churches use *The AMEC Bicentennial Hymnal* (Nashville, Tenn.: The African Methodist Episcopal Church, 1984); African Methodist Episcopal Zion churches use *The Songs of Zion* (Nashville, Tenn.: Abingdon Press, 1982); and Christian Methodist Episcopal churches use *The Hymnal of the Christian Methodist Episcopal Church* (Memphis, Tenn.: The CME Publishing House, 1987).

To indicate the order of the service:

A program will be provided and periodic announcements will be made by the pastor or another leader.

GUEST BEHAVIOR DURING THE SERVICE

Will a guest who is not a member of an African American Methodist denomination be expected to do anything other than sit?

Standing and kneeling with the congregation and reading prayers aloud and singing with congregants are all optional. Guests are welcome to participate if this does not compromise their personal beliefs. If guests do not wish to kneel or stand, they may remain seated at these times.

Are there any parts of the service in which a guest who is not a member of an African American Methodist denomination should *not* participate?

Yes. Methodists invite all to receive Holy Communion, but guests should be aware that partaking of communion is regarded as an act of identification with Christianity. Feel free to remain seated as others go forward for communion. Likewise, if communion bread and cups are passed among the pews, feel free to pass them along without partaking.

If not disruptive to the service, is it okay to:

- **Take pictures?** Possibly. Ask an usher.
- **Use a video camera?** Possibly. Ask an usher.
- **Use a flash camera?** Possibly. Ask an usher.
- **Use a tape recorder?** Possibly. Ask an usher.

(Note: Many African American Methodist churches have audio-visual ministries that enable congregants and guests to purchase copies of services at a modest cost. Information on obtaining these audio or video tapes is available from the offices of local churches.)

Will contributions to the church be collected at the service?

Yes. The offering plate will be passed through the congregation during the service. This usually occurs immediately before or after the sermon.

How much is customary to contribute?

The customary offering is about $10.

AFTER THE SERVICE

Is there usually a reception after the service?

Possibly. If so, it will be held in the church's reception area. It usually lasts less than 30 minutes and pastry, coffee and tea are ordinarily served.

Also, many congregations operate a kitchen after services, where low-cost meals can be purchased. These will be served in the church's dining area.

A brief prayer or blessing may be recited during the service or just before the meal in church dining area.

Is there a traditional form of address for clergy who may be at the reception?

"Reverend" or "Pastor."

Is it okay to leave early?

Yes.

GENERAL GUIDELINES AND ADVICE

The chief potential for mistake occurs during Holy Communion. Feel free not to partake if you cannot in good conscience do so. Christian guests should be aware that the African American Methodist denominations never refuse communion to anyone.

The cups at Holy Communion always contain grape juice, not wine. Children, as well as adults, are welcome to partake.

SPECIAL VOCABULARY

None provided.

DOGMA AND IDEOLOGY

African American Methodism teaches:

- The doctrine of the Trinity: God is the Father; the Son (embodied by Jesus Christ); and the Holy Spirit (the empowering spirit of God).
- The natural sinfulness of humanity.
- Humanity's fall from grace and the need for individual repentance.
- Freedom of will.
- In practice, Methodists are highly diverse in their beliefs and tend to emphasize right living more than orthodoxy of belief.

A basic book to which a guest can refer to learn more about the Methodist faith:

Directory of African American Religious Bodies: A Compendium by the Howard University School of Divinity, edited by Wardell J. Payne (Washington, D.C.: Howard University Press, 1995).

III · HOLY DAYS AND FESTIVALS

- *Advent.* Occurs four weeks before Christmas. The purpose is to begin preparing for Christmas and to focus on Christ. There is no traditional greeting for this holiday.
- *Christmas.* Occurs on the evening of December 24 and the day of December 25. Marks the birth and the incarnation of God as a man. The traditional greeting is "Merry Christmas."
- *Lent.* Begins on Ash Wednesday, which occurs six weeks before Easter. The purpose is to prepare for Easter. Between Lent and Easter, fasting and abstention from entertainment are encouraged, as is increased giving to the poor. Often, there are midweek worship services. There are no traditional greetings for this holiday.
- *Easter.* Always falls on the Sunday after the first full moon that occurs on or after March 21. Celebrates the Resurrection of Jesus Christ. The traditional greeting to Methodists is "Happy Easter!"
- *Pentecost Sunday.* The seventh Sunday after Easter. Celebrates the coming of the Holy Spirit, which is the empowering spirit of God in human life. This is often considered the birth of the Christian church. There are no traditional greetings for this holiday.

IV · LIFE CYCLE EVENTS

Birth Ceremony

Baptism initiates an infant into Christianity. It is administered once to each person, usually when they are an infant. The pastor sprinkles or pours water on the person's head or immerses the person in water. This signifies the washing away of sins. God is invoked to strengthen this new Christian, and the congregation, as well as the parent(s) and godparent(s), pledge to nurture him or her in the Christian faith and life.

Baptism is part of the larger weekly congregational Sunday morning service, which usually lasts about an hour.

BEFORE THE CEREMONY

Are guests usually invited by a formal invitation?

Yes.

If not stated explicitly, should one assume that children are invited?

Yes.

If one can't attend, what should one do?

Either of these is appropriate: Send flowers or a gift; or telephone the parents with your congratulations and your regrets that you can't attend.

APPROPRIATE ATTIRE

Men: A jacket and tie. No head covering is required.

Women: A dress. The arms do not necessarily have to be covered nor do hems have to be below the knees. Open-toed shoes and modest jewelry are permissible. No head covering is required.

There are no rules regarding colors of clothing.

GIFTS

Is a gift customarily expected?

No, but it is appropriate. Gifts such as U.S. savings bonds or baby clothes or toys are commonly given.

Should gifts be brought to the ceremony?

Usually gifts can be brought to the reception.

THE CEREMONY

Where will the ceremony take place?

In the parents' church.

When should guests arrive and where should they sit?

Arrive at the time for which the service has been called.

Ushers will indicate where to sit. There are usually no restrictions on where to sit.

If arriving late, are there times when a guest should *not* enter the ceremony?

Yes. Ushers will seat you when appropriate.

Are there times when a guest should *not* leave the ceremony?

No.

Who are the major officiants, leaders or participants at the ceremony and what do they do?

- *A pastor,* who will baptize the child.
- *The child and his or her parents.*

What books are used?

Books vary from congregation to congregation within each of the African American Methodist denominations, but the Bibles usually used are the King James Version, the New Revised Standard or the New International Version. Also, most African Methodist Episcopal churches use *The AMEC Bicentennial Hymnal* (Nashville, Tenn.: The African Methodist Episcopal Church, 1984); African Methodist Episcopal Zion churches use *The Songs of Zion* (Nashville, Tenn.: Abingdon Press, 1982); and Christian Methodist Episcopal churches use *The Hymnal of the Christian Methodist Episcopal Church* (Memphis, Tenn.: The CME Publishing House, 1987).

To indicate the order of the ceremony:

A program will be provided and periodic announcements will be made by the pastor or his or her assistant.

Will a guest who is not a member of an African American Methodist denomination be expected to do anything other than sit?

Standing and kneeling with the congregation and reading prayers aloud and singing with congregants are all optional. Guests are welcome to participate if this does not compromise their personal beliefs. If guests do not wish to kneel or stand, they may remain seated at these times.

Are there any parts of the ceremony in which a guest who is not a member of an African American Methodist denomination should *not* participate?

Yes. Methodists invite all to receive Holy Communion, but guests should be aware that partaking of communion is regarded as an act of identification with Christianity. Feel free to remain seated as others go forward for communion. Likewise, if communion bread and cups are passed among the pews, feel free to pass them along without partaking. Christian guests should be aware that the Methodist church never refuses communion to anyone. The cups at Holy Communion always contain grape juice, not wine. Children, as well as adults, are welcome to partake.

If not disruptive to the ceremony, is it okay to:

◙ **Take pictures?** Possibly. Ask ushers.
◙ **Use a video camera?** Possibly. Ask ushers.
◙ **Use a flash camera?** Possibly. Ask ushers.
◙ **Use a tape recorder?** Possibly. Ask ushers.

(Note: Many African American Methodist churches have audio-visual ministries that enable congregants and guests to purchase copies of services at a modest cost. Information on obtaining these audio or video tapes is available from the offices of local churches.)

Will contributions to the church be collected at the ceremony?

Yes. The offering plate will be passed through the congregation during the service. This usually occurs immediately before or after the sermon.

How much is customary to contribute?

The customary offering is about $10.

AFTER THE CEREMONY

Is there usually a reception after the ceremony?

Possibly. If so, it will be held in the church's reception area. It usually lasts less than 30 minutes and pastry, coffee and tea are ordinarily served.

Also, many congregations operate a kitchen after services, where low-cost meals can be purchased. These will be served in the church's dining area.

Would it be considered impolite to neither eat nor drink?

No.

Is there a grace or benediction before eating or drinking?

A brief prayer or blessing may be recited during the service or just before the reception or the meal.

Is there a grace or benediction after eating or drinking?

No.

Is there a traditional greeting for the family?

No. Just offer your congratulations.

Is there a traditional form of address for clergy who may be at the reception?

"Reverend" or "Pastor."

Is it okay to leave early?

Yes.

Initiation Ceremony

Confirmation is conferred to an early adolescent. It is a Methodist's first profession of faith. The candidates affirm for themselves the Christian faith and church into which they were baptized (usually as infants).

Teens participate in the ceremony with members of their confirmation class. The 15-minute ceremony is part of a larger Sunday morning service, which lasts about an hour.

BEFORE THE CEREMONY

Are guests usually invited by a formal invitation?

No.

If not stated explicitly, should one assume that children are invited?

Yes.

If one can't attend, what should one do?

Either of these is appropriate: Send flowers or a gift; or telephone the parents with your congratulations and your regrets that you can't attend.

APPROPRIATE ATTIRE

Men: A jacket and tie. No head covering is required.

Women: A dress. The arms do not necessarily have to be covered nor do hems have to be below the knees. Open-toed shoes and modest jewelry are permissible. No head covering is required.

There are no rules regarding colors of clothing.

GIFTS

Is a gift customarily expected?

No.

Should gifts be brought to the ceremony?

See above.

THE CEREMONY

Where will the ceremony take place?

Usually at the front of the main sanctuary of the church.

When should guests arrive and where should they sit?

Arrive at the time for which the service has been called.

An usher will indicate where to sit. There are usually no restrictions on where to sit.

If arriving late, are there times when a guest should *not* enter the ceremony?

Yes. Ushers will seat you when appropriate.

Are there times when a guest should *not* leave the ceremony?

No.

Who are the major officiants, leaders or participants at the ceremony and what do they do?

▪ *The pastor,* who confirms the teen(s).

▪ *The teen(s) being confirmed.*

What books are used?

Books vary from congregation to congregation within each of the African American Methodist denominations, but the Bibles usually used are the King James Version, the New Revised Standard or the New International Version. Also, most African Methodist Episcopal churches use *The AMEC Bicentennial Hymnal* (Nashville, Tenn.: The African Methodist Episcopal Church, 1984); African Methodist Episcopal Zion churches use *The Songs of Zion* (Nashville, Tenn.: Abingdon Press, 1982); and Christian Methodist Episcopal churches use *The Hymnal of the Christian Methodist Episcopal Church* (Memphis, Tenn.: The CME Publishing House, 1987).

To indicate the order of the ceremony:

A program will be provided, and periodic announcements will be made by the pastor or his assistant.

Will a guest who is not a member of an African American Methodist denomination be expected to do anything other than sit?

Standing and kneeling with the congregation and reading prayers aloud and singing with congregants are all optional. Guests are welcome to participate if this does not compromise their personal beliefs. If guests do not wish to kneel or stand, they may remain seated at these times.

Are there any parts of the ceremony in which a guest who is not a member of an African American Methodist denomination should *not* participate?

Yes. Methodists invite all to receive Holy Communion, but guests should be aware that partaking of communion is regarded as an act of identification with Christianity. Feel free to remain seated as others go forward for communion. Likewise, if communion bread and cups are passed among the pews, feel free to pass them along without partaking. Christian guests should be aware that the Methodist church never refuses communion to anyone. The cups at Holy Communion always contain grape juice, not wine. Children, as well as adults, are welcome to partake.

If not disruptive to the ceremony, is it okay to:

◙ **Take pictures?** Possibly. Ask ushers.

◙ **Use a video camera?** Possibly. Ask ushers.

◙ **Use a flash camera?** Possibly. Ask ushers.

◙ **Use a tape recorder?** Possibly. Ask ushers.

(Note: Many African American Methodist churches have audio-visual ministries that enable congregants and guests to purchase copies of services at a modest cost. Information on obtaining these audio or video tapes is available from the office of a local church.)

Will contributions to the church be collected at the ceremony?

Yes. The offering plate will be passed through the congregation during the service. This usually occurs immediately before or after the sermon.

How much is customary to contribute?

The customary offering is about $10.

AFTER THE CEREMONY

Is there usually a reception after the ceremony?

Possibly. If so, it will be held in the church's reception area. It usually lasts less than 30 minutes and pastry, coffee and tea are ordinarily served

Also, many congregations operate a kitchen after services, where low-cost meals can be purchased. These will be served in the church's dining area.

Would it be considered impolite to neither eat nor drink?

No.

Is there a grace or benediction before eating or drinking?

A brief prayer or blessing may be recited during the service or just before the reception or the meal.

Is there a grace or benediction after eating or drinking?

No.

Is there a traditional greeting for the family?

No. Just offer your congratulations.

Is there a traditional form of address for clergy who may be at the reception?

"Reverend" or "Pastor."

Is it okay to leave early?

Yes.

Marriage Ceremony

Marriage is the uniting of a man and a woman in a union which is intended—and which is pledged—to be lifelong. The marriage ceremony is a service unto itself. It may last between 15 and 30 minutes.

BEFORE THE CEREMONY

Are guests usually invited by a formal invitation?

Yes.

If not stated explicitly, should one assume that children are invited?

No.

If one can't attend, what should one do?

RSVP with your regrets and send a gift.

APPROPRIATE ATTIRE

Men: A jacket and tie. No head covering is required.

Women: A dress. The arms do not necessarily have to be covered nor do hems have to be below the knees. Open-toed shoes and modest jewelry are permissible. No head covering is required.

There are no rules regarding colors of clothing.

GIFTS

Is a gift customarily expected?

Yes. Such gifts as small appliances, sheets, towels or other household gifts are appropriate.

Should gifts be brought to the ceremony?

No, send them to the home of the newlyweds.

THE CEREMONY

Where will the ceremony take place?

Usually in the main sanctuary of a church.

When should guests arrive and where should they sit?

Arrive early. Depending on the setting, ushers may show guests where to sit.

If arriving late, are there times when a guest should *not* enter the ceremony?

Ushers will usually assist latecomers.

If arriving late, are there times when a guest should *not* leave the ceremony?

No.

Who are the major officiants, leaders or participants at the ceremony and what do they do?

◼ *The pastor,* who officiates.
◼ *The bride and groom and their wedding party.*

What books are used?

Books vary from congregation to congregation within each of the African American Methodist denominations, but the Bibles usually used are the King James Version, the New Revised Standard or the New International Version. Also, most African Methodist Episcopal churches use *The AMEC Bicentennial Hymnal* (Nashville, Tenn.: The African Methodist Episcopal Church, 1984); African Methodist Episcopal Zion churches use *The Songs of Zion* (Nashville, Tenn.: Abingdon Press, 1982); and Christian Methodist Episcopal churches use *The Hymnal of the Christian Methodist Episcopal Church* (Memphis, Tenn.: The CME Publishing House, 1987).

To indicate the order of the ceremony:

A program will be provided.

Will a guest who is not a member of an African American Methodist denomination be expected to do anything other than sit?

Standing and kneeling with the congregation and reading prayers aloud and singing with congregants are all optional. Guests are welcome to participate if this does not compromise their personal beliefs. If guests do not wish to kneel or stand, they may remain seated at these times.

Are there any parts of the ceremony in which a guest who is not a member of an African American Methodist denomination should *not* participate?

Yes. Holy Communion may be offered at the service. Methodists invite all to receive Holy Communion, but guests should be aware that partaking of communion is regarded as an act of identification with Christianity. Feel free to remain seated as others go forward for communion. Likewise, if communion bread and cups are passed among the pews, feel free to pass them along without partaking.

If not disruptive to the service, is it okay to:

◘ **Take pictures?** Possibly. Ask ushers.
◘ **Use a video camera?** Possibly. Ask ushers.
◘ **Use a flash camera?** Possibly. Ask ushers.
◘ **Use a tape recorder?** Possibly. Ask ushers.

Will contributions to the church be collected at the ceremony?
No.

AFTER THE CEREMONY

Is there usually a reception after the ceremony?

There is often a reception that may last one to two hours. It may be at a home, a catering facility or in the same building as the ceremony. Ordinarily, food and beverages are served and there is dancing and music. Alcoholic beverages may be served.

Would it be considered impolite to neither eat nor drink?
No.

Is there a grace or benediction before eating or drinking?
No.

Is there a grace or benediction after eating or drinking?

No.

Is there a traditional greeting for the family?

No. Just offer your congratulations.

Is there a traditional form of address for clergy who may be at the reception?

"Reverend" or "Pastor."

Is it okay to leave early?

Yes, but usually only after toasts have been made and the wedding cake has been served.

Funerals and Mourning

African American Methodist denominations affirm that life is eternal and that, in faith, one can look forward to life with God after death. African American Methodists have diverse beliefs about afterlife and are generally content to look forward to it as a glorious mystery. Funerals have as their purposes: 1) expressing grief and comforting one another in our bereavement; 2) celebrating the life of the deceased; and 3) affirming faith in life with God after death. Which of these is most emphasized at the funeral depends on the circumstances of the death and the extent of the faith of the deceased.

BEFORE THE CEREMONY

How soon after the death does the funeral usually take place?

Usually within two to three days.

What should one who is not a member of an African American Methodist denomination do upon hearing of the death of a member of that faith?

Telephone or visit the bereaved.

APPROPRIATE ATTIRE

Men: A jacket and tie. No head covering is required.

Women: A dress. Open-toed shoes and modest jewelry are permissible. No head covering is required.

There are no rules regarding colors of clothing, but somber, dark colors are recommended for men and women.

GIFTS

Is it appropriate to send flowers or make a contribution?

Yes. Send flowers to the home of the bereaved. Contributions are also optional. The recommended charity may be mentioned in the deceased's obituary.

Is it appropriate to send food?

Yes. Send it to the home of the bereaved.

THE CEREMONY

Where will the ceremony take place?

At a church or funeral home.

When should guests arrive and where should they sit?

Arrive early. Ushers will advise them where to sit.

If arriving late, are there times when a guest should *not* enter the ceremony?

No.

Will the bereaved family be present at the church or funeral home before the ceremony?

Possibly.

Is there a traditional greeting for the family?

Simply express your condolences.

Will there be an open casket?

Usually.

Is a guest expected to view the body?

This is entirely optional.

What is appropriate behavior upon viewing the body?

Silent prayer.

Who are the major officiants at the ceremony and what do they do?

◙ *A pastor,* who officiates.

To indicate the order of the ceremony:

A program will be provided.

Will a guest who is not a member of an African American Methodist denomination be expected to do anything other than sit?

No.

Are there any parts of the ceremony in which a guest who is not a member of an African American Methodist denomination should *not* participate?

No.

If not disruptive to the ceremony, is it okay to:

◙ **Take pictures?** No.
◙ **Use a video camera?** No.
◙ **Use a flash camera?** No.
◙ **Use a tape recorder?** No.

Will contributions to the church be collected at the ceremony?

No.

THE INTERMENT

Should guests attend the interment?

Yes.

Whom should one ask for directions?

The funeral director.

What happens at the graveside?

Prayers are recited by the pastor and the body is committed to the ground. If there has been a cremation, which is done privately before the service, the ashes are either buried or put in a vault.

Do guests who are not members of an African American Methodist denomination participate at the graveside ceremony?

No. They are simply present.

COMFORTING THE BEREAVED

Is it appropriate to visit the home of the bereaved after the funeral?

Yes, at any mutually convenient time. How long one stays depends on your closeness to the bereaved. Typically, one stays about 30 to 45 minutes.

Will there be a religious service at home of the bereaved?

No.

Will food be served?

No.

How soon after the funeral will a mourner usually return to a normal work schedule?

This is entirely at the discretion of the bereaved.

How soon after the funeral will a mourner usually return to a normal social schedule?

This is entirely at the discretion of the bereaved.

Are there mourning customs to which a friend who is not a member of an African American Methodist denomination should be sensitive?

No.

Are there rituals for observing the anniversary of the death?

There may be a service commemorating the deceased.

V · HOME CELEBRATIONS

Not applicable to African American Methodist denominations.

Chapter 2 Contents

2
Baha'i

I · HISTORY AND BELIEFS

The Baha'i religion sprang out of an Islamic movement known as the Babi faith, which was founded in the mid-19th century in Persia (now southern Iran) by Mirza Ali Muhammad, a direct descendent of the Prophet Muhammad. By proclaiming himself to be the Bab, which literally means "gate" or "door," Ali Muhammad announced that he was the forerunner of the Universal Messenger of God, who would usher in an era of justice and peace.

In 1850, the Bab was killed by a firing squad in Tabriz, Persia, upon the order of the grand vizier of the new Shah of Iran. The grand vizier was acting on behalf of traditional Islamic clergy in his country, who were alarmed at what they perceived to be the heretical doctrine being taught by the Bab and also by the fact that he was gaining followers.

In 1863, one of the Bab's 18 original closest disciples, Baha'u'llah, declared, while he was in exile in Iraq, that he was "He Whom God Shall Manifest," the messianic figure whom the Bab had predicted. He was soon banished by the Iraqi government to Istanbul and then to Adrianapole, where he stayed for five years.

Agitation from opponents caused the Turkish government to send the exiles to Acre, Palestine, where Baha'u'llah spent his last years. Upon his death, his eldest son, Abdu'l-Baha, "The Servant of Baha," led the faith, as had been determined in his father's will. With his death in 1921, leadership fell, as stipulated in Abdu'l-

Baha's will, to his eldest grandson, Shoghi Effendi, "The Guardian of the Cause of God," who devoted himself to expanding the world-wide Baha'i community, establishing its central administrative offices in Haifa, and translating the writings of his great-grandfather, Baha'u'llah.

Central to Baha'i beliefs is the unity of all religions and of all humanity. God, Baha'is teach, may be unknowable, but the divine presence manifests itself in various ways. Among these are the creation of the world and the prophets, beginning with Adam, and continuing through the Jewish prophets, Buddha, Krishna, Zoroaster, Jesus and Muhammad, who was succeeded by Baha'u'llah. Each prophet represents a divine message which was appropriate for the era in which he appeared. Baha'is believe that other prophets may come in the future, and that there is no last revelation or final prophet.

Members are elected to Baha'i's approximately 20,000 local spiritual councils, of which there are about 1,700 in the United States, and 324 in Canada. Members are also elected to 174 national spiritual assemblies throughout the world. These culminate in a Universal House of Justice, which has administrative, judicial and legislative functions and the authority to frame new rules for situations not provided for in the writings of Baha'u'llah.

There are now more than five million Baha'is in 233 countries and territories. Throughout the world, the Baha'i faith has only seven houses of worship, one on each continent. The house of worship in North America is in Wilmette, Illinois. Locally, Baha'is may meet for worship or for communal activities in homes or Baha'i centers. The minimum number of Baha'is that can comprise a local community is two, but nine are required for a local spiritual council.

U.S. communities: 7,000
U.S. membership: 130,000
(data from the Office of Public Information, Baha'is of the United States)

For more information, contact:
Office of Public Information
National Spiritual Assembly of the Baha'is of the United States
866 United Nations Plaza, Suite 120
New York, NY 10017-1822
(212) 803-2500

Canadian communities: 1,400
Canadian membership: 29,000
(data from the Office of Public Affairs, Baha'is of Canada)

For more information, contact:
Department of Public Affairs
Baha'i National Centre
7200 Leslie Street
Thornhill, ON L3T 6L8
(905) 889-8168

II · THE BASIC SERVICE

The centerpiece of the Baha'i community is the Nineteen Day Feast, which is held every 19 days and is the local community's regular worship gathering—and more. The feast day is held on the first day of each of the 19 months in the Baha'i calendar.

The Nineteen Day Feast helps sustain the unity of the local Baha'i community. While Baha'i feasts around the world adapt to local cultural and social needs, they always contain spiritual devotions, administrative consultation and fellowship.

The word "feast" is used to imply not that a large meal will be served, but that a "spiritual feast"—worship, companionship and unity—will be available.

During devotions, selections from the writings of the Baha'i faith and, often, other faiths will be read aloud. This is followed by a general discussion, which allows every member of the community to have a voice in community affairs.

Devotions plus the discussion that follows usually lasts about 90 minutes.

APPROPRIATE ATTIRE

Men: Personal preference for attire, plus one's own sense of reverence, are the only criteria. This may range from jacket and tie to slacks or jeans. No head covering is required.

Women: Personal preference for attire, plus one's own sense of reverence, are the only criteria. This may range from a dress or skirt to slacks or jeans. Clothing need not cover the arms or reach below the knees. No head covering is required. Women may wear open-toed shoes and/or modest jewelry.

There are no rules regarding colors of clothing.

THE SANCTUARY

What are the major sections of the house of worship?

The only Baha'i house of worship in North America is in Wilmette, Illinois, and has no "sanctuary." Instead, it has an entirely open, domed interior with a podium at the front. Elsewhere, Baha'is may meet in homes or in Baha'i community centers.

THE SERVICE

When should guests arrive and where should they sit?

Arrive at the time for which the service has been called. Guests may sit wherever they wish. There are no ushers to guide them to their seats.

If arriving late, are there times when a guest should *not* enter the service?

Yes. Do not enter during prayers.

Are there times when a guest should *not* leave the service?

No.

Who are the major officiants, leaders or participants and what do they do?

- *The chairperson or host*, who will conduct the flow of activities during the service. There are no clergy in the Baha'i faith. The method of selecting the host varies among Baha'i local communities. They are usually either elected or simply volunteer for the position. Often, the person in whose home a Nineteen Day Feast is held is the host for that occasion.

What are the major ritual objects of the service?

There are no ritual objects in the Baha'i faith.

What books are used?

A prayer book, which is usually *Baha'i Prayers* (Wilmette, Ill.: National Spiritual Assemblies of the Baha'is of the United States, 1991). This is a selection of writings by Baha'u'llah, Abdu'l Baha, and Shoghi Effendi. Also, readings from sacred Baha'i writings are often taken from *The Gleanings* by Baha'u'llah (Wilmette, Ill.: Baha'i Publishing Trust, 1976).

To indicate the order of the service:

Periodic announcements will be made by the chairperson or host.

GUEST BEHAVIOR DURING THE SERVICE

Will a guest who is not a Baha'i be expected to do anything other than sit?

No, although it is optional for guests to sing with the congregation.

Are there any parts of the service in which a guest who is not a Baha'i should *not* participate?

Yes. Guests should not participate in the business portion. Often, this will be suspended if guests are present out of consideration for them. The business portion consists of reports from the secretary and the treasurer, after which those present can make recommendations to the local spiritual council or the national spiritual assembly. Such recommendations may address any aspect of the Baha'i faith, from the secular to the religious. Members may, for example, express a desire to have more music during a worship service or to schedule a fund-raiser for the local religious school.

If not disruptive to the service, is it okay to:

◘ **Take pictures?** Yes.
◘ **Use a flash?** Yes.
◘ **Use a video camera?** Yes.
◘ **Use a tape recorder?** Yes.

Will contributions to the church be collected at the service?

No. But even if there were collections, only Baha'is may contribute to the Baha'i faith. The primary reason for this is to make Baha'is solely responsible for their faith. Also, contributing to the faith is considered a sacred privilege that rests on recognizing Baha'u'llah as the messiah.

AFTER THE SERVICE

Is there usually a reception after the service?

There may be a reception, depending on the customs of the individual community, each of which sets its own policy. If there is a reception, which is called the "social portion," it may last about 30 minutes to several hours. Food will definitely be served at a reception, but not alcoholic beverages, since alcohol is forbidden to Baha'is.

Is there a traditional form of address for clergy who may be at the reception?

No, since there are no clergy in the Baha'i faith.

Is it okay to leave early?

Yes.

GENERAL GUIDELINES AND ADVICE

None provided.

SPECIAL VOCABULARY

Key words or phrases which might be helpful for a visitor to know:

- *Baha'u'llah* ("Bah-HAH-oo-LAH"): Prophet. The founder of the Baha'i faith, whose name means "Glory of God."
- *Abdu'l-Baha* ("Ab-DOOL-bah-HAH"): Son of Baha'u'llah, whose name means "Servant of Baha."
- *Shoghi Effendi* ("SHOW-gey Eh-FEN-dee"): Grandson of Abdu'l-Baha, also called the "Guardian."
- *Allah'u'Abha* ("Ah-lah-oo-ab-HA"): "God is most glorious."
- *Baha'i* ("Ba-HIGH"): A follower of Baha'u'llah.

DOGMA AND IDEOLOGY

Baha'is believe:

- Humanity is one.
- Men and women are equal.
- Any apparent inequality between the capacities of men and women is due solely to the lack of educational opportunities currently available to women.
- Prejudice, religious intolerance and the extremes between wealth and poverty must be eliminated.
- In addition to the Ten Commandments, behavior should be guided by avoiding such activities as gambling, drinking alcohol, drug abuse, gossip and backbiting.
- Ethical work is a form of worship.
- In establishing a world federation and a world language.

◾ In universal education for all.

◾ That science and religion are in fundamental agreement about the cosmos since God would have not given humanity two systems that attempt to explain existence that are in conflict.

Some basic books to which a guest can refer to learn more about the Baha'i faith:

Baha'u'llah and the New Era by J.E. Esselmont (Wilmette, Ill.: Baha'i Publishing Trust, 1980).

The Baha'i Faith—An Introduction by Gloria Faizi (New Delhi, India: Baha'i Publications Trust, 1988).

The Proofs of Baha'u'llah's Mission: A Compilation from Baha'i Sacred Writings (Riviera Beach, Fla.: Palabra Publications, 1994).

The above books may be obtained from:

Baha'i Distribution Service
5397 Wilbanks Drive
Chattanooga, TN 37343
Phone: (800) 999-9019
Fax: (423) 843-0836

III · HOLY DAYS AND FESTIVALS

◾ *World Religion Day,* which occurs on the third Sunday in January. The purpose is to proclaim the oneness of religion and the belief that world religion will unify the peoples of the earth. There is no traditional greeting for this holiday.

◾ *Ayyam-i-ha* ("Ah-yam-ee-HAH") or "Days of Ha," which is celebrated from February 26 through March 1. The holiday is devoted to hospitality, charity and gift-giving and to spiritually preparing one's self for the annual fast for the entire length of the last month in the Baha'i calendar. The 19-day fast continues from sunrise to sundown for 19 days. Ayyam-i-ha is celebrated during the four days (five in a leap year) before the last month of the Baha'i year. There is no traditional greeting for this holiday.

◾ *Naw-Ruz* ("Naw-ROOZ"), the Baha'i New Year's Day which occurs on March 21. The day is astronomically fixed to commence the year on the first day of Spring. Baha'is attend neither work nor school on this day. While there are no set rituals for observing the holiday, it is often marked by prayers, feasts and possible festive communal field trips. There is no traditional greeting for this holiday.

■ *Festival of Ridvan* ("RIZ-von"), which is celebrated from April 21 through May 2. This 12-day holiday commemorates the 12 days from April 21-May 2, 1863, when Baha'u'llah, the prophet-founder of the Baha'i faith, publicly proclaimed in a garden in Baghdad his mission as God's messenger for this age. The garden was called "Ridvan." Three days during the Festival of Ridvan are holy days during which work and school are suspended: The first day (April 21); the ninth day (April 29) and the twelfth day (May 2). There is no traditional greeting for this holiday.

■ *The Declaration of the Bab* ("Bob"), which occurs on May 23. Commemorates the date in 1844 when the Bab, the prophet-herald of the Baha'i faith, announced in Shiraz, Persia, that he was the new herald of a new messenger of God. Work and school are suspended on this day, for which there is no traditional greeting.

■ *Race Unity Day,* which occurs on the second Sunday in June. A Baha'i-sponsored observance intended to promote racial harmony and understanding and the essential unity of humanity. Established in 1957 by the Baha'is of the United States. There is no traditional greeting for this holiday.

■ *The Martyrdom of the Bab* ("Bob"), which occurs on July 9, and commemorates the anniversary of the execution by a firing squad in Tabriz, Persia, of Mirza Ali Muhammad, the Bab, the prophet-herald of the Baha'i faith. The martyrdom is marked with prayers at noon, which is when the Bab was executed. There is no traditional greeting for this holiday.

■ *The Birth of the Bab* ("Bob"), which is celebrated on October 20. Commemorates the anniversary of the birth of the "Bab," which means "the Gate," and who was the prophet-founder of the Baha'i faith. The Bab was born with the name Siyyid Ali Muhammad in 1819. Work and school are suspended on this holiday. While there are no set rituals for observing the holiday, it is often marked by prayers, feasts and possibly festive communal field trips. There is no traditional greeting for this holiday.

■ *The Birth of Baha'u'llah* ("Bah-HAH-oo-LAH"), which is celebrated on November 12. Commemorates the birth of Baha'u'llah, who was born Mirza Husayn Ali in 1817 in Nur, Persia. Baha'u'llah, which means "Glory of God," was the prophet-founder of the Baha'i faith.

Work and school are suspended on this holiday. While there are no set rituals for observing the holiday, it is often marked by prayers, feasts and possibly festive communal field trips. There is no traditional greeting for this holiday.

■ *The Day of the Covenant,* which occurs on November 26. Commemorates Baha'u'llah's appointing his son, Abdu'l-Baha, as the Center of his Covenant. While there are no set rituals for observing the holiday, it is often marked by prayers, feasts and possibly festive communal field trips. There is no traditional greeting for this holiday.

IV · LIFE CYCLE EVENTS

Birth Ceremony

Not applicable to the Baha'i faith.

Initiation Ceremony

Not applicable to the Baha'i faith.

Marriage Ceremony

The Baha'i faith teaches that the family is the basic unit of society and that monogamous marriage is the foundation of family life. Also, preparation for marriage is essential for ensuring a happy marriage. Preparation includes parental approval for the choice of a spouse. This does not mean that Baha'i marriages are arranged since Baha'is marry the person of their choice. But once the choice is made, parents have the right and the obligation to weigh carefully whether to give their consent and, thus, to guide their offspring in one of life's most important decisions.

Baha'is encourage interracial marriages since these stress humanity's essential oneness. The faith also does not discourage interfaith marriages.

The Baha'i faith allows divorce, although it strongly discourages it. If a Baha'i couple decides to seek a divorce, they must live apart from each other for at least one year—the "year of patience"—while they attempt to reconcile. If they still desire a divorce after those 12 months, it is granted.

The Baha'i faith does not have a standard wedding service. Its only stipulation for a wedding is that the bride and groom must exchange vows in front of two witnesses designated by the local Baha'i spiritual council. The vow repeated by the bride and groom is, "We will all verily abide by the Will of God." For a Baha'i, that Will implies all of the commitments associated with marriage, including to love, honor and cherish; to care for each other, regardless of health or wealth; and to share with and serve each other.

Other than meeting the criteria regarding witnesses and the bride and groom reciting the vows, a Baha'i wedding may be as simple or elaborate as a couple wishes.

The length of the wedding varies, depending on its content.

BEFORE THE CEREMONY

Are guests usually invited by a formal invitation?

Either by a written invitation or a telephone call.

If not stated explicitly, should one assume that children are invited?

Yes.

If one can't attend, what should one do?

Depending on one's personal preference, one may send flowers or a gift to the couple along with writing or telephoning your regrets that you cannot attend.

APPROPRIATE ATTIRE

Men: A jacket and tie. No head covering is required.

Women: A dress. Clothing need not cover the arms or reach below the knees. No head covering is required. Women may wear open-toed shoes and/or modest jewelry.

There are no rules regarding colors of clothing.

GIFTS

Is a gift customarily expected?

Yes. Appropriate gifts are whatever is the norm in one's culture.

Should gifts be brought to the ceremony?

They may be brought to the ceremony or the reception or sent to the home of the newlyweds.

THE CEREMONY

Where will the ceremony take place?

Baha'i weddings may be held wherever the bride and groom desire.

When should guests arrive and where should they sit?

Arrive at the time for which the service has been called. At some weddings, there may be ushers to advise guests on where to sit.

If arriving late, are there times when a guest should *not* enter the ceremony?

No.

Are there times when a guest should *not* leave the ceremony?

No.

Who are the major officiants, leaders or participants at the ceremony and what do they do?

◨ *The bride, the groom and two witnesses approved by the local spiritual council and who need not be Baha'is.*

What books are used?

There are no standard readings at Baha'i weddings. Whatever is read is chosen by the bride and groom and usually includes writings from Baha'i and other faiths, and other poetry and prose.

To indicate the order of the ceremony:

There may be a program or periodic announcements.

Will a guest who is not a Baha'i be expected to do anything other than sit?

No.

Are there any parts of the ceremony in which a guest who is not a Baha'i should *not* participate?

No.

If not disruptive to the ceremony, is it okay to:

◨ **Take pictures?** Yes.
◨ **Use a flash?** Yes.
◨ **Use a video camera?** Yes.
◨ **Use a tape recorder?** Yes.

Will contributions to the house of worship be collected at the ceremony?

No.

AFTER THE CEREMONY

Is there usually a reception after the ceremony?

Possibly, depending on personal preference. If there is a reception, there will probably be food, but no alcoholic beverages, since members of the Baha'i faith do not drink alcohol. There may also be music and dancing at the reception.

Would it be considered impolite to neither eat nor drink?

No.

Is there a grace or benediction before eating or drinking?

No.

Is there a grace or benediction after eating or drinking?

No.

Is there a traditional greeting for the family?

No.

Is there a traditional form of address for clergy who may be at the reception?

No, since there are no clergy in the Baha'i faith.

Is it okay to leave early?

Yes.

Funerals and Mourning

The Baha'i faith teaches that there is a separate, rational soul for every human. It provides the underlying animation for the body and is our real self. Upon the death of the body, the soul is freed from its ties with the physical body and the surrounding physical world, and begins its journey through the spiritual world. Baha'is understand the spiritual world to be a timeless, placeless extension of our own universe, and not a physically remote or removed place.

Heaven is envisioned partly as a state of nearness to God; hell is a state of remoteness from God. Each state is a natural consequence of the efforts of an individual—or the lack of them—to develop spiritual-ly. The key to spiritual progress is to follow the path outlined by the various Prophets of God, who include Adam, Moses, Buddha, Krishna, Zoroaster, Jesus and Muhammad, and Baha'u'llah.

Beyond this, the exact nature of afterlife remains a mystery.

While the Baha'i faith is relatively free of teachings regarding the actual rituals of funerals, it does advise that the deceased should not be embalmed, unless it is required by state law. Also the deceased should be buried within one hour's travel time from the place of death since the Baha'i faith teaches that we are all world citizens and should not be attached to any particular geographic site.

BEFORE THE CEREMONY

How soon after the death does the funeral usually take place?

Usually within two or three days.

What should a non-Baha'i do upon hearing of the death of a member of that faith?

Convey your condolences to the bereaved either by telephone or a visit to their home.

APPROPRIATE ATTIRE

Men: Personal preference for attire, and one's own sense of reverence, are the only criteria. This may range from jacket and tie to slacks or jeans. No head covering is required.

Women: Personal preference for attire, and one's own sense of rever-ence, are the only criteria. This may range from a dress or skirt to slacks or jeans. Clothing need not cover the arms or reach below the knees. No head covering is required. Women may wear open-toed shoes and/or modest jewelry.

There are no rules regarding colors of clothing, but these should con-form to social and cultural custom.

GIFTS

Is it appropriate to send flowers or make a contribution?

Yes. Flowers may be sent either to the home of the bereaved before or after the funeral or to the funeral itself. Contributions may be made to a fund or charity designated by the bereaved or before death by the deceased, but non-Baha'is cannot contribute to a Baha'i fund.

Is it appropriate to send food?

Food may be sent to the home of the bereaved before or after the funeral. No specific types of food are best to send or are prohibited.

THE CEREMONY

Where will the ceremony take place?

At the local house of worship or at a funeral home.

When should guests arrive and where should they sit?

Arrive early or at the time for which the service has been called. Ushers may be available to advise guests on where to sit.

If arriving late, are there times when a guest should *not* enter the ceremony?

No.

Will the bereaved family be present before the ceremony?

Possibly.

Is there a traditional greeting for the family?

No. Simply express your condolences.

Will there be an open casket?

Rarely, since the Baha'i faith does not allow embalming.

Is a guest expected to view the body?

This is entirely optional.

What is appropriate behavior upon viewing the body?

The Baha'i faith does not ordain certain behavior at such moments since open caskets are so rare.

Who are the major officiants at the ceremony and what do they do?

Whoever the family asks to officiate. They will see that the service is carried out according to the family's wishes.

What books are used?

A prayer book, which is usually *Baha'i Prayers* (Wilmette, Ill.: National Spiritual Assemblies of the Baha'is of the United States, 1991). This is a selection of writings by Baha'u'llah, Abdu'l Baha, and Shoghi Effendi. Readings from sacred Baha'i writings are often taken from *The Gleanings* by Baha'u'llah (Wilmette, Ill.: Baha'i Publishing Trust, 1976). Other religious writings, prose or poetry may be also be read.

To indicate the order of the ceremony:

There may be periodic announcements or a program may be distributed.

Will a guest who is not a Baha'i be expected to do anything other than sit?

No.

Are there any parts of the ceremony in which a guest who is not a Baha'i should *not* participate?

No.

If not disruptive to the ceremony, is it okay to:

- **Take pictures?** Possibly, depending on the preference of the family members.
- **Use a flash?** Possibly, depending on the preference of the family members.
- **Use a video camera?** Possibly, depending on the preference of the family members.
- **Use a tape recorder?** Possibly, depending on the preference of the family members.

Will contributions to the house of worship be collected at the ceremony?

No.

THE INTERMENT

Should guests attend the interment?

Yes.

Whom should one ask for directions?

Family members or the funeral director.

What happens at the graveside?

A particular Baha'i prayer for the deceased may be recited at the grave-side.

Do guests who are not Baha'is participate at the graveside ceremony?

Depending on a guest's relationship with the deceased, the bereaved family may possibly ask a guest to read aloud some prayers to those gathered at the funeral.

COMFORTING THE BEREAVED

Is it appropriate to visit the home of the bereaved after the funeral?

Yes. The timing of the visit entirely depends on the personal preference of the visitor and the bereaved.

Will there be a religious service at the home of the bereaved?

No.

Will food be served?

Probably.

How soon after the funeral will a mourner usually return to a normal work schedule?

The Baha'i faith ordains no particular mourning period. The length of a mourner's absence from work depends entirely on the individual mourner.

How soon after the funeral will a mourner usually return to a normal social schedule?

The Baha'i faith ordains no particular mourning period. The length of a mourner's absence from social events depends entirely on the individual mourner.

Are there mourning customs to which a friend who is not a Baha'i should be sensitive?

No, since the Baha'i faith ordains no particular mourning customs.

Are there rituals for observing the anniversary of the death?

No.

V · HOME CELEBRATIONS

Not applicable to the Baha'i faith.

Chapter 3 Contents

3

Christian and Missionary Alliance

I · HISTORY AND BELIEFS

The Christian and Missionary Alliance is literally an *alliance* of evangelical believers, who have joined together, through their local churches and their own personal lives, to bring the gospel and the life of Jesus Christ to all peoples and all nations.

In the United States, the denomination has its roots in two groups—the Christian Alliance and the Evangelical Missionary Alliance—both of which were founded in 1887 by Dr. Albert B. Simpson, a Presbyterian minister motivated by the spiritual needs of urban residents in the United States, as well as by the unevangelized peoples in other lands. These two organizations' underlying thrust was Jesus' comment in Matthew (24:14): "The gospel of the kingdom will be preached in the whole world as a testimony to all nations, and then the end will come." In Canada, a movement that was begun in 1887 by Rev. John Salmon joined the Christian Alliance in 1889, becoming the Auxiliary of the Christian Alliance, Toronto.

The two groups that had been founded by Dr. Simpson were combined in 1897 to form the Christian and Missionary Alliance, which now has a worldwide membership of 2.4 million and ministries devoted to evangelism for Christ in 56 countries and territories. In 1981, the Canadian districts became autonomous and formed the Christian and Missionary Alliance in Canada. Its General Assembly is held every two years.

Presently, more than 1,169 missionaries are taking the Christian gospel to almost 150 "unsaved people groups" around the globe. The church defines a "people group" as "a distinct group of individuals having no community of Christians able to evangelize its people without outside help." For example, the Church has two missionaries evangelizing Moslems residing in Great Britain, six to Chinese living in Australia, four to Native Americans living in urban areas in the United States, and two to North American Jews.

The Church believes that Jesus Christ is the living Word of God, the supreme Revelation of divine love, the sacrificial Lamb of God who alone provides salvation for humanity and every need of body and soul, and is the only hope for a world of lost people. Baptism and the Lord's Supper are recognized as the two ordinances of the Church. These are not related to individual salvation, but are outward signs of an inward commitment to Christ. Baptism by immersion is taught and practiced. The Lord's Supper is administered regularly in church services.

Church policies, which are set by an annual General Council, are administered by a 28-member Board of Managers and are implemented by the staff of the national office and district offices. Each local church sends its pastor and lay delegates to General Council and district conferences so it can have a voice in shaping policy.

U.S. churches: 1,850
U.S. membership: 311,600
(data from the 1998 Yearbook of American and Canadian Churches)

For more information, contact:
The Christian and Missionary Alliance
P.O. Box 35000
Colorado Springs, CO 80935-3500
(719) 599-5999

Canadian churches: 376
Canadian membership: 87,197
(data from the 1998 Yearbook of American and Canadian Churches)

For more information, contact:
Christian and Missionary Alliance in Canada
#510–105 Gordon Baker Road
North York, ON M2H 3P8
(905) 771-6747

II · THE BASIC SERVICE

The majority of churches in the Christian and Missionary Alliance have services Sunday morning and Sunday evening; some have services only on Sunday morning. Since individual churches in the Alliance have considerable autonomy, the worship service may vary from church to church. But services invariably have music, prayer and a sermon. Some churches also have a "mission moment," in which a report is made to congregants on missionary work in North America and overseas.

The service, whether it be in the morning or the evening, usually lasts more than one hour.

APPROPRIATE ATTIRE

Men: Jacket and tie or more casual clothing. Standards and expectations for attire vary from church to church. No head covering is required.

Women: A skirt and blouse are usually worn. Hems need not reach below the knees nor must clothing cover the arms. Open-toed shoes and modest jewelry are permissible. No head covering is required.

There are no rules regarding colors of clothing.

THE SANCTUARY

What are the major sections of the church?

Since churches belonging to the Christian and Missionary Alliance are autonomous, there is no particular architectural or ritualistic pattern to them. All have a sanctuary where the services are held.

THE SERVICE

When should guests arrive and where should they sit?

Arrive early. In some churches, ushers will direct congregants and visitors to their seats. Otherwise, sit wherever you wish.

If arriving late, are there times when a guest should *not* enter the service?

Do not enter while prayers are being recited.

Are there times when a guest should *not* leave the service?

No.

Who are the major officiants, leaders or participants and what do they do?

- *The pastor,* who gives the pastoral prayers and messages.
- *The worship leader,* who leads the service.
- *The musicians,* who provide music for the service.

What are the major ritual objects of the service?

No particular ritual objects are necessary for services. Most churches, though, have pitchers and cups that hold the grape juice used in communion to symbolize the blood of Christ on the cross. These may be highly decorated or as simple as paper cups. To represent the body of Christ during communion, churches ordinarily offer wafers or crackers. A few offer matzah, the flat, unleavened bread which Jews use at their Passover seder to commemorate their Exodus from bondage in Egypt.

What books are used?

A hymnal and a Bible. The autonomy of individual churches precludes having standard hymnals and Bibles throughout the Church.

To indicate the order of the service:

A program will be provided.

GUEST BEHAVIOR DURING THE SERVICE

Will a guest who is not a member of the Christian and Missionary Alliance be expected to do anything other than sit?

Yes. Stand with the congregants for prayer or to sing hymns.

Are there any parts of the service in which a guest who is not a member of the Christian and Missionary Alliance should *not* participate?

Non-Christians do not receive the Lord's Supper, which is also known as communion. All Christians, whether or not they are members of the Christian and Missionary Alliance, may receive communion in the Church.

If not disruptive to the service, is it okay to:

- **Take pictures?** Only under certain circumstances and with the prior permission of the pastor.

◘ **Use a flash?** No.
◘ **Use a video camera?** Only under certain circumstances and with the prior permission of the pastor.
◘ **Use a tape recorder?** Yes.

Will contributions to the church be collected at the service?

Yes.

How much is customary to contribute?

The Church encourages members to follow the Bible's tithing of 10 percent. As for non-members, contributions are entirely optional. While the amount of the contribution is at the discretion of the congregants or vistors, contributions between $1 and $5 are common.

AFTER THE SERVICE

Is there usually a reception after the service?

No.

Is there a traditional form of address for clergy whom a guest may meet?

"Pastor."

GENERAL GUIDELINES AND ADVICE

None provided.

SPECIAL VOCABULARY

Key words or phrases which might be helpful for a visitor to know:

◘ *The Fourfold Gospel:* Refers to Jesus Christ as Savior, Sanctifier, Healer and the Coming King.
◘ *Bring Back the King:* Reaching the unreachable throughout the world with the gospel to hurry the return of Jesus Christ.

DOGMA AND IDEOLOGY

Members of the Christian and Missionary Alliance believe:

◘ There is one God who is infinitely perfect and exists eternally in three persons: Father, Son and Holy Spirit.

■ The Holy Spirit is a divine person, sent to guide, teach and empower the believer.

■ Jesus Christ is true God and true man. He was conceived by the Holy Spirit and born of the Virgin Mary. He died upon the cross for the unjust. He arose from the dead and is now at the right hand of God as our great High Priest. He will return to establish His Kingdom of righteousness and peace.

■ The Old and New Testaments were verbally inspired by God and are a complete revelation of His will for the salvation of humanity.

■ Mankind was originally created in God's image, but fell into disobedience, thus incurring physical and spiritual death. Each person is born with a sinful nature, and can only be saved through the atoning work of Jesus Christ.

■ The redemptive work of Jesus Christ provides for the healing of the physical body. Prayer for the sick and anointing with oil are taught in the Scriptures and practiced by the Church. There shall be a bodily resurrection of the just, who will be eternally resurrected into life; and for the unjust, who will be eternally separated from God.

■ The Second Coming of Jesus Christ is imminent. It will be personal and visible.

Some basic books to which a guest can refer to learn more about the Christian and Missionary Alliance:

All for Jesus by Robert L. Niklaus, John S. Sawin, and Samuel J. Stoesz (Camp Hill, Pa.: Christian Publications, Inc., 1986).

To All Peoples by Robert L. Niklaus (Camp Hill, Pa.: Christian Publications, Inc., 1980).

The Best of A.B. Simpson, compiled by Keith Bailey (Camp Hill, Pa.: Christian Publications, Inc., 1987).

The Pursuit of God by A. W. Tozer (Camp Hill, Pa.: Christian Publications, Inc., 1948).

III · HOLY DAYS AND FESTIVALS

■ *Christmas,* celebrated on December 25. Marks the birth of Jesus Christ. Church members and non-church members can greet each other with "Merry Christmas!"

■ *Good Friday.* The date of observance varies, although it usually occurs in April and is always the Friday before Easter. It marks the crucifixion of Christ in Jerusalem. There is no traditional greeting for this holiday.

- ▣ *Easter*. The date of observance varies, but it usually occurs in April and is always on the Sunday after the first full moon that occurs on or after the spring equinox of March 21. Commemorates the resurrection of Jesus Christ after His crucifixion. The traditional greeting is "Happy Easter!"

IV · LIFE CYCLE EVENTS

Birth Ceremony

This ritual is called an "Infant Dedication." It is a simple 10-minute ceremony in which the parents of the newborn promise before God and before their congregation that they will raise this child for God. There is no set age at which an infant will have a Dedication. It is done anytime the child's parents request it.

The ceremony is usually part of the regular Sunday morning worship service, which may last over an hour.

BEFORE THE CEREMONY

Are guests usually invited by a formal invitation?

No.

If not stated explicitly, should one assume that children are invited?

Yes.

If one can't attend, what should one do?

RSVP with regrets.

APPROPRIATE ATTIRE

Men: Jacket and tie or more casual attire. Standards and expectations for attire vary from church to church. No head covering is required.

Women: A skirt and blouse are usually worn. Hems need not reach below the knees nor must clothing cover the arms. Open-toed shoes and modest jewelry are permissible. No head covering is required.

There are no rules regarding colors of clothing.

GIFTS

Is a gift customarily expected?

No.

Should gifts be brought to the ceremony?

See above.

THE CEREMONY

Where will the ceremony take place?

In the church sanctuary.

When should guests arrive and where should they sit?

Arrive early. In some churches, ushers will direct congregants and visitors to their seats. Otherwise, sit wherever you wish.

If arriving late, are there times when a guest should *not* enter the ceremony?

Do not enter while prayers are being recited.

Are there times when a guest should *not* leave the ceremony?

No.

Who are the major officiants, leaders or participants at the ceremony and what do they do?

- *The pastor*, who will present the baby to God and take the vows from the parents.
- *The parents and child.*

What books are used?

A hymnal and a Bible are used for the Sunday morning service of which the Dedication is a component. The autonomy of individual churches precludes having standard hymnals and Bibles throughout the Church.

To indicate the order of the ceremony:

A program will be provided.

Will a guest who is not a member of the Christian and Missionary Alliance be expected to do anything other than sit?

Guests are expected to stand with the congregants while they are singing and praying, although they are not obliged to engage in prayer and song if these violate their religious beliefs.

Are there any parts of the ceremony in which a guest who is not a member of the Christian and Missionary Alliance should *not* participate?

Non-Christians do not receive the Lord's Supper, which is also known as communion. All Christians, whether or not they are members of the Christian and Missionary Alliance, may receive communion in the Church.

If not disruptive to the ceremony, is it okay to:

■ **Take pictures?** Only under certain circumstances and with the prior permission of the pastor.
■ **Use a flash?** No.
■ **Use a video camera?** Only under certain circumstances and with the prior permission of the pastor.
■ **Use a tape recorder?** Yes.

Will contributions to the church be collected at the ceremony?

Yes.

How much is customary to contribute?

The Church encourages members to follow the Bible's tithing of 10 percent. Non-members are not obligated to contribute, but are welcome to do so. While the amount of the contribution is at the discretion of the guest, contributions between $1 and $5 are common.

AFTER THE CEREMONY

Is there usually a reception after the ceremony?

No.

Is there a traditional greeting for the family?

"Congratulations."

Is there a traditional form of address for clergy whom a guest may meet?

"Pastor."

Initiation Ceremony

Babies are not baptized in the Christian and Missionary Alliance since the Church believes that one must have a personal relationship with Jesus Christ before baptism. Baptism, then, is usually held when a child is 10 to 12 years. The ceremony is an outward sign of an inner commitment to Christ.

The baptism may be part of a larger service, or may be a ceremony unto itself. A baptismal ceremony may be held for a single youth or for as many as 15 or 20, depending on circumstances and how many ask to be baptized at a given date. The baptism may last about 15 to 30 minutes, depending on the number of persons being baptized.

BEFORE THE CEREMONY

Are guests usually invited by a formal invitation?
No. They are invited orally.

If not stated explicitly, should one assume that children are invited?
Yes.

If one can't attend, what should one do?
RSVP with regrets.

APPROPRIATE ATTIRE

Men: Jacket and tie. More casual attire is appropriate if the baptism is held outdoors. Standards and expectations for attire vary from church to church. No head covering is required.

Women: A skirt and blouse are usually worn. More casual attire is appropriate if the baptism is held outdoors. Hems need not reach below the knees nor must clothing cover the arms. Open-toed shoes and modest jewelry are permissible. No head covering is required.

There are no rules regarding colors of clothing.

GIFTS

Is a gift customarily expected?
No.

Should gifts be brought to the ceremony?
See above.

THE CEREMONY

Where will the ceremony take place?

In the baptistery, if the church has one. If not, the ceremony may be held in the baptistery of a nearby church. Some baptisms are held at rivers. The site of a baptism is chosen by the person being baptized or by his or her family.

When should guests arrive and where should they sit?

Arrive early. If held in a church, ushers may direct congregants and visitors to their seats. Otherwise, sit wherever you wish.

If arriving late, are there times when a guest should *not* enter the ceremony?

Do not enter while prayers are being recited.

Are there times when a guest should *not* leave the ceremony?

No.

Who are the major officiants, leaders or participants at the ceremony and what do they do?

- *The pastor,* who performs the baptism.
- *The person being baptized.*

What books are used?

A hymnal and a Bible. The autonomy of individual churches precludes having standard hymnals and Bibles throughout the Church.

To indicate the order of the ceremony:

A program may be distributed if the baptism is held in a church.

Will a guest who is not a member of the Christian and Missionary Alliance be expected to do anything other than sit?

If the ceremony is held in a church, guests are expected to stand with the congregants while they are singing and praying, although they are not obliged to engage in prayer and song if these violate their religious beliefs. If it is held outdoors, guests will probably stand throughout the relatively brief ceremony.

Are there any parts of the ceremony in which a guest who is not a member of the Christian and Missionary Alliance should *not* participate?

If the baptism is a ceremony unto itself, guests who are not members of the Christian and Missionary Alliance do not participate. If it is part of a worship service, non-Christians do not receive the Lord's Supper, which is also known as communion. All Christians, whether or not they are members of the Christian and Missionary Alliance, may receive communion in the Church.

If not disruptive to the ceremony, is it okay to:

◾ **Take pictures?** Only under certain circumstances and with the prior permission of the pastor.

◾ **Use a flash?** No.

◾ **Use a video camera?** Only under certain circumstances and with the prior permission of the pastor.

◾ **Use a tape recorder?** Yes.

Will contributions to the church be collected at the ceremony?

Contributions will be collected if the baptism is part of a larger worship service.

How much is customary to contribute?

The Church encourages members to follow the Bible's tithing of 10 percent. Non-members are not obligated to contribute, but are welcome to do so. Although the amount of the contribution is at the discretion of the congregants or visitors, contributions between $1 and $5 are common.

AFTER THE CEREMONY

Is there usually a reception after the ceremony?

No.

Is there a traditional greeting for the family?

"Congratulations."

Is there a traditional form of address for clergy whom a guest may meet?

"Pastor."

Marriage Ceremony

God instructed that man and woman should marry when He said in Genesis (2:24), "For this reason a man will leave his father and mother and be united to his wife, and they will become one flesh."

In Matthew (19:6), Jesus quoted this passage from Genesis, adding,

"Therefore, what God has joined together, let man not separate."

Genesis (2:18) further states, "It is not good that man should be alone." By this statement, God shows the incompleteness of man and woman apart from one another. Hence, marriage becomes the means to achieve completeness. From this physical and spiritual union, the home and family are established, which become the foundation of society and the well-being of the human race.

The 30- to 60-minute wedding service is a service unto itself.

BEFORE THE CEREMONY

Are guests usually invited by a formal invitation?

Yes.

If not stated explicitly, should one assume that children are invited?

Yes.

If one can't attend, what should one do?

RSVP with regrets and send a gift.

APPROPRIATE ATTIRE

Men: Jacket and tie or more casual clothing. Standards and expectations for attire vary from church to church. No head covering is required.

Women: A dress. Hems need not reach below the knees nor must clothing cover the arms. Open-toed shoes and modest jewelry are permissible. No head covering is required.

There are no rules regarding colors of clothing.

GIFTS

Is a gift customarily expected?

Yes. Cash, small household appliances, and household furnishings, such as sheets or towels are customary.

Should gifts be brought to the ceremony?

Yes.

THE CEREMONY

Where will the ceremony take place?

In the main sanctuary of the church.

When should guests arrive and where should they sit?

Arrive early. Ushers will advise you where to sit.

If arriving late, are there times when a guest should *not* enter the ceremony?

Do not enter when the bride and her wedding party are marching down the aisle.

Are there times when a guest should *not* leave the ceremony?

Do not leave during the processional or recessional of the wedding party or during the recitation of the wedding vows.

Who are the major officiants, leaders or participants at the ceremony and what do they do?

◼ *The pastor,* who leads the service.
◼ *The bride and groom and members of the wedding party.*

What books are used?

A hymnal and Bible. The autonomy of individual churches precludes having standard hymnals and Bibles throughout the Church.

To indicate the order of the ceremony:

A program will be provided.

Will a guest who is not a member of the Christian and Missionary Alliance be expected to do anything other than sit?

No.

Are there any parts of the ceremony in which a guest who is not a member of the Christian and Missionary Alliance should *not* participate?

No.

If not disruptive to the ceremony, is it okay to:

◼ **Take pictures?** Yes.
◼ **Use a flash?** Sometimes, but only with prior permission of the pastor.
◼ **Use a video camera?** Yes.
◼ **Use a tape recorder?** Yes.

Will contributions to the church be collected at the ceremony?

No.

AFTER THE CEREMONY

Is there usually a reception after the ceremony?

Yes. This may last two hours or more. Anything from light snack food to a complete dinner will be served. Alcoholic beverages are not served.

Would it be considered impolite to neither eat nor drink?

No.

Is there a grace or benediction before eating or drinking?

Yes.

Is there a grace or benediction after eating or drinking?

Possibly.

Is there a traditional greeting for the family?

"Congratulations."

Is there a traditional form of address for clergy who may be at the reception?

"Pastor."

Is it okay to leave early?

Yes.

Funerals and Mourning

As portrayed in both the Old and the New Testaments, death is the result of sin. The Christian and Missionary Alliance believes that in its spiritual aspects, death is a separation from God; in its physical aspects, it shows that man is mortal. Therefore, death is seen as the most fearsome of enemies since all humans must die.

Jesus came to give life both immediately and in the future. Christians are still mortal since they die physically, but they die "in Christ." By His death and His resurrection, Jesus conquered death and His victory becomes the believer's victory. As I Corinthians (15:57) states, "But thanks be to God! He gives us the victory through our Lord Jesus Christ!"

The ceremony may last 45 to 60 minutes.

BEFORE THE CEREMONY

How soon after the death does the funeral usually take place?

Within two to three days.

What should someone who is not a member of the Christian and Missionary Alliance do upon hearing of the death of a member of that faith?

Telephone or visit the bereaved. Let them know of your concern for them and offer any help you can give them.

APPROPRIATE ATTIRE

Men: A jacket and tie. No head covering is required.

Women: A dress. Hems need not reach below the knees nor must clothing cover the arms. Open-toed shoes and modest jewelry are permissible. No head covering is required.

Dark, somber colors are advised, but not required.

GIFTS

Is it appropriate to send flowers or make a contribution?

Yes. Flowers may be sent to the home of the bereaved upon hearing of the death, to the funeral itself, or to the home of the bereaved after the funeral.

The family may designate certain charities to which contributions may be donated.

Is it appropriate to send food?

Yes. Food may be sent to the home of the bereaved upon hearing of the death or after the funeral.

THE CEREMONY

Where will the ceremony take place?

Usually in a church.

When should guests arrive and where should they sit?

Arrive early. Usually ushers will advise you where to sit.

If arriving late, are there times when a guest should *not* enter the ceremony?

Do not enter while prayers are being recited.

Are there times when a guest should *not* leave the ceremony?

No.

Will the bereaved family be present at the church before the ceremony?

Possibly. If so, let them know of your concern for them and offer any help you can give.

Is there a traditional greeting for the family?

Offer your condolences.

Will there be an open casket?

Usually.

Is a guest expected to view the body?

This is optional.

What is appropriate behavior upon viewing the body?

Spend a few moments in silence as you stand in front of the casket.

Who are the major officiants at the ceremony and what do they do?

- *The pastor,* who will officiate.
- *The musicians,* who will provide music.

What books are used?

A hymnal and Bible. The autonomy of individual churches precludes having standard hymnals and Bibles throughout the Church.

To indicate the order of the ceremony:

A program will be provided.

Will a guest who is not a member of the Christian and Missionary Alliance be expected to do anything other than sit?

No.

Are there any parts of the ceremony in which a guest who is not a member of the Christian and Missionary Alliance should *not* participate?

No.

If not disruptive to the ceremony, is it okay to:

◘ **Take pictures?** No.

◘ **Use a flash?** No.

◘ **Use a video camera?** No.

◘ **Use a tape recorder?** Yes.

Will contributions to the church be collected at the ceremony?
No.

THE INTERMENT

Should guests attend the interment?

Yes.

Whom should one ask for directions?

Ask the ushers.

What happens at the graveside?

Prayers are recited, Scripture is read and a short service is held.

Do guests who are not members of the Christian and Missionary Alliance participate at the graveside ceremony?

They may participate if requested to do so by the family.

COMFORTING THE BEREAVED

Is it appropriate to visit the home of the bereaved after the funeral?

Yes, but limit your visit to 30 minutes or less.

Will there be a religious service at the home of the bereaved?

Very rarely is a service held at home.

Will food be served?

Yes, but no alcoholic beverages.

How soon after the funeral will a mourner usually return to a normal work schedule?

This is entirely at the discretion of the bereaved.

How soon after the funeral will a mourner usually return to a normal social schedule?

This is entirely at the discretion of the bereaved.

Are there mourning customs to which a friend who is not a member of the Christian and Missionary Alliance should be sensitive?

No.

Are there rituals for observing the anniversary of the death?

No.

V · HOME CELEBRATIONS

Not applicable to the Christian and Missionary Alliance.

Chapter 4 Contents

The Christian Congregation

(Also known as The Christian Church.
Since local churches are semi-autonomous, they are sometimes known as
Independents or Universalists. This latter term should not
be confused with Unitarian Universalism.)

I · HISTORY AND BELIEFS

The Christian Congregation originated in the late 18th century along the frontier near the Ohio River. It was incorporated in 1887 when several ministers formally constituted the Church because they sought greater cooperation with each other.

The Church considers itself to be a progressive organization that places greater emphasis on ethical behavior than on strict adherence to doctrine. Its guiding principle is John 13:34-35: "A new commandment I give to you, that you love one another, even as I have loved you, that you also love one another. By this, all men will know that you are My disciples, if you have love for one another." Essential to Church belief is the conviction that all wars are unjust, and that war itself is an obsolete means to resolve disputes. Its doctrinal positions are intended to transcend racial distinctions and national identities and to foster a creative activism.

The Christian Congregation is an evangelistic association whose local churches are semi-autonomous.

Number of U.S. churches: 1,437
Number of U.S. members: 114,700
(data from the 1998 Yearbook of American and Canadian Churches*)*

For more information, contact:
The Christian Congregation, Inc.
804 West Hemlock Street
LaFollette, TN 37766
(423) 562-8511

II · THE BASIC SERVICE

Worship is a congregation's encounter and communion with God and with one another in God's name. It includes praise and prayer, scripture readings, a sermon and sometimes Holy Communion. Most services last slightly more than one hour.

APPROPRIATE ATTIRE

Men: A jacket and tie or slightly more casual attire. No head covering is required.

Women: A dress or a skirt and blouse or a pants suit. Shorts are not appropriate. Arms do not have to be covered nor do hems have to be below the knees. Open-toed shoes and modest jewelry are permissible. No head covering is required.

There are no rules regarding colors of clothing.

THE SANCTUARY

What are the major sections of the church?

Since local congregations are semi-autonomous, architecture varies among churches. But usually each church has:
- *A podium:* A raised section at the front of the church where the minister conducts services and a song leader leads congregants in singing.
- *A large assembly room:* Where congregants and guests sit on pews.

THE SERVICE

When should guests arrive and where should they sit?

Arrive shortly before the time for which the service has been called.

Ushers may be present to indicate where to sit. If not, sit wherever you wish.

If arriving late, are there times when a guest should *not* enter the service?

Do not enter during prayers.

Are there times when a guest should *not* leave the service?

Do not leave during prayers.

Who are the major officiants, leaders or participants and what do they do?

- *The minister,* who conducts the service.
- *The song leader,* who is in charge of music.
- *The choir,* which sings hymns and psalms.

What are the major ritual objects of the service?

Since local congregations are semi-autonomous, each has considerable latitude in the conduct and the contents of their services. Communion is held at the option of each local church, and consists of:

- *Wafers,* which are eaten during Holy Communion and signify the body of Jesus Christ.
- *Grape juice,* which the minister presents to congregants to drink and which signifies the blood of Jesus Christ.

What books are used?

The Christian Congregation has no official Bible translation. Each church chooses the hymnal and the translation of the Bible it will use.

To indicate the order of the service:

A program will be provided and periodic announcements will be made by the minister or another leader.

GUEST BEHAVIOR DURING THE SERVICE

Will a guest who is not a member of The Christian Congregation be expected to do anything other than sit?

Standing and kneeling with the congregation and reading prayers aloud and singing with congregants are all optional. Guests are welcome to participate if this does not compromise their personal beliefs. Anyone present at a service of The Christian Congregation can participate in communion, the accepting of which does not signal that one embraces Jesus Christ as his or her personal savior, but rather that one understands and accepts the ethical principles that motivated Jesus, and that these are compatible with how that person lives.

Are there any parts of the service in which a guest who is not a member of The Christian Congregation should *not* participate?

No.

If not disruptive to the service, is it okay to:

◼ **Take pictures?** Yes.
◼ **Use a video camera?** Yes.
◼ **Use a flash camera?** Yes.
◼ **Use a tape recorder?** Yes.

Will contributions to the church be collected at the service?

Yes. The offering plate will be passed through the congregation during the service.

How much is customary to contribute?

The customary offering is from $1 to $4.

AFTER THE SERVICE

Is there usually a reception after the service?

Yes. This may be in the church's reception area. It usually lasts less than 30 minutes and pastry, coffee and tea are ordinarily served. No alcoholic beverages are ever served at a church function. It is not considered impolite to neither eat nor drink. There is no grace or benediction before or after eating or drinking.

Is there a traditional form of address for clergy who may be at the reception?

"Reverend." "Doctor" may be used if the minister has a Ph.D. or an honorary doctorate.

Is it okay to leave early?

Yes.

GENERAL GUIDELINES AND ADVICE

None provided.

SPECIAL VOCABULARY

None provided.

DOGMA AND IDEOLOGY

Members of The Christian Congregation believe:

- There is a Supreme Being because there cannot be a creation without a Creator.
- Jesus was completely human and became divine through living an ethical life.
- Each of us can become immortal by living an ethical life.
- The Church does not subscribe to the concept of the Trinity in which God is the Father; the Son (embodied by Jesus Christ); and the Holy Spirit (the empowering spirit of God). However, individuals or individual churches are given the latitude to follow such belief.
- Each person is responsible for his or her own mistakes; the entire human race did not fall from God's grace because of the mistakes of Adam and Eve or of anyone else in a previous or present generation.
- Each person has freedom of will and freedom of conscience.
- All warfare, capital punishment and abortion on demand should be opposed. This is based on John 13:34-35: "A new commandment I give to you, that you love one another, even as I have loved you, that you also love one another. By this, all men will know that you are My disciples, if you have love for one another."

A basic book to which a guest can refer to learn more about The Christian Congregation:

The 1998 Yearbook of American and Canadian Churches, edited by Eileen W. Lindner (Nashville, Tenn.: Abingdon Press, 1998).

III · HOLY DAYS AND FESTIVALS

While the Christian Congregation considers every day to be a holy day, it is optional for individual churches to celebrate specific holidays. These may include:

- *Advent.* Occurs four weeks before Christmas. The purpose is to begin preparing for Christmas and to focus on Christ. There is no traditional greeting for this holiday.
- *Christmas.* Occurs on the evening of December 24 and the day of

December 25. Marks the birth of Jesus. The traditional greeting is "Merry Christmas."

■ *Lent.* Begins on Ash Wednesday, which occurs six weeks before Easter. The purpose is to prepare for Easter. Between Lent and Easter, fasting and abstention from entertainment are encouraged, as is increased giving to the poor. Often, there are midweek worship services. There is no traditional greeting for this holiday.

■ *Easter.* Always falls on the Sunday after the first full moon that occurs on or after the spring equinox of March 21. Celebrates the resurrection of Jesus Christ. The traditional greeting is "Happy Easter!"

IV · LIFE CYCLE EVENTS

Birth Ceremony

At the dedication ceremony, the parents of a newborn infant present the child to the minister, who represents the congregation. The parents pledge to nurture the child in the Christian faith and life, and the church commits itself to guide the child as he or she grows and develops.

A chief component of the ceremony is John 13:34-35, which is a prime tenet of The Christian Congregation: "A new commandment I give to you, that you love one another, even as I have loved you, that you also love one another. By this, all men will know that you are My disciples, if you have love for one another."

The 10-minute ceremony is part of the larger weekly congregational Sunday morning service, which usually lasts slightly more than one hour.

BEFORE THE CEREMONY

Are guests usually invited by a formal invitation?

No. The ceremony is part of the Sunday worship service and is open to all.

If not stated explicitly, should one assume that children are invited?

Yes.

If one can't attend, what should one do?

RSVP with regrets.

APPROPRIATE ATTIRE

Men: A jacket and tie or slightly more casual attire. No head covering is required.

Women: A dress or a skirt and blouse or a pants suit. Shorts are not appropriate. Arms do not have to be covered nor do hems have to be below the knees. Open-toed shoes and modest jewelry are permissible. No head covering is required.

There are no rules regarding colors of clothing.

GIFTS

Is a gift customarily expected?
No.

Should gifts be brought to the ceremony?
See above.

THE CEREMONY

Where will the ceremony take place?
Usually in the parents' church. Sometimes at the parents' home, if they prefer this.

When should guests arrive and where should they sit?
Arrive shortly before the time for which the service has been called. Ushers may be present to indicate where to sit. If not, sit wherever you wish.

If arriving late, are there times when a guest should *not* enter the ceremony?
Do not enter during prayers or during a processional.

Are there times when a guest should *not* leave the ceremony?
Do not leave during prayers or during a processional.

Who are the major officiants, leaders or participants at the ceremony and what do they do?
- *The minister*, who conducts the ceremony.
- *The infant*, whom parents and congregants pledge to nurture in wholesome growth.
- *The infant's parents.*

What books are used?

Only the minister uses a book for the ceremony. A hymnal and Bible are used during the rest of the service. The Christian Congregation has no official Bible translation. Each church chooses the hymnal and the translation of the Bible it will use.

To indicate the order of the ceremony:

A program will be provided or periodic announcements will be made by the minister.

Will a guest who is not a member of The Christian Congregation be expected to do anything other than sit?

Standing and kneeling with the congregation and reading prayers aloud and singing with congregants are all optional. Guests are welcome to participate if this does not compromise their personal beliefs. Anyone present at a service of The Christian Congregation can participate in communion, the accepting of which does not signal that one embraces Jesus Christ as his or her personal savior, but rather that one understands and accepts the ethical principles that motivated Jesus, and that these are compatible with how that person lives.

Are there any parts of the ceremony in which a guest who is not a member of The Christian Congregation should *not* participate?

No.

If not disruptive to the ceremony, is it okay to:

- **Take pictures?** Yes.
- **Use a video camera?** Yes.
- **Use a flash camera?** Yes.
- **Use a tape recorder?** Yes.

Will contributions to the church be collected at the ceremony?

Yes. The offering plate will be passed through the congregation during the service.

How much is customary to contribute?

The customary offering is from $1 to $4.

AFTER THE CEREMONY

Is there usually a reception after the ceremony?

This may be a reception after the worship service in the church's reception area. Ordinarily, pastry, coffee and tea are served. No alcoholic beverages are ever served at a church function. A reception usually lasts less than 30 minutes.

Would it be considered impolite to neither eat nor drink?

No.

Is there a grace or benediction before eating or drinking?

No.

Is there a grace or benediction after eating or drinking?

No.

Is there a traditional greeting for the family?

Just offer your congratulations.

Is there a traditional form of address for clergy who may be at the reception?

"Reverend." "Doctor" may be used if the minister has a Ph.D. or an honorary doctorate.

Is it okay to leave early?

Yes.

Initiation Ceremony

Not applicable to The Christian Congregation.

Marriage Ceremony

Marriage is the uniting of a man and a woman in a union which is intended—and which is pledged—to be lifelong. The marriage ceremony is a service unto itself. It may last between 15 and 30 minutes.

BEFORE THE CEREMONY

Are guests usually invited by a formal invitation?

Yes.

If not stated explicitly, should one assume that children are invited?

Yes.

If one can't attend, what should one do?

RSVP with regrets.

APPROPRIATE ATTIRE

Men: A jacket and tie or slightly more casual attire. No head covering is required.

Women: A dress or a skirt and blouse or a pants suit. Shorts are not appropriate. Arms do not have to be covered nor do hems have to be below the knees. Open-toed shoes and modest jewelry are permissible. No head covering is required.

There are no rules regarding colors of clothing.

GIFTS

Is a gift customarily expected?

Yes, ordinarily cash or such items for the household as small appliances, dishes, towels or blankets.

Should gifts be brought to the ceremony?

Gifts are usually given to the newlyweds at the reception or are sent to their home.

THE CEREMONY

Where will the ceremony take place?

In the family's church.

When should guests arrive and where should they sit?

Arrive shortly before the time for which the service has been called. Ushers may be present to indicate where to sit. If not, sit wherever you wish.

If arriving late, are there times when a guest should *not* enter the ceremony?

Do not enter during prayers or during the processional or recessional.

Are there times when a guest should *not* leave the ceremony?

Do not leave during prayers or during the processional or recessional.

Who are the major officiants, leaders or participants at the ceremony and what do they do?

- *The minister,* who conducts the ceremony.
- *The bride and groom and their wedding party.*
- *The choir,* which sings.
- *The minister of music,* who directs the music.

What books are used?

Only the minister uses a book; guests do not.

To indicate the order of the ceremony:

A program will be provided and periodic announcements will be made by the minister.

Will a guest who is not a member of The Christian Congregation be expected to do anything other than sit?

No.

Are there any parts of the ceremony in which a guest who is not a member of The Christian Congregation should *not* participate?

No.

If not disruptive to the ceremony, is it okay to:

- **Take pictures?** Only with prior permission of the family.
- **Use a video camera?** Only with prior permission of the family.
- **Use a flash camera?** Only with prior permission of the family.
- **Use a tape recorder?** Only with prior permission of the family.

Will contributions to the church be collected at the ceremony?

No.

AFTER THE CEREMONY

Is there usually a reception after the ceremony?

Yes. This may be in the same building as the marriage ceremony, in a catering hall or in a home. It usually consists of light food, such as sandwiches, soft drinks and cookies, but never alcoholic beverages. The reception, which is an opportunity for fellowship and congratulating the newlyweds and taking their photos, may last about 60 minutes.

Would it be considered impolite to neither eat nor drink?

No.

Is there a grace or benediction before eating or drinking?

No.

Is there a grace or benediction after eating or drinking?

No.

Is there a traditional greeting for the family?

Just offer your congratulations.

Is there a traditional form of address for clergy who may be at the reception?

"Reverend." "Doctor" may be used if the minister has a Ph.D. or an honorary doctorate.

Is it okay to leave early?

Yes, but usually only after the wedding cake has been served.

Funerals and Mourning

The Christian Congregation affirms that, in faith, one can look forward to life with God after death. The Church does not believe that one necessarily has an immortal soul, but that one can become immortal by living an ethical life. If one does not achieve immortality, then he or she does not endure everlasting punishment in the equivalent of hell, but is eventually extinguished and ceases to exist in any form.

The funeral is a ceremony unto itself and usually lasts about 15 to 30 minutes.

BEFORE THE CEREMONY

How soon after the death does the funeral usually take place?

Usually within two to three days.

What should someone who is not a member of The Christian Congregation do upon hearing of the death of a member of that faith?

Telephone or visit the bereaved. Express your condolences, and mostly listen to the mourner if that person wants to talk.

APPROPRIATE ATTIRE

Men: A jacket and tie. No head covering is required.

Women: A dress or a skirt and blouse. Arms do not have to be covered nor do hems have to be below the knees. Open-toed shoes and modest jewelry are permissible. No head covering is required.

There are no rules regarding colors of clothing, but somber, dark colors are recommended for men and women.

GIFTS

Is it appropriate to send flowers or make a contribution?

Flowers may be sent to the home of the bereaved. Contributions are optional, but are not ordinarily encouraged.

Is it appropriate to send food?

Yes. This may be sent to the home of the bereaved upon hearing of the news of the death or after the funeral.

THE CEREMONY

Where will the ceremony take place?

At a church or funeral home. Sometimes the funeral will be at the home of the bereaved.

When should guests arrive and where should they sit?

Arrive early. Ushers will advise guests where to sit.

If arriving late, are there times when a guest should *not* enter the ceremony?

Do not enter during prayer.

Will the bereaved family be present at the church or funeral home before the ceremony?

Possibly. If so, briefly express your condolences.

Will there be an open casket?

Usually.

Is a guest expected to view the body?

This is entirely optional.

What is appropriate behavior upon viewing the body?

Stand silently near the casket and view the body. You are seeing a friend for the last time in this earthly sphere.

Who are the major officiants at the ceremony and what do they do?

- *The minister,* who officiates.
- *Musicians or singers,* who provide music.

What books are used?

A hymnal and a Bible. (The Christian Congregation has no official Bible translation. Each church chooses the hymnal and the translation of the Bible it will use.)

To indicate the order of the ceremony:

A program will be provided or the officiating minister may make announcements.

Will a guest who is not a member of The Christian Congregation be expected to do anything other than sit?

No.

Are there any parts of the ceremony in which a guest who is not a member of The Christian Congregation should *not* participate?

No.

If not disruptive to the ceremony, is it okay to:

- **Take pictures?** Yes.
- **Use a video camera?** Yes.
- **Use a flash camera?** No.
- **Use a tape recorder?** Yes.

Will contributions to the church be collected at the ceremony?

No.

THE INTERMENT

Should guests attend the interment?

This is optional.

Whom should one ask for directions?

The funeral director.

What happens at the graveside?

Scriptures and prayers are recited by the minister and the body is committed to the ground.

Do guests who are not members of The Christian Congregation participate at the graveside ceremony?

No. They are simply present.

COMFORTING THE BEREAVED

Is it appropriate to visit the home of the bereaved after the funeral?

Yes, at any mutually convenient time. It is best to visit two or three days after the funeral. The length of the visit depends on your closeness to the bereaved. Typically, one stays about 20 to 30 minutes.

Will there be a religious service at the home of the bereaved?

No.

Will food be served?

This is unlikely. What is certain is that no alcoholic beverages will be served.

How soon after the funeral will a mourner usually return to a normal work schedule?

Usually within three days after the funeral.

How soon after the funeral will a mourner usually return to a normal social schedule?

Usually within a week after the funeral.

Are there mourning customs to which a friend who is not a member of The Christian Congregation should be sensitive?

No.

Are there rituals for observing the anniversary of the death?

No.

V · HOME CELEBRATIONS

Not applicable to The Christian Congregation.

Chapter 5 Contents

5

Church of the Brethren

I · HISTORY AND BELIEFS

The Church of the Brethren began in 1708 in an obscure German principality, Sayn-Wittgenstein-Hohenstein, when five men and three women pledged to base their lives on biblical lessons and truths and "to take up all the commandments of Jesus Christ as an easy yoke." They criticized the Church as inattentive to the Bible and too concerned with maintaining itself as an institution. They also believed that baptism was not for infants, but for believers who had reached a mature age of accountability and could decide for themselves to embrace Christian precepts.

By denying the validity of the baptism each member of this small group had received as infants, they implicitly challenged the authority of the existing Church. Since churches in Germany were closely identified with the state, adult baptism was considered to be not only religious heresy, but also treason. Soon, members of this expanding group were persecuted by the state, not only for their stance on baptism, but also because they refused to take oaths or serve in the military.

In 1719, some Brethren fled Europe for Pennsylvania. Four years later, the entire male membership in the Germantown, Pennsylvania, congregation began an evangelistic mission to preach, baptize and form new congregations throughout the colonies. By the middle of the next century, there were new churches as far as California.

The original members of the Church in Germany had simply

called themselves "brethren," which meant brothers and sisters. But in 1836, legal papers in the United States listed the group as the Fraternity of German Baptists. This became the German Baptist Brethren in 1871, although they were also nicknamed "Dunkers" because of adult baptism by immersion.

In 1908, the German identification disappeared and the name was changed to the Church of the Brethren. There have been recent murmurings about again changing the Church's name since "brethren" generally refers only to males in today's usage. For now, "brethren" is being retained to remind members of the deep connections they have—as sisters and brothers—in their faith.

Church members affirm their belief in Jesus Christ as the Lord and Savior and promise to turn from sin and live in faithfulness to God and to the Church, taking Jesus as their model. The Church insists that members not thoughtlessly adopt the habits and ways of others, and encourages members to think carefully about how to live comfortably, but not ostentatiously, in an affluent society; to be aware of the environment and limited resources in a global community; and to engage in creative efforts to achieve peace and reconciliation. The Church condemns gambling and urges members to refrain from alcohol, drug and tobacco use. Brethren are encouraged to practice nonresistance in the face of violence, and discouraged from engaging in military service since the Church has declared all war to be sin.

Oath-taking is discouraged because the Church of the Brethren believes that Jesus advocated completely abolishing such practices (James 5:12) since persons should always be truthful, not just at particular moments. Taking an oath implies an erratic attitude toward truthfulness since it suggests that, this time, one is being truthful, yet is not truthful at other times. Jesus, according to the Church, taught that a true Christian knows the will of God and is true to it at all times. Indecisiveness, which is fostered by the devil, erodes one's credibility.

The Church also discourages members from resorting to civil court when injured by another because, as Peter Nead, the leading Brethren theologian of the 19th century, wrote, the doctrine taught by Jesus does not allow Christians "to retaliate or seek redress for their grievances. Under the law, retaliation was allowable, but not so under the Gospel of Jesus Christ." Instead, wrote Nead, when a Christian is injured by another, his only recourse is to suffer since that is what Jesus did and that is what anyone wishing to be a child of God must do.

But in a statement written in 1920, the Church slightly relaxed its proscription against members participating in proceedings in a civil court. The statement cited Matthew 5:40-41 and Luke 6:30 to show that Jesus taught that if the legal process cannot be avoided, then the Christian should do more than is required by secular law. The statement gave permission to Brethren to comply with civil law if three preconditions were met: Such action did not violate such Christian principles as nonresistance; one Brethren had not resorted to civil law without the permission of another Brethren whom he was contesting in a court action; and the church's counsel is sought before resorting to civil law.

At least once a year, each church celebrates a "love feast," which may also be called an "agape (pronounced 'ah-GAH-pay') meal." The ceremony includes a mutual footwashing between two congregants of the same gender, who then embrace and give each other a "holy kiss." This is followed by communion and a simple meal. The ritual echoes Jesus' washing of the feet of His disciples at the Last Supper, where He sought to draw them closer into the fold of His love.

Individual Brethren congregations have considerable autonomy. Each sets its own budget and chooses its own pastor, a moderator who conducts the gatherings when Brethren meet to do church business, and a board of administration. Each also belongs to one of the 23 districts that comprise the Annual Conference, which meets each year to make decisions about the future of the Church. Each church can send at least one delegate to the conference.

U.S. churches: 1,106
U.S. membership: 141,800
(data from the 1998 Yearbook of American and Canadian Churches)

For more information, contact:
The Church of the Brethren General Offices
1451 Dundee Avenue
Elgin, IL 60120-1694
(847) 742-5100

II · THE BASIC SERVICE

To Brethren, worship is a meaningful and genuine meeting with God and with Christian sisters and brothers, and is a time to gather to celebrate and affirm the good news of Jesus Christ.

Brethren strive for a balance of emphasis between the communal dimension of worship—the fellowship of those gathered together—and the transcendent nature of worship—standing in awe of the mysterious, transcendent God.

The form or structure of Brethren worship varies from one church to another and from Sunday to Sunday. Although no creed is said, many congregations incorporate elements of more liturgical worship, such as affirmations of faith, litanies of confession, assurances of pardon, readings in unison, and choral anthems. Music, especially congregational singing, is a vital part of worship. Story time with children and the sharing of congregational joys and concerns are also often part of the service.

In virtually all Brethren churches, services are held on Sunday mornings. A small minority may also have services on Wednesday evenings. All services last slightly more than one hour.

APPROPRIATE ATTIRE

Men: A jacket and tie. More casual attire, if modest, is especially appropriate in warm weather. No head covering is required.

Women: A dress or a skirt and blouse or a pants suit. Hems need not reach below the knees nor must clothing cover the arms. Open-toed shoes and modest jewelry are permissible. Some congregations prefer that a small head covering be worn. Traditionally, this "prayer covering" is a symbol of prayer and submission for women. It relates to Paul's admonition in I Corinthians 11:5-7, which states, in part, "...Every woman who has her head uncovered while praying or prophesying disgraces her head." Nevertheless, in recent years, increasingly fewer women have worn "prayer coverings." In those churches where head coverings are still customary, they will not be provided by the church. Guests may want to bring their own head covering—a scarf or a small hat.

There are no rules regarding colors of clothing.

THE SANCTUARY

What are the major sections of the church?

- *The chancel,* from which the pastor leads the service.
- *The baptistery,* where baptism by immersion is performed.
- *The pews,* where congregants and guests are seated.
- *The choir loft or choir section,* where the choir is seated.

THE SERVICE

When should guests arrive and where should they sit?

Arrive at the time for which the service has been called or shortly before that time. Ushers may assist guests with seating. If no ushers are present, sit wherever you wish.

If arriving late, are there times when a guest should *not* enter the service?

Do not enter during times of prayer.

Are there times when a guest should *not* leave the service?

Do not leave during prayer.

Who are the major officiants, leaders or participants and what do they do?

- *The pastor,* who delivers a sermon and may lead the worship.
- *The worship leader,* who directs the worship.
- *The choir director,* who directs the choir.
- *The organist and/or pianist,* who accompany the choir and lead congregational singing.

What are the major ritual objects of the service?

- *The altar or worship center,* which (through flowers or banners or such symbols as a cross or a lit candle) helps focus worshippers' attention on the biblical text or on spiritual matters.

What books are used?

Since each congregation chooses the translation of the Bible it will use, different translations are used throughout the Church. Among the more common translations used is the New Revised Standard Version. Texts also used in services are a worship bulletin published by the local church, and *Hymnal: A Worship Book* (Elgin, Ill.: Brethren Press, 1992).

To indicate the order of the service:

A program or bulletin is commonly distributed or a display near the front of the sanctuary will announce the order of the hymns and readings. The bulletin is usually available from the ushers.

GUEST BEHAVIOR DURING THE SERVICE

Will a guest who is not a member of the Church of the Brethren be expected to do anything other than sit?

It is expected that guests stand, sing and read prayers aloud with the congregation, if they are so inclined. In a few local churches, congregants kneel; in those churches where this occurs, it is expected for guests to do so also, unless this violates their own religious beliefs. Guests who choose not to kneel may remain seated while congregants are kneeling.

Are there any parts of the service in which a guest who is not a member of the Church of the Brethren should *not* participate?

Guests are welcome to participate in all aspects of the service except for possibly the Eucharist. A few churches restrict participation in the Eucharist to church members. Individual churches also determine whether children who have not been baptized may partake of the Eucharist.

If not disruptive to the service, is it okay to:

- **Take pictures?** Yes, if done discreetly.
- **Use a flash?** No.
- **Use a video camera?** Yes.
- **Use a tape recorder?** Yes.

Will contributions to the church be collected at the service?

Yes. The offering plate will be passed through the congregation during the service.

How much is customary to contribute?

It is entirely optional for guests to contribute. If they choose to do so, they may contribute whatever amount they choose. Contributions of $1 to $5 are common.

AFTER THE SERVICE

Is there usually a reception after the service?

There may be a 15-to 30-minute break for coffee and tea between worship and church school.

Is there a traditional form of address for clergy whom a guest may meet?

"Pastor."

GENERAL GUIDELINES AND ADVICE

In some churches, guests may be introduced to congregants by the minister or their host or hostess.

SPECIAL VOCABULARY

Key words or phrases which might be helpful for a visitor to know:

- *Anointing:* The prayerful, loving application of oil to the forehead of someone in physical or spiritual need. Most often done at home or in small group settings, although some congregations have anointings in public worship.
- *Conversation:* Considered to be at the heart of what it means to be a Brethren, who expect to receive new revelations as they discuss the Bible and try to remain open to fresh interpretations of it.
- *Love Feast:* Also called an "agape (pronounced 'ah-GAH-pay') meal." Held at least once a year in each church, this ceremony includes a mutual footwashing between two congregants of the same gender, who then embrace and give each other a "holy kiss." This is followed by a simple meal and communion. The ritual echoes Jesus' washing of the feet of His disciples at the Last Supper, where He sought to draw them closer into the fold of His love and to demonstrate the love and regard they have for one another.
- *Offertory:* The portion of the service set apart for the collection of contributions from the congregation. Also, a musical composition played or sung during an offertory.
- *Pastoral Prayer:* Prayer offered in public worship by the pastor during which the pastor prays on behalf of the entire congregation.

DOGMA AND IDEOLOGY

Members of the Church of the Brethren believe:

◘ Being a disciple of Christ affects all that one says or does.

◘ God, the Creator, is the source of all that exists.

◘ Jesus Christ's death on the cross and subsequent burial were a sacrifice for the sin and for the transgressions of humanity. Christ rose from the dead and ascended into heaven, where He will intercede for all humanity until He judges all humanity when He returns at the end of time.

◘ The Old and New Testaments comprise the Holy Scriptures and the inspired written Word of God. In both Testaments, life is offered to humanity through Christ, who is the only mediator between God and man.

◘ One should live simply, but not austerely; refuse to take oaths or serve in the military; and confront violence with nonresistance.

◘ One should dress modestly, abstain from gambling and tobacco and from using alcohol and drugs, other than for medical purposes.

◘ Their covenant with Christ extends beyond the boundary of their denomination. Thus, Church members follow Christ's compassion by supporting soup kitchens, day care centers and homeless shelters that have no restrictions on whom they serve, and Christ's love by perceiving no enemies and engaging in neither war nor violence.

Some basic books and pamphlets to which a guest can refer to learn more about the Church of the Brethren:

For All Who Minister: A Worship Manual for the Church of the Brethren (Elgin, Ill.: Brethren Press, 1992).

Who Love These Brethren? by Joan Decter (Elgin, Ill.: Brethren Press, 1995).

Church of the Brethren: Another Way of Living and *There Am I in the Midst of Them.* Both of these pamphlets can be obtained from:

The Church of the Brethren General Offices
1451 Dundee Avenue
Elgin, IL 60120-1694

III · HOLY DAYS AND FESTIVALS

◘ *Thanksgiving,* celebrated on the fourth Thursday in November. Celebrates harvest and home, sometimes with a church service that emphasizes thanksgiving and a traditional Thanksgiving dinner at home. There is no traditional greeting for this holiday.

- *Advent,* which begins four Sundays prior to Christmas, during which one prepares for Christ's Coming with His birth at Christmas. There is no traditional greeting for this holiday.

- *Christmas Eve and Christmas,* which always fall on the evening of December 24 and the day of December 25. Celebrates the birth of Christ. Special worship services are held in many congregations on Christmas Eve. The traditional greeting is "Merry Christmas."

- *Ash Wednesday,* which occurs 40 days before Easter, and commemorates the beginning of Lent, which is a season for preparation and penitence before Easter itself. Celebrated only by some congregations. There is no traditional greeting for this holiday.

- *Maundy Thursday,* which always falls on the evening before Good Friday, the day that Christ was crucified. Commemorates the institution of the Eucharist (also known as Communion) and Jesus' subsequent arrest and trial. A church service reenacts the Last Supper with footwashing, a meal and the Eucharist. Some congregations include the Holy Kiss, which may also be called the "Kiss of Peace," and which emulates Jesus' efforts at His Last Supper to draw His disciples closer into His fold of love.

  In a few congregations, one must be a member of the Church of the Brethren to participate in the service. There is no traditional greeting for this holiday.

- *Easter,* which always falls on the Sunday after the first full moon that occurs on or after the Spring equinox of March 21. Commemorates the death and resurrection of Christ. The traditional greeting is "Happy Easter" or "Christ is risen." A guest may respond with "Christ is risen, indeed," or simply with a handshake.

- *World Communion Sunday,* which always falls on the first Sunday of October. Participants in this global observance of the Eucharist join through communion with Christians around the world. There is no traditional greeting for this holiday.

IV · LIFE CYCLE EVENTS

Birth Ceremony

Called a "child's dedication" or a "child's consecration," this ceremony has three emphases: to consecrate or bless the child to the Lord; to consecrate the parents, including a charge for them to be Christian parents; and to consecrate the congregation to be the spiritual family that nurtures and supports the child.

The ceremony may consecrate one or more children and their families. The congregation may present each child and his or her family with a rose or another gift.

Children may be consecrated anytime between infancy and the time of their baptism, which usually occurs in early adolescence. The ceremony is most often part of a regularly scheduled Sunday worship service.

BEFORE THE CEREMONY

Are guests usually invited by a formal invitation?

The family of the child commonly invite relatives and friends orally either on the telephone or in person.

If not stated explicitly, should one assume that children are invited?

Yes.

If one can't attend, what should one do?

RSVP with regrets.

APPROPRIATE ATTIRE

Men: A jacket and tie. No head covering is required.

Women: A dress or a skirt and blouse or a pants suit. Hems need not reach below the knees nor must clothing cover the arms. Open-toed shoes and modest jewelry are permissible. Some congregations prefer that a small head covering be worn. Traditionally, this "prayer covering" is a symbol of prayer and submission for women. It relates to Paul's admonition in I Corinthians 11:5-7, which states, in part, "...Every woman who has her head uncovered while praying or prophesying disgraces her head." In recent years, increasingly fewer women have worn "prayer coverings." In those churches where head coverings are still customary, they will not be provided by the church. Guests may want to bring their own head covering—a scarf or a small hat.

There are no rules regarding colors of clothing.

GIFTS

Is a gift customarily expected?

No.

Should gifts be brought to the ceremony?

See above.

THE CEREMONY

Where will the ceremony take place?

In the main sanctuary of the parents' church.

When should guests arrive and where should they sit?

Arrive at the time for which the service has been called or shortly before that time. Ushers may advise guests where to sit or the family may designate where guests should sit. If no ushers or family members are present, sit wherever you wish.

If arriving late, are there times when a guest should *not* enter the ceremony?

Do not enter during prayer.

Are there times when a guest should *not* leave the ceremony?

Do not leave during prayer.

Who are the major officiants, leaders or participants at the ceremony and what do they do?

- *The pastor,* who leads the service and blesses the child.
- *A deacon,* who may be present to assist the pastor.
- *The child and his or her parents.* Siblings of the child being baptized may also participate.

What books are used?

Since each congregation chooses the translation of the Bible it will use, different translations are used throughout the Church. Among the more common translations used is the New Revised Standard Version. Texts also used in services are a worship bulletin published by the local church, and *Hymnal: A Worship Book* (Elgin, Ill.: Brethren Press, 1992).

To indicate the order of the ceremony:

The ceremony will be incorporated into the regular Sunday morning service. For the rest of the service, a program or bulletin is commonly distributed or a display near the front of the sanctuary will announce the order of the hymns and readings. The bulletin is usually available from the ushers.

Will a guest who is not a member of the Church of the Brethren be expected to do anything other than sit?

The family of the child being consecrated may request close friends or relatives to come with them and the child to the front of the church to symbolize the support the child will receive from them. It is appropriate for guests to stand, sing and read prayers aloud with the congregation. In a few local churches during the rest of the service, congregants may kneel. In those churches where this is done, it is expected for a guest to do so, unless this violates their own religious beliefs. Guests who do not kneel may remain seated while congregants are kneeling.

Are there any parts of the ceremony in which a guest who is not a member of the Church of the Brethren should *not* participate?

Guests are welcome to participate in all aspects of the service except for possibly the Eucharist. A few churches restrict participation in the Eucharist to church members. Individual churches also determine whether children who have not been baptized may partake of the Eucharist.

If not disruptive to the ceremony, is it okay to:

■ **Take pictures?** Yes, if done discreetly.
■ **Use a flash?** No.
■ **Use a video camera?** Yes.
■ **Use a tape recorder?** Yes.

Will contributions to the church be collected at the ceremony?

There will be no collection during the consecration ceremony, but an offering plate will be passed through the congregation during the rest of the service.

How much is customary to contribute?

It is entirely optional for guests to contribute. If they choose to do so, they may contribute whatever amount they choose. Contributions of $1 to $5 are common.

AFTER THE CEREMONY

Is there usually a reception after the ceremony?

Possibly. If there is one, it will probably be in the family's home or a catering hall and may include light foods or a complete meal, but not alcoholic beverages. There may be secular music, but there is usually no dancing. The reception may last one to two hours.

Would it be considered impolite to neither eat nor drink?

No.

Is there a grace or benediction before eating or drinking?

Grace will probably be said.

Is there a grace or benediction after eating or drinking?

No.

Is there a traditional greeting for the family?

Just offer your congratulations.

Is there a traditional form of address for clergy who may be at the reception?

"Pastor."

Is it okay to leave early?

Yes.

Initiation Ceremony

Called "baptism," this connotes a commitment to Jesus Christ as one's personal Lord and Savior. Candidates for baptism must be instructed in Christian belief and in the history, beliefs and practices of the Church of the Brethren.

Brethren believe that baptism is a response to God's saving of humanity through the life, death and resurrection of Jesus Christ; that it symbolizes spiritual cleansing and a new life; and is an outward sign of an inner experience.

Baptism in the Church is by full immersion three times, after which the pastor lays his or her hands on the candidate's head and prays for forgiveness of sin and the gift of the Holy Spirit, which is the presence of Christ to guide and empower an individual.

Youths as young as eight or nine years of age, as well as adults, are eligible for baptism, which may be performed for individuals or for an entire class of religious school students. The 15-to 30-minute ceremony is usually part of a larger Sunday morning service. The service itself lasts slightly more than one hour.

BEFORE THE CEREMONY

Are guests usually invited by a formal invitation?

The person being baptized or his or her family may invite guests either on the telephone or in person.

If not stated explicitly, should one assume that children are invited?

Yes.

If one can't attend, what should one do?

RSVP with regrets.

APPROPRIATE ATTIRE

Men: A jacket and tie, or modest casual clothing, especially in warm weather. No head covering is required.

Women: A dress or a skirt and blouse or a pants suit. Hems need not reach below the knees nor must clothing cover the arms. Open-toed shoes and modest jewelry are permissible. Some congregations prefer that a small head covering be worn. Traditionally, this "prayer covering" is a symbol of prayer and submission for women. It relates to Paul's admonition in I Corinthians 11:5-7, which states, in part, "...Every woman who has her head uncovered while praying or prophesying disgraces her head." Nevertheless, in recent years, increasingly fewer women have worn "prayer coverings." In those churches where head coverings are still customary, they will not be provided by the church. Guests may want to bring their own head covering—a scarf or small hat.

There are no rules regarding colors of clothing.

GIFTS

Is a gift customarily expected?

No.

Should gifts be brought to the ceremony?

See above.

THE CEREMONY

Where will the ceremony take place?

Usually at the baptistery in the individual's church; sometimes at a special time other than Sunday morning at a stream, a pond, a lake or the ocean.

When should guests arrive and where should they sit?

Arrive at the time for which the service has been called or shortly before that time. If the ceremony is held at a church, ushers may advise guests where to sit. If no ushers are present, sit wherever you wish.

If arriving late, are there times when a guest should *not* enter the ceremony?

Do not enter during the baptismal ceremony or during prayer.

Are there times when a guest should *not* leave the ceremony?

Do not leave during the baptismal ceremony or during prayer.

Who are the major officiants, leaders or participants in the ceremony and what do they do?

- *The pastor,* who leads the service and blesses the person being baptized.
- *A deacon,* who may be present to assist the pastor.
- *The youth or adult being baptized.*

What books are used?

Since each congregation chooses the translation of the Bible it will use, different translations are used throughout the Church. Among the more common translations used is the New Revised Standard Version. Texts also used in services are a worship bulletin published by the local church, and *Hymnal: A Worship Book* (Elgin, Ill.: Brethren Press, 1992).

To indicate the order of the ceremony:

Most often, the ceremony is incorporated into the regular Sunday morning service. For the rest of the service, a program will be distributed or a display near the front of the sanctuary will announce the order of the hymns. These may also be included in a printed bulletin that is distributed at the service.

Will a guest who is not a member of the Church of the Brethren be expected to do anything other than sit?

It is expected for guests to stand, sing and read prayers aloud with the congregation. In a few local churches, congregants kneel; in those churches where this is done, it is expected for a guest to do so also, unless this violates their own religious beliefs. Guests who choose not to kneel may remain seated while congregants are kneeling.

Are there any parts of the service in which a guest who is not a member of the Church of the Brethren should *not* participate?

Guests are welcome to participate in all aspects of the service except for possibly the Eucharist. A few churches restrict participation in the Eucharist to church members. Individual churches also determine whether children who have not been baptized may partake of the Eucharist.

If not disruptive to the ceremony, is it okay to:

◘ **Take pictures?** Yes, if done discreetly.
◘ **Use a flash?** No.
◘ **Use a video camera?** Yes.
◘ **Use a tape recorder?** Yes

Will contributions to the church be collected at the ceremony?

There will be no collection during the baptism, but an offering plate will be passed through the congregation during the rest of the service.

How much is customary to contribute?

It is entirely optional for guests to contribute. If they choose to do so, they may contribute whatever amount they choose. Contributions of $1 to $5 are common.

AFTER THE CEREMONY

Is there usually a reception after the ceremony?

Possibly. If there is one, it will probably be in the same building as the baptism or in a catering hall. The reception, which is an opportunity to extend your best wishes to the newly-baptized person(s), may include light foods, fruit, tea and coffee, but no alcoholic beverages. There will be no music or dancing. The reception may last less than half an hour.

Would it be considered impolite to neither eat nor drink?
No.

Is there a grace or benediction before eating or drinking?
A grace or blessing may be said.

Is there a grace or benediction after eating or drinking?
No.

Is there a traditional greeting for the family?
Just offer your congratulations.

Is there a traditional form of address for clergy who may be at the reception?
"Pastor."

Is it okay to leave early?
Yes.

Marriage Ceremony

A wedding ceremony recognizes the commitment of two people who agree to love each other faithfully and to live together within God's love to their mutual benefit. God joins the couple, but those who attend the wedding agree, by their presence, to offer them encouragement and support.

The wedding ceremony is a ceremony unto itself. It may last from 30 to 60 minutes.

BEFORE THE CEREMONY

Are guests usually invited by a formal invitation?
Yes.

If not stated explicitly, should one assume that children are invited?
Yes.

If one can't attend, what should one do?
RSVP with regrets.

APPROPRIATE ATTIRE

Men: A jacket and tie or more casual attire, depending on local custom. No head covering is required.

Women: A dress or a skirt and blouse or a pants suit. Hems need not reach below the knees nor must clothing cover the arms. Open-toed shoes and modest jewelry are permissible. Some congregations prefer that a small head covering be worn. Traditionally, this "prayer covering" is a symbol of prayer and submission for women. It relates to Paul's admonition in I Corinthians 5-7, which states, in part, "... Every woman who has her head uncovered while praying or prophesying disgraces her head." Nevertheless, in recent years, increasingly fewer women have worn "prayer coverings." In those churches where head coverings are still customary, they will not be provided by the church. Guests may want to bring their own head covering—a scarf or small hat.

There are no rules regarding colors of clothing.

GIFTS

Is a gift customarily expected?

Usually, unless stipulated otherwise.

Should gifts be brought to the ceremony?

Local customs vary, but it is always correct to send gifts to the bride's home in advance of the wedding.

THE CEREMONY

Where will the ceremony take place?

Locations vary. The ceremony may be in a church, a home or outdoors.

When should guests arrive and where should they sit?

Arrive shortly before the time for which the ceremony has been called. Ushers will advise guests where to sit.

If arriving late, are there times when a guest should *not* enter the ceremony?

Do not enter during the processional of the wedding party or while prayers or marriage vows are being recited.

Are there times when a guest should *not* leave the ceremony?

Do not leave during the prayers or marriage vows or the recessional of the wedding party.

Who are the major officiants, leaders or participants at the ceremony and what do they do?

- *The pastor(s),* who officiates at the ceremony and witnesses the vows of the bride and groom.
- *The bride and groom and their wedding party.*
- *An instrumentalist, a vocalist and/or a choir.*

What books are used?

Since each congregation chooses the translation of the Bible it will use, different translations are used throughout the Church. Among the more common translations used is the New Revised Standard Version. Texts also used in services are a worship bulletin published by the local church, and *Hymnal: A Worship Book* (Elgin, Ill.: Brethren Press, 1992).

To indicate the order of the ceremony:

A program will usually be distributed or there will be periodic instructions by the pastor.

Will a guest who is not a member of the Church of the Brethren be expected to do anything other than sit?

It is expected for each guest to stand, sing and read prayers aloud with other guests if these do not violate their religious beliefs.

Are there any parts of the ceremony in which a guest who is not a member of the Church of the Brethren should *not* participate?

No.

If not disruptive to the ceremony, is it okay to:

- **Take pictures?** Only with prior permission of the family and pastor.
- **Use a flash?** No.
- **Use a video camera?** Only with prior permission of the family and pastor.
- **Use a tape recorder?** Only with prior permission of the family and pastor.

Will contributions to the church be collected at the ceremony?

No.

AFTER THE CEREMONY

Is there usually a reception after the ceremony?

There is usually a reception. This may be held in the church reception hall, in a catering hall or at a home. There may be light food served or a complete meal, but no alcoholic beverages if the reception is held in a church building. There may be a nonalcoholic toast to the newlyweds, and sometimes music and possibly dancing. Gifts are sometimes opened at the reception, which may last for one to two hours.

Would it be considered impolite to neither eat nor drink?

No.

Is there a grace or benediction before eating or drinking?

Grace is usually said.

Is there a grace or benediction after eating or drinking?

No.

Is there a traditional greeting for the family?

Just offer your congratulations.

Is there a traditional form of address for clergy who may be at the reception?

"Pastor."

Is it okay to leave early?

Yes.

Funerals and Mourning

The Brethren funeral service or memorial service celebrates the resurrection promised by Jesus Christ: "I am the resurrection and the life. Those who believe in Me, even though they die, will live, and everyone who lives and believes in Me will never die."

The service also celebrates the individual who has died, and is an opportunity to reflect upon the meaning of his or her life.

The funeral ceremony is a ceremony unto itself and may last about 30 to 60 minutes.

BEFORE THE CEREMONY

How soon after the death does the funeral or memorial service usually take place?

Two to three days. If a memorial service is held instead of a funeral, it may be held from one to three weeks after the death itself.

What should someone who is not a member of the Church of the Brethren do upon hearing of the death of a member of that faith?

If the deceased was a close friend or a relative, telephone or visit the bereaved to express your condolences. If a "visitation" or a "wake" is scheduled, visit then if you can.

APPROPRIATE ATTIRE

Men: A jacket and tie or more casual attire, depending on local custom. No head covering is required.

Women: A dress or a skirt and blouse or a pants suit. Hems need not reach below the knees nor must clothing cover the arms. Open-toed shoes and modest jewelry are permissible. No head covering is required.

There are no rules regarding colors of clothing.

GIFTS

Is it appropriate to send flowers or make a contribution?

Flowers may be sent to the funeral service or to the home of the bereaved upon hearing of the death of the deceased or before or after the funeral. In lieu of flowers, contributions may be made to a fund or charity designated by the family of the deceased.

Is it appropriate to send food?

Yes. This may be sent to the home of the bereaved upon hearing of the death or after the funeral.

THE CEREMONY

Where will the ceremony take place?

In a church or a funeral home.

When should guests arrive and where should they sit?

Arrive at the time for which the ceremony has been called. Ushers may advise guests where to sit. If there are no ushers, sit wherever you wish.

If arriving late, are there times when a guest should *not* enter the ceremony?

Ushers will advise you when to enter.

Will the bereaved family be present at the church before the ceremony?

Possibly.

Is there a traditional greeting for the family?

Just express your sympathy for the bereaved.

Will there be an open casket?

Possibly.

Is a guest expected to view the body?

This is entirely optional.

What is appropriate behavior upon viewing the body?

Be quiet and respectful. Gaze silently at the deceased for a brief moment.

Who are the major officiants at the ceremony and what do they do?

- *The pastor,* who officiates.
- *The eulogist(s),* who delivers a eulogy about the deceased.
- *A choir, a vocal ensemble, or a soloist,* who may be present to sing.
- *An organist or a pianist,* who provides music.

What books are used?

Since each congregation chooses the translation of the Bible it will use, different translations are used throughout the Church. Among the more common translations used is the New Revised Standard Version. Also used will be *Hymnal: A Worship Book* (Elgin, Ill.: Brethren Press, 1992).

To indicate the order of the ceremony:

A program may be provided.

Will a guest who is not a member of the Church of the Brethren be expected to do anything other than sit?

No. It is entirely optional for guests to stand, kneel, read prayers aloud and sing with other guests.

Are there any parts of the ceremony in which a guest who is not a member of the Church of the Brethren should *not* participate?

No.

If not disruptive to the ceremony, is it okay to:

- **Take pictures?** No.
- **Use a flash?** No.
- **Use a video camera?** No.
- **Use a tape recorder?** Only with prior approval of the bereaved.

Will contributions to the church be collected at the ceremony?

No.

THE INTERMENT

Should guests attend the interment?

This is entirely optional.

Whom should one ask for directions?

The funeral director or a member of the family of the deceased.

What happens at the graveside?

Scripture is read, usually Isaiah 40:6b, 8 or 66:13; or Psalm 46:1-2a, 103-13-14, or 121:1-2, 7b-8. Prayers are then invoked and the body is committed to the ground.

Do guests who are not members of the Church of the Brethren participate at the graveside ceremony?

No. They are simply present.

COMFORTING THE BEREAVED

Is it appropriate to visit the home of the bereaved after the funeral?

Yes. It is recommended that the visit be brief. When visiting, express your sympathy to the bereaved and offer specific help to them.

Will there be a religious service at the home of the bereaved?

This is rare.

Will food be served?

In many congregations, a fellowship meal is served in the church to guests, family, and friends after the funeral or memorial service.

How soon after the funeral will a mourner usually return to a normal work schedule?

This varies according to one's personal needs. There is no doctrine on mourning.

How soon after the funeral will a mourner usually return to a normal social schedule?

This varies according to one's personal needs. There is no doctrine on mourning.

Are there mourning customs to which a friend who is not a member of the Church of the Brethren should be sensitive?

No, but the thoughtful and compassionate reflections of friends is encouraged.

Are there rituals for observing the anniversary of the death?

No.

V · HOME CELEBRATIONS

Anointing

When does it occur?

When a congregant is ill, physically or spiritually. Brethren may ask for anointing before surgery or during serious illness, or in times of grief, emotional turmoil or broken relationships.

What is its significance?

Anointing is a way for God's grace and blessing to restore wholeness and health.

What is the proper greeting to the celebrants?

Express your prayerful support for them, perhaps using such phrases as "God's blessing upon you" or "May the peace of God be upon you."

BEFORE THE CEREMONY

Are guests usually invited by formal invitation?

Yes.

If not stated explicitly, should one assume children are invited?

No.

If one can't attend, what should one do?

Inform the person who will be anointed of your inability to attend with a call or a note.

APPROPRIATE ATTIRE

Men: A jacket and tie. More casual attire, if modest, is especially appropriate in warm weather. No head covering is required.

Women: A dress or a skirt and blouse or a pants suit. Hems need not reach below the knees, but it is preferable that clothing cover the arms. Open-toed shoes and modest jewelry are permissible. If the anointing is held in a church, some congregations prefer that a head covering be worn. Traditionally, this "prayer covering" is a symbol of prayer and submission for women. It relates to Paul's admonition in I Corinthians 11: 5-7, which states, in part, "...Every woman who has her head uncovered while praying or prophesying disgraces her head." Nevertheless, in recent years, increasingly fewer women have worn "prayer coverings." In those churches where head coverings are still customary, they will not be provided by the church. Guests may want to bring their own head covering—a scarf or small hat.

There are no rules regarding colors of clothing.

GIFTS

Is a gift customarily expected?

No.

If one decides to give a gift, is a certain type of gift appropriate?

See above.

THE CEREMONY

Anointing is a practice based on Hebrew and Christian scripture (Genesis 5:1-32; Genesis 12:1-3; Mark 14:24; Corinthians 11:25). Anointing with oil is associated in these texts with the covenant relationship throughout the Old Testament; with priests and kings who were anointed for their special tasks; with the cleansing of lepers; and with receiving comfort and strength.

The anointing ceremony is most often done at home or in small group settings, although some congregations have anointings in public worship. A time is provided for the person being anointed to make a confession, and then the minister or another representative of the church applies oil three times to the forehead. This symbolizes forgiveness of sin, strengthening of faith, and healing of mind, body and spirit. Finally, the minister or church representative lays hands on the one to be anointed, sometimes inviting others to do the same, and prays specifically for this person's expressed concern. The laying on of hands is a reminder that the whole congregation, whether present or not, joins in prayer and support.

The ceremony may last 10 to 15 minutes.

What are the major ritual objects of the ceremony?

- *Oil*, which is applied with love and a prayer to the forehead of the person in physical or spiritual need.

What books are used?

The New Revised Standard Version of the Bible or another translation; and possibly *Hymnal: A Worship Book* (Elgin, Ill.: Brethren Press, 1992).

Will a guest who is not a member of the Church of the Brethren be expected to do anything other than sit?

Sometimes each participant joins in an oral prayer.

Are there any parts of the ceremony in which a guest who is not a member of the Church of the Brethren should *not* participate?

No.

If not disruptive to the ceremony, is it okay to:

- **Take pictures?** No.
- **Use a flash?** No.
- **Use a video camera?** No.
- **Use a tape recorder?** No.

EATING AND DRINKING

Is a meal part of the celebration?
No.

Will there be alcoholic beverages?
No.

Would it be considered impolite to neither eat nor drink?
See above.

Will there be:
◘ **Dancing?** No.
◘ **Music?** No.

GENERAL GUIDELINES AND ADVICE

Those present at an anointing that is held at a home or a hospital room should leave promptly after the ceremony and after giving words of encouragement and support, so the person anointed has time for personal reflection and prayer.

Chapter 6 Contents

6

Church of the Nazarene

I · HISTORY AND BELIEFS

The distant roots of Church of the Nazarene are in Methodism; its more recent roots are in the teachings of John Wesley, who led a revival centered around the doctrines of Holiness and sanctification in 18th-century England; and its most recent roots are in three churches that merged in 1907 and 1908: The Association of Pentecostal Churches, which was based in New York and New England; the Holiness Church of Christ, which was based in the South; and the Church of the Nazarene, based in California.

The church's doctrine centers around "sanctification," which is a feeling of grace stemming from "regeneration." This latter term refers to the sense of being made anew through faith in Jesus Christ. All pastors (who may also be called "ministers") and local church officials must profess this experience. Other prime doctrines are that the Scriptures contain all truths necessary to Christian faith and living; that through His death, Christ atoned for the sins of humanity; and that upon Christ's return, the dead will be resurrected.

Tobacco and alcohol use are prohibited. Church members believe in divine healing, but not to the exclusion of medical aid.

Each of the Church's 85 districts in the United States and Canada is supervised by a district superintendent, who is elected for a four-year term by members of the district assembly. Internationally, the Church is administered by a general board, which consists of an equal number of lay members and ministers.

The Church emphasizes evangelism, and more than 650 missionaries conduct missionary work around the globe.

Worldwide, there are almost 850,000 Nazarenes (as members of the Church of the Nazarene are called) in more than 8,600 churches.

U.S. churches: 5,135
U.S. membership: 608,000
(data from the 1998 Yearbook of American and Canadian Churches*)*

For more information, contact:
The Church of the Nazarene
6401 The Paseo
Kansas City, MO 64131
(816) 333-7000

Canadian churches: 182
Canadian membership: 11,931
(data from the 1998 Yearbook of American and Canadian Churches)

For more information, contact:
Church of the Nazarene Canada
20 Regan Road, Unit 9
Brampton, ON L7A 1C3
(905) 846-4220

II · THE BASIC SERVICE

The worship service usually begins with prayers, singing of hymns and/or praise choruses (brief verses, usually from the Scriptures, that celebrate God) and scripture readings. The sermon, which usually addresses practical aspects of life, is the primary focus of the service.

Churches observe communion, also called the Lord's Supper, at least once during each quarter of the year. It may be offered more frequently at the discretion of the pastor and each local congregation. These symbols of Christ's body and blood—bread and grape juice—may be received by all believers in Christ regardless of their particular church affiliation.

Most churches have services on Sunday mornings and evenings. A few have them on Saturday night, as well. Services usually last about 60 to 75 minutes.

APPROPRIATE ATTIRE

Men: A jacket and tie or more casual attire, depending on the specific church and season. No head covering is required.

Women: A dress or skirt and blouse is most common. Hems need not reach below the knees nor must clothing cover the arms. Open-toed shoes and modest jewelry are permissible. No head covering is required.

There are no rules regarding colors of clothing.

THE SANCTUARY

What are the major sections of the church?

- *The foyer or narthex,* the entry area of the church where congregants and guests are greeted and may have "fellowship," or a reception, after the service.
- *The sanctuary or chapel,* where the congregation is seated and the service is conducted.
- *The chancel,* the platform area on which is located the pulpit and/or lectern and from which the service is led by musicians and pastors.

THE SERVICE

When should guests arrive and where should they sit?

Arrive early or at the time for which the service has been called. There is no designated or assigned seating. Ushers will assist in seating people where they feel most comfortable.

If arriving late, are there times when a guest should not enter the service?

Do not enter during prayers. Ushers are usually present to advise congregants and guests when to enter.

Are there times when a guest should not leave the service?

Do not leave during the sermon or the benediction.

Who are the major officiants, leaders or participants and what do they do?

- *The pastor,* who presides during the service and preaches the sermon.
- *The music minister,* who leads the congregational singing and directs the choir.

■ *The choir or worship team,* which provides music during the service.
■ *Greeters/ushers,* who welcome congregants and guests and assist them as needed.

What are the major ritual objects of the service?

■ *Grape juice and bread,* which comprise the elements of communion (the Lord's Supper). They are considered to be a memorial to the body and blood of Jesus Christ and are also a reminder of His Second Coming.

What books are used?

Hymnals are placed in the pew racks. These are usually *Sing to the Lord* edited by Ken Bible (Kansas City, Mo.: Lillenas Publishing Co., 1993). Worshippers bring their own Bibles. Several translations of the Bible may be used by congregants at the same service. The most common are the King James version, the New International Version, and the New Revised Standard Version.

To indicate the order of the service:

A program is often distributed.

GUEST BEHAVIOR DURING THE SERVICE

Will a guest who is not a Nazarene be expected to do anything other than sit?

Guests are expected to also stand when the congregation rises.

Are there any parts of the service in which a non-Nazarene guest should *not* participate?

Christians who are not Nazarenes may receive communion. It is inappropriate for guests who are not professing Christians to do so.

If not disruptive to the service, is it okay to:

■ **Take pictures?** Only with prior permission of the pastor.
■ **Use a flash?** Only with prior permission of the pastor.
■ **Use a video camera?** Only with prior permission of the pastor.
■ **Use a tape recorder?** Only with prior permission of the pastor.

Will contributions to the church be collected at the service?

Yes.

How much is customary to contribute?

Most Nazarenes support the Church with tithes and offerings. It is entirely optional for guests to contribute. While the amount of the contribution is completely at the discretion of congregants or visitors and the Church of the Nazarene is not comfortable recommending specific amounts to guests, contributions between $1 and $5 are common.

AFTER THE SERVICE

Is there usually a reception after the service?

There is often an informal reception called a "fellowship," at which coffee, tea, cake and cookies—but no alcoholic beverages—will be served. A prayer is often said before eating. There is no concluding ritual after eating. "Fellowship" may last about 30 minutes.

Is there a traditional form of address for clergy whom a guest may meet at the fellowship?

"Pastor."

Is it okay to leave early?

No.

GENERAL GUIDELINES AND ADVICE

None provided.

SPECIAL VOCABULARY

Key words or phrases which might be helpful for a visitor to know:

- *Sanctification:* A feeling of grace.
- *Regeneration:* A sense of being made anew through faith in Jesus Christ.

DOGMA AND IDEOLOGY

Nazarenes believe:

- There is one God—the Father, the Son and the Holy Spirit.
- The Old and the New Scriptures were given by general inspiration and contain all truth necessary to faith and Christian living.
- Man is born with a fallen nature and is, therefore, inclined to evil.
- Atonement through Jesus Christ is for the entire human race; and

that whoever repents and believes in the Lord Jesus Christ is saved from sin.

▪ Believers are to be sanctified wholly, subsequent to regeneration, through faith in the Lord Jesus Christ.

▪ The Holy Spirit bears witness to the new birth and to the entire sanctification of believers.

▪ When Jesus Christ returns, the dead will be raised and the final judgment of all humanity will take place.

A basic book to which a guest can refer to learn more about the Church of the Nazarene:

The Manual of the Church of the Nazarene (available from the Nazarene Publishing House, 6401 The Paseo, Kansas City, Mo. 64131) contains the church's history, constitution, governance and rituals.

III · HOLY DAYS AND FESTIVALS

▪ *Christmas,* celebrated on December 25. Marks the birth of Jesus Christ. Church members and non-church members greet each other with "Merry Christmas!"

▪ *Good Friday.* The date of observance varies, although it usually occurs in April and is always the Friday before Easter. Marks the crucifixion of Christ in Jerusalem. There is no traditional greeting for this holiday.

▪ *Easter.* The date of observance varies, but it usually occurs in April and is always on the Sunday after the first full moon that occurs on or after the spring equinox of March 21. Commemorates the resurrection of Jesus Christ after His crucifixion. The traditional greeting is "He is risen!" The response to this among Nazarenes is "He is risen, indeed!" A non-believer may respond silently with a handshake.

▪ *Pentecost.* Occurs 50 days after Easter because this is when the Holy Spirit (the spirit of Jesus) descended on His apostles. Celebrates the power of the Holy Spirit and its manifestation in the early Christian church. There is no traditional greeting for this holiday.

IV · LIFE CYCLE EVENTS

Birth Ceremony

The age for the birth ceremony can range from infancy until about five years of age. During the service, parents acknowledge before the congregation the gift of a new life and profess their commitment to "raise the child in the nurture and admonition of the Lord."

The dedication, which is the same for males and females, usually lasts about 10 to 15 minutes. It may be part of a Sunday morning worship service that lasts about 60 minutes.

BEFORE THE CEREMONY

Are guests usually invited by a formal invitation?

They are ordinarily invited orally over the telephone or in person.

If not stated explicitly, should one assume that children are invited?

Yes.

If one can't attend, what should one do?

RSVP with regrets. Gifts are not expected.

APPROPRIATE ATTIRE

Men: A jacket and tie or more casual attire, depending on the specific church and season. No head covering is required.

Women: A dress or skirt and blouse is most common. Hems need not reach below the knees nor must clothing cover the arms. Open-toed shoes and modest jewelry are permissible. No head covering is required.

There are no rules regarding colors of clothing.

GIFTS

Is a gift customarily expected?

No.

Should gifts be brought to the ceremony?

See above.

THE CEREMONY

Where will the ceremony take place?

In the church sanctuary.

When should guests arrive and where should they sit?

Arrive early or at the time for which the service has been called. There is no designated or assigned seating. Ushers will assist in seating people where they feel most comfortable.

If arriving late, are there times when a guest should *not* enter the ceremony?

Do not enter during prayers. Ushers are usually present to advise congregants and guests when to enter.

Are there times when a guest should *not* leave the ceremony?

Do not leave during the sermon or the benediction.

Who are the major officiants, leaders or participants at the ceremony and what do they do?

- *The pastor,* who presides during the dedication service and the entire worship service.
- *The parents and their child.*

What books are used?

For the dedication ceremony, only the pastor uses a book. For the rest of the service of which the dedication ceremony is a part, congregants use a hymnal and Bible. Hymnals are placed in the pew racks. These are usually *Sing to the Lord* edited by Ken Bible (Kansas City, Mo.: Lillenas Publishing Co., 1993). Worshippers bring their own Bibles. Several translations of the Bible may be used by congregants at the same service. The most common are the King James version, the New International Version, and the New Revised Standard Version.

To indicate the order of the ceremony:

A program is often distributed.

Will a guest who is not a Nazarene be expected to do anything other than sit?

Guests are expected to stand when the congregation rises.

Are there any parts of the ceremony in which a non-Nazarene guest should *not* participate?

Christians who are not Nazarenes may receive communion. It is inappropriate for guests who are not professing Christians to do so.

If not disruptive to the ceremony, is it okay to:

◨ **Take pictures?** Only with prior permission of the pastor.
◨ **Use a flash?** Only with prior permission of the pastor.
◨ **Use a video camera?** Only with prior permission of the pastor.
◨ **Use a tape recorder?** Only with prior permission of the pastor.

Will contributions to the church be collected at the ceremony?

Yes.

How much is customary to contribute?

Most Nazarenes support the Church with tithes and offerings. While the amount of the contribution is completely at the discretion of congregants or visitors and the Church of the Nazarene is not comfortable recommending specific amounts to guests, contributions between $1 and $5 are common.

AFTER THE CEREMONY

Is there usually a reception after the ceremony?

Possibly. If there is a reception, it may be held at the home of the parents of the newborn or at the church fellowship hall. Usually, the food served consists of cake and cookies and non-alcoholic beverages.

Would it be considered impolite to neither eat nor drink?

No.

Is there a grace or benediction before eating or drinking?

Yes.

Is there a grace or benediction after eating or drinking?

No.

Is there a traditional greeting for the family?

Just offer your congratulations.

Is there a traditional form of address for clergy who may be at the reception?

"Pastor."

Is it okay to leave early?

Yes.

Initiation Ceremony

During this ceremony, which is called a baptism, an individual is completely immersed into the baptismal waters. The ceremony represents an active, volitional, public declaration of one's commitment to the Lord. One's downward movement in the baptismal waters symbolizes the death of Jesus; the upward movement symbolizes His resurrection. Baptism occurs at the "age of accountability," which the Church has not defined, but which is assumed to usually occur between the ages of 10 to 15 years old. The actual baptism takes about five to ten minutes, although the larger basic service of which it is a part lasts about one hour.

BEFORE THE CEREMONY

Are guests usually invited by a formal invitation?

They are ordinarily invited orally over the telephone or in person.

If not stated explicitly, should one assume that children are invited?

Yes.

If one can't attend, what should one do?

RSVP with regrets. Gifts are not expected.

APPROPRIATE ATTIRE

Men: A jacket and tie or more casual attire, depending on the specific church and season. No head covering is required.

Women: A dress or skirt and blouse is most common. Hems need not reach below the knees nor must clothing cover the arms. Open-toed shoes and modest jewelry are permissible. No head covering is required.

There are no rules regarding colors of clothing.

GIFTS

Is a gift customarily expected?

No.

Should gifts be brought to the ceremony?

See above.

THE CEREMONY

Where will the ceremony take place?

In the church sanctuary.

When should guests arrive and where should they sit?

Arrive early or at the time for which the service has been called. There is no designated or assigned seating. Ushers will assist in seating people where they feel most comfortable.

If arriving late, are there times when a guest should *not* enter the ceremony?

Do not enter during prayers. Ushers usually are present to advise congregants and guests when to enter.

Are there times when a guest should *not* leave the ceremony?

Do not leave during the sermon or the benediction.

Who are the major officiants, leaders or participants at the ceremony and what do they do?

- *The pastor,* who presides during the baptism and the entire worship service.
- *The person being baptized.*

What books are used?

For the baptism ceremony, only the pastor uses a book. For the rest of the service of which the baptism is a part, congregants use a hymnal and Bible. Hymnals are placed in the pew racks. These are usually *Sing to the Lord* edited by Ken Bible (Kansas City, Mo.: Lillenas Publishing Co., 1993). Worshippers bring their own Bibles. Several translations of the Bible may be used by congregants at the same service. The most common are the King James version, the New International Version, and the New Revised Standard Version.

To indicate the order of the ceremony:

A program is often distributed.

Will a guest who is not a Nazarene be expected to do anything other than sit?

Guests are expected to stand when the congregation rises.

Are there any parts of the service in which a non-Nazarene guest should *not* participate?

Christians who are not Nazarenes may receive communion. It is inappropriate for guests who are not professing Christians to do so.

If not disruptive to the ceremony, is it okay to:

◘ **Take pictures?** Only with prior permission of the pastor.
◘ **Use a flash?** Only with prior permission of the pastor.
◘ **Use a video camera?** Only with prior permission of the pastor.
◘ **Use a tape recorder?** Only with prior permission of the pastor.

Will contributions to the church be collected at the ceremony?

Yes.

How much is customary to contribute?

Most Nazarenes support the Church with tithes and offerings. While the amount of the contribution is completely at the discretion of congregants or visitors and the Church of the Nazarene is not comfortable recommending specific amounts to guests, contributions between $1 and $5 are common.

AFTER THE CEREMONY

Is there usually a reception after the ceremony?

Possibly. If there is a reception, the food served there usually consists of cake and cookies and non-alcoholic beverages.

Would it be considered impolite to neither eat nor drink?

No.

Is there a grace or benediction before eating or drinking?

Yes.

Is there a grace or benediction after eating or drinking?

No.

Is there a traditional greeting for the family?

Just offer your congratulations.

Is there a traditional form of address for clergy who may be at the reception?

"Pastor."

Is it okay to leave early?

Yes.

Marriage Ceremony

Marriage is the uniting of a man and a woman in a union which is intended—and which is pledged—to be lifelong. The marriage ceremony is a service unto itself. It may last between 15 and 30 minutes.

BEFORE THE CEREMONY

Are guests usually invited by a formal invitation?

Yes, although sometimes the invitation to the wedding may also be published in the church bulletin.

If not stated explicitly, should one assume that children are invited?

Yes.

If one can't attend, what should one do?

RSVP with regrets and send a gift if you have received a formal invitation to the wedding.

APPROPRIATE ATTIRE

Men: A suit and tie or a sport jacket, slacks and a tie. No head covering is required.

Women: A dress or a business suit appropriate to the season and the time of day for which the wedding has been called. Arms do not have to be covered nor do hems need to reach below the knees. Open-toed shoes and modest jewelry are permissible. No head covering is required.

There are no rules regarding colors of clothing.

GIFTS

Is a gift customarily expected?

Only if you have received a formal invitation to the wedding. Such gifts as small household appliances, sheets or towels or other household goods are appropriate.

Should gifts be brought to the ceremony?

Gifts may be brought to the ceremony itself, to the reception afterward or sent to the home of the newlyweds.

THE CEREMONY

Where will the ceremony take place?

In the church chapel or sanctuary.

When should guests arrive and where should they sit?

Arrive shortly before the time for which the wedding has been called and in time to sign the guest registry, which will be in the church foyer. Ushers will advise you where to sit.

If arriving late, are there times when a guest should *not* enter the ceremony?

Ushers will advise you about when to enter the service.

Are there times when a guest should *not* leave the ceremony?

Do not leave during the processional or recessional of the wedding party.

Who are the major officiants, leaders or participants at the ceremony and what do they do?

▪ *The pastor(s).*
▪ *The bride and groom and members of their wedding party.*

What books are used?

Only the pastor uses a text.

To indicate the order of the ceremony:

A program may be distributed.

Will a guest who is not a Nazarene be expected to do anything other than sit?

While it is customary for all guests to stand for the bride's entrance, they should stand only if the mother of the bride stands.

Are there any parts of the ceremony in which a guest who is not a Nazarene should *not* participate?

No.

If not disruptive to the ceremony, is it okay to:

◘ **Take pictures?** Only with prior permission of the pastor.

◘ **Use a flash?** Only with prior permission of the pastor.

◘ **Use a video camera?** Only with prior permission of the pastor.

◘ **Use a tape recorder?** Only with prior permission of the pastor.

Will contributions to the church be collected at the ceremony?

No.

AFTER THE CEREMONY

Is there usually a reception after the ceremony?

Yes. It may be held at any location chosen by the couple, possibly the church fellowship hall, a catering hall, a country club or a garden setting at a home. Light food, such as punch and cookies or cake, may be served. In some instance, there may be a full meal, but never alcoholic beverages. The reception may last up to two hours.

Would it be considered impolite to neither eat nor drink?

No.

Is there a grace or benediction before eating or drinking?

No.

Is there a grace or benediction after eating or drinking?

No.

Is there a traditional greeting for the family?

Just offer your congratulations.

Is there a traditional greeting for clergy who may be at the reception?

"Pastor."

Is it okay to leave early?

Yes.

Funerals and Mourning

The Church of the Nazarene affirms that life is eternal and that, through faith in Christ, one can look forward to life with God after death. Death may be a time of separation from the body, but the soul and new body will be reunited upon the coming of Christ and the final judgment. Funerals have as their purposes: 1) expressing grief and comforting one another in our bereavement; 2) celebrating the life of the deceased; and 3) affirming faith in life with God after death. Which of these is most emphasized at the funeral depends on the circumstances of the death and the extent of the faith of the deceased.

The funeral lasts about 30 to 60 minutes.

BEFORE THE CEREMONY

How soon after the death does the funeral usually take place?

Within three to six days.

What should a non-Nazarene do upon hearing of the death of a member of that faith?

Express your condolences to the bereaved family through a telephone call or a card or letter.

APPROPRIATE ATTIRE

Men: A suit and tie or a sport jacket, slacks and a tie. No head covering is required.

Women: A dress or a business suit. Arms do not have to be covered nor do hems need to reach below the knees. Open-toed shoes and modest jewelry are permissible. No head covering is required.

Dark, somber colors are recommended.

GIFTS

Is it appropriate to send flowers or make a contribution?

Yes. Often family members request that such contributions be made to the deceased's favorite charity in memory of the deceased.

Is it appropriate to send food?

Those who are especially close to the bereaved family often do so.

THE CEREMONY

Where will the ceremony take place?

In the church sanctuary or a funeral home.

When should guests arrive and where should they sit?

Arrive a few minutes before the time for which the service has been called. An usher will suggest where to sit.

If arriving late, are there times when a guest should *not* enter the ceremony?

Ushers will advise you when to enter.

Will the bereaved family be present at the church or funeral home before the ceremony?

Members of the bereaved family will arrive shortly before the funeral begins.

Is there a traditional greeting for the family?

Sincerely express your love and sympathy.

Will there be an open casket?

This is done entirely at the option of the family.

Is a guest expected to view the body?

No. One may exit the location of the funeral without passing by an open casket.

What is appropriate behavior upon viewing the body?

Pause briefly in front of the casket.

Who are the major officiants at the ceremony and what do they do?

- *The pastor(s)*, who direct the service.
- *The musician(s)*, who provide music.

What books are used?

For the funeral ceremony, only the pastor uses a book.

To indicate the order of the ceremony:

A program may be provided.

Will a guest who is not a Nazarene be expected to do anything other than sit?

No.

Are there any parts of the ceremony in which a guest who is not a Nazarene should *not* participate?

No.

If not disruptive to the ceremony, is it okay to:

◙ **Take pictures?** Only with prior permission of the pastor.

◙ **Use a flash?** Only with prior permission of the pastor.

◙ **Use a video camera?** Only with prior permission of the pastor.

◙ **Use a tape recorder?** Only with prior permission of the pastor.

Will contributions to the church be collected at the ceremony?

No.

THE INTERMENT

Should guests attend the interment?

Yes, unless it is announced that it will be a private interment.

Whom should one ask for directions?

The funeral director.

What happens at the graveside?

Prayers and words of committal are recited. Sometimes a song is sung.

Do guests who are not Nazarenes participate at the graveside ceremony?

No. The officiating pastor is the only participant.

COMFORTING THE BEREAVED

Is it appropriate to visit the home of the bereaved after the funeral?

Yes.

Will there be a religious service at the home of the bereaved?

No.

Will food be served?

No.

How soon after the funeral will a mourner usually return to a normal work schedule?

Absence from work is at the sole discretion of the mourner, but usually a few days, depending upon individual preference.

How soon after the funeral will a mourner usually return to a normal social schedule?

Absence from socializing is at the sole discretion of the mourner, but usually a few days, depending upon individual preference.

Are there mourning customs to which a friend who is not a Nazarene should be sensitive?

No.

Are there rituals for observing the anniversary of the death?

No.

V · HOME CELEBRATIONS

Not applicable to the Church of the Nazarene.

Chapter 7 Contents

Evangelical Free Church

I · HISTORY AND BELIEFS

The Evangelical Free Church is an association of autonomous churches that are united by a commitment to serve Jesus Christ. "Evangelical" refers to Church members' commitment to the proclamation of the Gospel and the authority of the Scriptures as the only sufficient guide to faith and practice. "Free" refers to the church government that assures local churches are independent of a central controlling body. Evangelical Free Churches depend upon the active participation of pastors and laity to make decisions that direct their local church.

The Evangelical Free Church of America was formed in 1950 by the merger of the Swedish Evangelical Free Church and the Norwegian-Danish Evangelical Free Church Association. The two denominations had a total of 275 local churches, and both had originated in the revival movements of the late nineteenth century.

A partner Church, The Evangelical Free Church of Canada, also of Scandinavian heritage, was incorporated under federal charter in 1967, although it traces its history to Enchant, Alberta, where the first formally organized congregation opened its doors in 1917.

From its inception, the Evangelical Free Church has been committed to being actively involved in the mission of Jesus Christ. Internationally, this dates from one of its two original Churches—

the Swedish Evangelical Free Church—sending the first missionaries to China in 1887.

The Evangelical Free Church has national church bodies in 16 nations and plans to expand to another 15 countries. Domestically, the Church is committed to "planting" 1,000 new local churches by the year 2001.

U.S. churches: 1,224
U.S. membership: 242,619
(*data from the* 1998 Yearbook of American and Canadian Churches)

For more information, contact:
The Evangelical Free Church of America
901 East 78th Street
Minneapolis, MN 55420-1300
(612) 854-1300

Canadian churches: 135
Canadian membership: 7,315
(*data from the* Evangelical Free Church of Canada 1998–1999 Directory)

For more information, contact:
Evangelical Free Church of Canada
Box 56109, Valley Centre P.O.
Langley, BC V3A 8B3
(604) 888-8668

II · THE BASIC SERVICE

Within the Evangelical Free Church are found a variety of styles of worship services. Common to more traditional services is congregational singing of several hymns related to the "message," which is gleaned from the reading of text from Scripture. Music is presented by a choir and/or a special musical offering is presented by a soloist. A pastoral prayer for the needs of the congregation is usually given by the pastor.

During more contemporary services, congregants are led by a worship team that sings "praise sings" to God. Musical instruments might include drums, stringed instruments, a piano and/or an electronic synthesizer. The pastor is the designated speaker at such services, but laity are very involved in leading the service, which may even include an occasional play.

Services are God-directed in their adoration to the divinity, and evangelistic in developing congregants' commitment to Christ.

The worship service, which is on Sunday mornings, usually lasts between one hour to one hour and a half.

APPROPRIATE ATTIRE

Men: Attire for men varies and most styles are acceptable, from a jacket and tie to more casual clothes. No head covering is required.

Women: Attire for women varies and most styles are acceptable, from a dress to a skirt and blouse to a pants suit or more casual clothes. Open-toed shoes and modest jewelry are permissible. Clothing need not cover the arms nor hems reach below the knees. No head covering is required.

There are no rules regarding colors of clothing.

THE SANCTUARY

What are the major sections of the church?

- *The pews,* where members and visitors sit for worship. There are no special or specific sections in the pews.
- *The pulpit area,* where song and prayer leaders and the pastor sit and from where the service is led.

THE SERVICE

When should guests arrive and where should they sit?

Arrive early or at the time for which the service has been called. Sit wherever you wish.

If arriving late, are there times when a guest should *not* enter the service?

Do not enter while prayers are being recited.

Are there times when a guest should *not* leave the service?

No.

Who are the major officiants, leaders or participants and what do they do?

- *The pastor,* who preaches and leads the congregation in prayer.
- *The worship leader,* who leads the congregation in worship through song.

What are the major ritual objects of the service?

◘ *Grape juice and unleavened bread,* used during communion to symbolize the body and blood of Jesus Christ. In most churches, communion is offered once a month.

◘ *A communion table,* the site from which the Lord's Supper (communion) is served and which has an open Bible on it.

◘ *A baptismal tank* for the immersion of believers.

What books are used?

Most congregations use either the New International Version or the New American Standard translations of the Bible. Instead of hymnals, many churches use overhead projectors to project the words of hymns for congregants to sing.

To indicate the order of the service:

Periodic announcements are usually made by the pastor. Occasionally, they will be made by an associate pastor or a lay member.

GUEST BEHAVIOR DURING THE SERVICE

Will a guest who is not a member of the Evangelical Free Church be expected to do anything other than sit?

Standing and reading prayers aloud and singing with the congregation are all entirely optional. Kneeling is rarely done during a worship service. If congregants should kneel, visitors may remain seated.

Are there any parts of the service in which a guest who is not a member of the Evangelical Free Church should *not* participate?

Non-believers in Christ should not receive communion.

If not disruptive to the service, is it okay to:

◘ **Take pictures?** Yes.
◘ **Use a flash?** No.
◘ **Use a video camera?** Yes.
◘ **Use a tape recorder?** Yes.

Will contributions to the church be collected at the service?

Yes. The offertory takes place during the service when the offering plate is passed throughout the congregation.

How much is customary to contribute?

While guests are not expected or required to make a contribution, donations between $1 and $4 are appropriate.

AFTER THE SERVICE

Is there usually a reception after the service?

Yes. This is usually held in the church's reception area and may last about 15 to 30 minutes. Sometimes, coffee and light pastries are served.

Is there a traditional form of address for clergy who may be at the reception?

Yes. "Pastor."

Is it okay to leave early?

Yes.

GENERAL GUIDELINES AND ADVICE

Evangelical Free Church services are very informal and relaxed, and a visitor should be, also.

SPECIAL VOCABULARY

Key words or phrases which might be helpful for a visitor to know:

- *Gospel:* As used during worship, this means a reading from one of the accounts of Jesus as written in the New Testament by four of His apostles.
- *Communion or Lord's Supper:* The common meal instituted by Jesus Christ at the Last Supper.

DOGMA AND IDEOLOGY

Members of the Evangelical Free Church of North America believe:

- The Old and New Testaments are the inspired Word of God and without error in the original writings. They are the complete revelation of God's will for the salvation of humanity and the divine and final authority for Christian faith and life.
- In one God, the Creator of all things, exist three persons: the Father, the Son and the Holy Spirit.

◾ Jesus Christ is true God and true man, having been conceived of Holy Spirit and born of the Virgin Mary. He died on the cross as a sacrifice for the sins of humanity. Upon rising bodily from the dead, He ascended into heaven, where He presides as the right hand of God as our High Priest and Advocate.

◾ The ministry of the Holy Spirit is to glorify Jesus Christ, and to regenerate the believing sinner, and guide, instruct and empower the believer for godly living and service.

◾ Humanity was created in the image of God, but, upon falling into sin, was lost. Only through regeneration by the Holy Spirit can salvation and spiritual life be obtained.

◾ Baptism through water and offering the Lord's Supper are practices the Church observes in the present age. They are not regarded as means of salvation.

◾ Every church has the right, under Christ, to decide and govern its own affairs.

Basic books and pamphlets to which a guest can refer to learn more about the Evangelical Free Church:

A Living Legacy compiled by Dr. Thomas McDill (Minneapolis, Mn.: Free Church Press, 1990).

Believers Only by Dr. Arnold T. Olson (Minneapolis, Minn.: Free Church Press, 1964).

This We Believe by Dr. Arnold T. Olson (Minneapolis, Minn.: Free Church Press, 1961).

This is the Evangelical Free Church of America, a pamphlet published by the Evangelical Free Church of America, and which can be obtained by writing to the Church at 901 East 78th Street, Minneapolis, MN 55420-1300.

III · HOLY DAYS AND FESTIVALS

◾ *Christmas*, celebrated on December 25. Marks the birth of Jesus Christ. Church members and non-church members can greet each other with "Merry Christmas!"

◾ *Good Friday.* The date of observance varies, although it usually occurs in April and always the Friday before Easter. Marks the crucifixion of Christ in Jerusalem. There is no traditional greeting for this holiday.

◾ *Easter.* The date of observance varies, but it usually occurs in April and always on the Sunday after the first full moon that occurs on or after the spring equinox of March 21. Commemorates the resurrection of Jesus Christ after His crucifixion. The traditional greeting is "Happy Easter!"

IV · LIFE CYCLE EVENTS

Birth Ceremony

The Baby Dedication is usually part of a regular Sunday worship service. It includes a short challenge to parents and congregants to dedicate the new child to Christ, as well as a prayer by the pastor that this be done. The entire worship service will last more than one hour.

BEFORE THE CEREMONY

Are guests usually invited by a formal invitation?

No. The parents of the newborn informally let family and friends know of the Baby Dedication by telephoning them about it or mentioning it to them face-to-face.

If not stated explicitly, should one assume that children are invited?

Yes.

If one can't attend, what should one do?

RSVP with regrets.

APPROPRIATE ATTIRE

Men: Attire for men varies and most styles are acceptable, from a jacket and tie to more casual clothes. No head covering is required.

Women: Attire for women varies and most styles are acceptable, from a dress to a skirt and blouse to a pants suit or more casual clothes. Open-toed shoes and modest jewelry are permissible. Clothing need not cover the arms nor hems reach below the knees. No head covering is required.

There are no rules regarding colors of clothing.

GIFTS

Is a gift customarily expected?

No.

Should gifts be brought to the ceremony?

See above.

THE CEREMONY

Where will the ceremony take place?

In the main sanctuary of the church.

When should guests arrive and where should they sit?

Arrive early or at the time for which the service has been called. Sit wherever you wish.

If arriving late, are there times when a guest should *not* enter the ceremony?

Do not enter while prayers are being recited.

Are there times when a guest should *not* leave the ceremony?

No.

Who are the major officiants, leaders or participants at the ceremony and what do they do?

◾ *The pastor,* who dedicates the child to Christ.
◾ *The child and his or her parents.*

What books are used?

Most congregations use either the New International Version or the New American Standard translations of the Bible. Instead of hymnals, most churches use overhead projectors to project the words of hymns for congregants to sing.

To indicate the order of the ceremony:

Periodic announcements are usually made by the pastor. Occasionally, they will be made by an associate pastor or a lay member.

Will a guest who is not a member of the Evangelical Free Church be expected to do anything other than sit?

Standing and reading prayers aloud and singing with the congregation are all entirely optional. Kneeling is rarely done during a worship service. If congregants should kneel, visitors may remain seated.

Are there any parts of the ceremony in which a guest who is not a member of the Evangelical Free Church should *not* participate?

Non-believers in Christ should not receive communion.

If not disruptive to the ceremony, is it okay to:

▪ **Take pictures?** Yes.
▪ **Use a flash?** No.
▪ **Use a video camera?** Yes.
▪ **Use a tape recorder?** Yes.

Will contributions to the church be collected at the ceremony?

Yes. The offertory takes place during the service when the offering plate is passed throughout the congregation.

How much is customary to contribute?

While guests are not expected or required to make a contribution, donations between $1 and $4 are appropriate.

AFTER THE CEREMONY

Is there usually a reception after the ceremony?

Yes. This is the usual after-worship reception held in the church's reception area. It may last about 15 to 30 minutes. Sometimes, coffee and light pastries are served.

Would it be considered impolite to neither eat nor drink?

No.

Is there a grace or benediction before eating or drinking?

No.

Is there a grace or benediction after eating or drinking?

No.

Is there a traditional greeting for the family?

"Congratulations."

Is there a traditional form of address for clergy who may be at the reception?

"Pastor."

Is it okay to leave early?

Yes.

Initiation Ceremony

Some churches have a short graduation service for young people, who are usually in seventh or eighth grade, who have completed their Bible instruction classes. The service is part of the regular Sunday worship service.

BEFORE THE CEREMONY

Are guests usually invited by a formal invitation?

Guests are usually invited with an oral invitation.

If not stated explicitly, should one assume that children are invited?

Yes.

If one can't attend, what should one do?

RSVP with regrets.

APPROPRIATE ATTIRE

Men: Attire for men varies and most styles are acceptable, from a jacket and tie to more casual clothes. No head covering is required.

Women: Attire for women varies and most styles are acceptable, from a dress to a skirt and blouse to a pants suit or more casual clothes. Open-toed shoes and modest jewelry are permissible. Clothing need not cover the arms nor hems reach below the knees. No head covering is required.

There are no rules regarding colors of clothing.

GIFTS

Is a gift customarily expected?

No.

Should gifts be brought to the ceremony?

See above.

THE CEREMONY

Where will the ceremony take place?

In the main sanctuary of the church.

When should guests arrive and where should they sit?

Arrive early or at the time for which the service has been called. Sit wherever you wish.

If arriving late, are there times when a guest should *not* enter the ceremony?

Do not enter while prayers are being recited.

Are there times when a guest should *not* leave the ceremony?

No.

Who are the major officiants, leaders or participants at the ceremony and what do they do?

◾ *The pastor,* who speaks to the graduation class.
◾ *Members of the graduation class.*

What books are used?

Most congregations use either the New International Version or the New American Standard translations of the Bible. Instead of hymnals, most churches use overhead projectors to project the words of hymns for congregants to sing.

To indicate the order of the ceremony:

Periodic announcements are usually made by the pastor. Occasionally, they will be made by an associate pastor or a lay member.

Will a guest who is not a member of the Evangelical Free Church be expected to do anything other than sit?

Standing and reading prayers aloud and singing with the congregation are all entirely optional. Kneeling is rarely done during a worship service. If congregants should kneel, visitors may remain seated.

Are there any parts of the ceremony in which a guest who is not a member of the Evangelical Free Church should *not* participate?

Non-believers in Christ should not receive communion.

If not disruptive to the ceremony, is it okay to:
- **Take pictures?** Yes.
- **Use a flash?** No.
- **Use a video camera?** Yes.
- **Use a tape recorder?** Yes.

Will contributions to the church be collected at the ceremony?

Yes. The offertory takes place during the service when the offering plate is passed throughout the congregation.

How much is customary to contribute?

While guests are not expected or required to make a contribution, donations between $1 and $4 are appropriate.

AFTER THE CEREMONY

Is there usually a reception after the ceremony?

Yes. This is the usual after-worship reception held in the church's reception area. It may last about 15 to 30 minutes. Sometimes, coffee and light pastries are served.

Would it be considered impolite to neither eat nor drink?

No.

Is there a grace or benediction before eating or drinking?

No.

Is there a grace or benediction after eating or drinking?

No.

Is there a traditional greeting for the family?

"Congratulations."

Is there a traditional form of address for clergy who may be at the reception?

Yes. "Pastor."

Is it okay to leave early?

Yes.

Marriage Ceremony

Marriage is considered to be a sacred union since it is an institution ordained by God in Genesis and affirmed by Jesus in the Gospels. The sacredness of the marriage ceremony and the relationship between man and wife are based upon the Scriptures and the teaching that marriage represents our relationship to Jesus Christ.

The wedding ceremony usually lasts between 30 and 60 minutes. It is a service unto itself.

BEFORE THE CEREMONY

Are guests usually invited by a formal invitation?

Yes.

If not stated explicitly, should one assume that children are invited?

No.

If one can't attend, what should one do?

RSVP with regrets and send a gift to the newlyweds.

APPROPRIATE ATTIRE

Men: A jacket and tie. No head covering is required.

Women: A dress or a skirt and blouse. Open-toed shoes and modest jewelry are permissible. Clothing need not cover the arms nor hems reach below the knees. No head covering is required.

There are no rules regarding colors of clothing.

GIFTS

Is a gift customarily expected?

Cash or U.S. savings bonds or small household items are most frequently given.

Should gifts be brought to the ceremony?

Gifts may be brought to the ceremony, to the reception afterward or sent to the home of the newlyweds.

THE CEREMONY

Where will the ceremony take place?

The ceremony may be in the main sanctuary of the church or in another appropriate setting, such as a catering hall or even outdoors.

When should guests arrive and where should they sit?

Arrive early. Ushers will advise guests about where to sit.

If arriving late, are there times when a guest should *not* enter the ceremony?

Do not enter during the processional by the wedding party.

Are there times when a guest should *not* leave the ceremony?

Do not leave until the service is over.

Who are the major officiants, leaders or participants at the ceremony and what do they do?

▪ *The pastor,* who performs the ceremony.
▪ *The bride and groom and members of their wedding party.*

What books are used?

Instead of hymnals, most churches use overhead projectors to project the words of hymns for guests to sing.

To indicate the order of the ceremony:

A program will be provided.

Will a guest who is not a member of the Evangelical Free Church be expected to do anything other than sit?

Stand with the other guests. It is entirely optional for non-church members to sing and read prayers aloud with church members.

Are there any parts of the ceremony in which a guest who is not a member of the Evangelical Free Church should *not* participate?

No.

If not disruptive to the ceremony, is it okay to:

▪ **Take pictures?** Yes.
▪ **Use a flash?** No.
▪ **Use a video camera?** Yes.
▪ **Use a tape recorder?** Yes.

Will contributions to the church be collected at the ceremony?

No.

AFTER THE CEREMONY

Is there usually a reception after the ceremony?

Yes. This may be held in the church's reception hall, in a catering facility, in a home or outdoors. Food (often a complete meal) is usually served, although no alcoholic beverages will be served. There may be music, but no dancing. The length of the reception varies, but it may last two hours or more.

Would it be considered impolite to neither eat nor drink?

No.

Is there a grace or benediction before eating or drinking?

No.

Is there a grace or benediction after eating or drinking?

Possibly.

Is there a traditional greeting for the family?

"Congratulations."

Is there a traditional form of address for clergy who may be at the reception?

"Pastor."

Is it okay to leave early?

Yes.

Funerals and Mourning

Members of the Evangelical Free Church believe that upon the coming of Jesus Christ, the dead will be resurrected, and believers will receive everlasting blessedness and unbelievers will receive everlasting conscious punishment.

A ceremony unto itself, the funeral service lasts about 30 and 60 minutes.

BEFORE THE CEREMONY

How soon after the death does the funeral usually take place?

Usually within two to three days, but sometimes as long as one week.

What should one who is not a member of the Evangelical Free Church do upon hearing of the death of a member of that faith?

Telephone or visit the bereaved and express one's condolences and concern.

APPROPRIATE ATTIRE

Men: A jacket and tie. No head covering is required.

Women: A dress or a skirt and blouse. Open-toed shoes and modest jewelry are permissible. Clothing need not cover the arms nor hems reach below the knees. No head covering is required.

There are no rules regarding colors of clothing, but dark, somber colors are recommended.

GIFTS

Is it appropriate to send flowers or make a contribution?

Yes. Flowers may be sent to the home of the bereaved upon hearing of the death, or they may be sent to the funeral home or the church where the funeral will be held. Contributions may be made to a memorial fund designated by family members.

Is it appropriate to send food?

Yes. This may be sent to the home of the bereaved.

THE CEREMONY

Where will the ceremony take place?

Either in a church or a funeral home.

When should guests arrive and where should they sit?

Arrive early. Ushers usually advise guests where to sit.

If arriving late, are there times when a guest should *not* enter the ceremony?

Do not enter while prayers are being recited.

Will the bereaved family be present at the church or funeral home before the ceremony?

Possibly.

Is there a traditional greeting for the family?

Express your condolences.

Will there be an open casket?

Sometimes.

Is a guest expected to view the body?

This is entirely optional.

What is appropriate behavior upon viewing the body?

Pause briefly in front of the casket, then take a seat in the church sanctuary or the room in the funeral home where the service will be held.

Who are the major officiants at the ceremony and what do they do?

- *The pastor,* who reads from the Scriptures.
- *Family and/or friends,* who may deliver a eulogy.

What books are used?

Most congregations use either the New International Version or the New American Standard translations of the Bible.

To indicate the order of the ceremony:

A program will be provided and periodic announcements will also be made by the pastor.

Will a guest who is not a member of the Evangelical Free Church be expected to do anything other than sit?

Stand with the other guests. It is entirely optional for non-church members to sing and read prayers aloud with church members.

Are there any parts of the ceremony in which a guest who is not a member of the Evangelical Free Church should *not* participate?

No.

If not disruptive to the ceremony, is it okay to:

- **Take pictures?** No.
- **Use a flash?** No.
- **Use a video camera?** No.
- **Use a tape recorder?** Possibly.

Will contributions to the church be collected at the ceremony?

No.

THE INTERMENT

Should guests attend the interment?

Only if they are invited to do so. Some interments are public; some are private.

Whom should one ask for directions?

The funeral director, the ushers or family members.

What happens at the graveside?

Prayers are recited and the pastor reads from the Bible.

Do guests who are not members of the Evangelical Free Church participate at the graveside ceremony?

No. They are simply present.

COMFORTING THE BEREAVED

Is it appropriate to visit the home of the bereaved after the funeral?

Yes.

Will there be a religious service at the home of the bereaved?

No.

Will food be served?

Invariably after a funeral and the graveside service that follows, family and friends are invited back to the church for a lunch. Occasionally, the church will serve lunch to the family of the deceased and their close friends at the home of the bereaved.

How soon after the funeral will a mourner usually return to a normal work schedule?

This depends entirely on one's individual preference. The Church has no set tradition.

How soon after the funeral will a mourner usually return to a normal social schedule?

This depends entirely on one's individual preference. The Church has no set tradition.

Are there mourning customs to which a friend who is not a member of the Evangelical Free Church should be sensitive?

No. The Church has no rituals of mourning.

Are there rituals for observing the anniversary of the death?

No.

V · HOME CELEBRATIONS

Not applicable to the Evangelical Free Church.

Chapter 8 Contents

8

International Church of the Foursquare Gospel

I · HISTORY AND BELIEFS

The International Church of the Foursquare Gospel was founded in 1923 in Los Angeles by Aimee Semple McPherson. The new Church was an outgrowth of the revival movement in the United States that had begun at the turn of the century. Many involved in the movement spoke "in tongues" (in a language unknown to those speaking it), and claims were made of divine healing that saved lives. Since many of these experiences were associated with the coming of the Holy Spirit (the empowering quality of God) on the Day of Pentecost, participants in the revival were called Pentecostals.

"Foursquare" is a biblical term used in the Book of Exodus to refer to the tabernacle, in the Book of Ezekiel to refer to the Temple of the Lord, and in the Book of Revelations to refer to Heaven. Aimee Semple McPherson first used the term "Foursquare Gospel" during an evangelical campaign in Oakland, California, in 1922. It represents that which is equally balanced on all sides, and which is established and enduring. Such confidence in the power of the Gospel is also expressed by a New Testament verse (Hebrews 13:8) that is displayed in Foursquare churches: "Jesus Christ the Same, Yesterday, Today, and Forever."

The "Foursquare Gospel" presents Jesus Christ as Savior of the world, Baptizer with the Holy Spirit, the Great Physician, and the Soon-Coming King. It shares with the entire Pentecostal movement the concept that the truth of the Baptism is proven when the Holy Spirit empowers one to speak in tongues, a phenomenon whose task is to present Christ in the language, culture and understanding of the hearer.

The Church also shares the core Pentecostal belief in bodily healing rooted in individual atonement.

Men and women participate equally at all levels of the Church.

Official business of the International Church of the Foursquare Gospel is conducted by a president, a board of directors that is called the Foursquare Cabinet and an executive council. The Church's highest authority is its annual convention, which has the sole authority to make or amend the Church's by-laws.

District supervisors are appointed by the president, with the approval of the board of directors for districts in the United States. They are ratified by the pastors of their respective districts every four years. The ministry of each local congregation is cared for by a pastor, a church council, deacons and deaconesses and elders. Each church is expected to contribute monthly to missionary work in the United States and abroad.

In Canada, a national church, the Foursquare Gospel Church of Canada, was formed in 1981.

The Church's strong emphasis on missionary work has produced more than 80 Hispanic churches in North America and at least four major churches that minister to African-Americans. Abroad, 17,226 congregations serve 1.8 million adherents.

U.S. churches: 1,773
U.S. membership: 229,600
(*data from the* 1998 Yearbook of American and Canadian Churches)

For more information, contact:
The International Church of the Foursquare Gospel
1910 West Sunset Boulevard, Suite 200, P.O. Box 26902
Los Angeles, CA 90026-0176
(213) 484-2400
www.foursquare.org

Canadian churches: 54
Canadian membership: 3,063
(*data from the* 1998 Yearbook of American and Canadian Churches)

For more information, contact:
Foursquare Gospel Church of Canada
8459–160th Street #100
Surrey, BC V3S 3T9
(604) 543-8414

II · THE BASIC SERVICE

Worship in the International Church of the Foursquare Gospel is marked by spontaneity and freedom of expression, and especially by exuberant prayer, music and Scripture reading, and "speaking in tongues." "Praying in tongues" means that one is able to pray according to the will of God without the interference of one's natural desire. "Praising in tongues" lets the worshipper be free to express his or her love for God without the inhibitions of his natural language. This is the outward manifestation of the presence of the Holy Spirit.

All churches have services on Sunday morning. In addition to these, some churches have services either on Saturday evening or Sunday evening. The worship service lasts slightly more than one hour.

APPROPRIATE ATTIRE

Men: A jacket and tie or more casual attire, such as slacks and a shirt. No headcovering is required.

Women: A dress or a skirt and blouse or a pants suit or other casual attire. Halters and jeans are frowned upon. Clothing need not cover the arms and hems need not reach below the knees. Open-toed shoes and modest jewelry are permissible. No head covering is required.

There are no rules regarding colors of clothing.

THE SANCTUARY

What are the major sections of the church?
- *The foyer,* where congregants and guests are greeted upon arrival.
- *The auditorium,* where congregants and guests are seated.

◼ *The platform or pulpit,* where the service leaders lead prayer or read scriptures and preach.

THE SERVICE

When should guests arrive and where should they sit?

Arrive at the time for which the service has been called. Ushers will advise congregants and guests where to sit.

If arriving late, are there times when a guest should *not* enter the service?

Do not enter during prayers.

Are there times when a guest should *not* leave the service?

Do not leave during prayers.

Who are the major officiants, leaders or participants and what do they do?

◼ *The pastor,* who delivers a sermon.
◼ *The worship leader,* who leads musical worship.

What are the major ritual objects of the service?

There are none. Most churches have little, if any, adornment and lack statues and stained glass windows. The cross is the most commonly displayed symbol.

What books are used?

Several translations of the Old and New Testaments are used throughout the Church. Most commonly used is the New International Version of the King James translation of the Bible. Most churches no longer use a hymnal since the service emphasizes worship choruses.

To indicate the order of the service:

Periodic announcements will be made by the pastor or worship leader.

GUEST BEHAVIOR DURING THE SERVICE

Will a guest who is not a member of the International Church of the Foursquare Gospel be expected to do anything other than sit?

Yes. It is expected for guests to stand with the congregants. If it does not violate their religious beliefs, it is entirely optional for guests to kneel and sing with the congregants and to pray aloud with them.

Are there any parts of the service in which a guest who is not a member of the International Church of the Foursquare Gospel should *not* participate?

If not a Christian, do not take communion, which is also known as the Lord's Supper.

If not disruptive to the service, is it okay to:

◗ **Take pictures?** No.
◗ **Use a flash?** No.
◗ **Use a video camera?** No.
◗ **Use a tape recorder?** No.

Will contributions to the church be collected at the service?

Yes.

How much is customary to contribute?

Contributions are entirely optional. While the amount of the contribution is entirely at the discretion of congregants or visitors, contributions between $1 and $5 are common.

AFTER THE SERVICE

Is there usually a reception after the service?

Yes, although no food or beverages will be served. The reception will usually be in either the church sanctuary or in the church's reception area.

Is there a traditional form of address for clergy whom a guest may meet?

"Reverend."

Is it okay to leave early?

Yes.

GENERAL GUIDELINES AND ADVICE

None provided.

SPECIAL VOCABULARY

Key words or pharases which might be helpful for a visitor to know:

- *Anointing with oil:* An ancient Christian practice in which the sick are anointed with oil in the name of the Lord. Prayers are also made for their healing.
- *Lifting up of hands:* Holding up one's hands during prayer and praise in anticipation of receiving the presence and power of the Holy Spirit.

DOGMA AND IDEOLOGY

Members of the International Church of the Foursquare Gospel believe:

- The Old and New Testaments are "true, immutable, steadfast and as unchangeable as...[their] author, the Lord Jehovah."
- God is a trinity in unity, consisting of the Father, the Son and the Holy Spirit.
- Jesus Christ was born of a virgin birth, lived a sinless life, performed miracles, atoned for the sins of others when placed upon the cross, and was resurrected bodily to be at the right hand of God, the Father.
- Regeneration by the Holy Ghost is absolutely essential for the salvation of the lost and sinful.
- All churches water baptize by immersion and administer the Lord's Supper.
- Those who are physically sick are healed as an answer to their faithful prayers.
- Jesus Christ will imminently and bodily return to resurrect the dead. The believed who are resurrected will return to life; sinners will be resurrected to damnation.

Basic books to which a guest can refer to learn more about the International Church of the Foursquare Gospel:

The Vine: The Branches by Nathaniel Van Cleave (Los Angeles: International Church of the Foursquare Gospel, 1992).

Dictionary of Pentecostal and Charismatic Movements by Stanley M. Burgess, Gary B. McGee and Patrick H. Alexander (Grand Rapids, Mich.: Zondervan Publishing House, 1988).

III · HOLY DAYS AND FESTIVALS

■ *Christmas*, celebrated on December 25. Marks the birth of Jesus Christ. Church members and non-church members greet each other with "Merry Christmas!"

■ *Good Friday.* The date of observance varies, although it usually occurs in April and is always the Friday before Easter. Marks the crucifixion of Christ in Jerusalem. There is no traditional greeting for this holiday.

■ *Easter.* The date of observance varies, but it usually occurs in April and always on the Sunday after the first full moon that occurs on or after the spring equinox of March 21. Commemorates the resurrection of Jesus Christ after His crucifixion. The traditional greeting is "Happy Easter!"

■ *Pentecost.* Occurs 50 days after Easter because this is when the Holy Spirit (the spirit of Jesus) descended on His apostles. Celebrates the power of the Holy Spirit and its manifestation in the early Christian church. There is no traditional greeting for this holiday.

IV · LIFE CYCLE EVENTS

Birth Ceremony

This ceremony, which is called a dedication, is based on the biblical account of Jesus calling young children to Him and blessing them. The Church does not believe that the dedication constitutes salvation, but rather that it lets the child's parents publicly commit themselves to their intentions to raise the child in the teachings of Jesus.

During the dedication, which is for infants or young children, the pastor asks the parents to pledge to live in such a way that, at an early age, their child will become a Christian. They respond with, "We do." Some pastors also charge the congregation to help the parents by role-modeling Christian living for the child.

The dedication ceremony, which is the same for males and females, usually lasts about three to five minutes. It is part of a larger service (usually a Sunday morning worship service) that lasts slightly more than one hour.

BEFORE THE CEREMONY

Are guests usually invited by a formal invitation?

No. They are personally invited by the parents.

If not stated explicitly, should one assume that children are invited?

Yes.

If one can't attend, what should one do?

RSVP orally with regrets.

APPROPRIATE ATTIRE

Men: A jacket and tie or more casual attire, such as slacks and a shirt. No headcovering is required.

Women: A dress or a skirt and blouse or a pants suit or other casual attire. Halters and jeans are frowned upon. Clothing need not cover the arms and hems need not reach below the knees. Open-toed shoes and modest jewelry are permissible. No head covering is required.

There are no rules regarding colors of clothing.

GIFTS

Is a gift customarily expected?

No.

Should gifts be brought to the ceremony?

See above.

THE CEREMONY

Where will the ceremony take place?

In the main auditorium of the church.

When should guests arrive and where should they sit?

Arrive at the time for which the service has been called. Ushers will advise congregants and guests where to sit.

If arriving late, are there times when a guest should *not* enter the ceremony?

Do not enter during prayer.

Are there times when a guest should *not* leave the ceremony?

Do not leave during prayers.

Who are the major officiants, leaders or participants at the ceremony and what do they do?

- *The pastor,* who delivers a sermon.
- *The worship leader,* who leads musical worship.
- *The child's parents.*
- *The child.*

What books are used?

No books are used during the dedication itself. During the rest of the worship service, a Bible is used. Several translations of the Old and New Testaments are used throughout the Church. Most commonly used is the New International Version of the King James translation of the Bible. Most churches no longer use a hymnal since the service emphasizes worship choruses.

To indicate the order of the ceremony:

Periodic announcements will be made by the pastor or worship leader.

Will a guest who is not a member of the International Church of the Foursquare Gospel be expected to do anything other than sit?

It is expected for guests to stand with the congregants. If it does not violate their religious beliefs, it is entirely optional for guests to kneel and sing with the congregants and pray aloud with them.

Are there any parts of the ceremony in which a guest who is not a member of the International Church of the Foursquare Gospel should *not* participate?

If not a Christian, do not take communion, which is also known as the Lord's Supper.

If not disruptive to the ceremony, is it okay to:

- **Take pictures?** Yes.
- **Use a flash?** No.
- **Use a video camera?** Yes.
- **Use a tape recorder?** No.

Will contributions to the church be collected at the ceremony?

Contributions will not be collected at the dedication itself, but they will be collected during the rest of the worship service.

How much is customary to contribute?

Contributions are entirely optional. While the amount of the contribution is at the discretion of congregants or visitors, contributions between $1 and $5 are common.

AFTER THE CEREMONY

Is there usually a reception after the ceremony?

Yes, although no food or beverages will be served. The reception will usually be in either the church sanctuary or in the church's reception area.

Is there a traditional greeting for the family?

"Congratulations."

Is there a traditional form of address for clergy who may be at the reception?

"Reverend."

Is it okay to leave early?

Yes.

Initiation Ceremony

The baptism ceremony, which is the same for males and females, is considered to be an outward testimony of one's acceptance of Christ as Savior. During it, new believers are fully immersed in the baptismal waters. Baptism is necessary because all people are born in a sinful condition and it signifies the purging, cleansing and zeal of the Holy Spirit, the empowering quality of God.

Baptism is a public testimony of the death of the individual's sinful nature and of one's new birth in the spirit of Jesus. It endows believers with the power to serve others, to dedicate themselves to the work of God, to have a more intense love for Jesus, and to have certain spiritual gifts. Baptism, which is performed once for any individual, can occur at any time during one's life.

The baptismal service is usually part of a regular Sunday worship service. The baptism itself lasts a few minutes.

BEFORE THE CEREMONY

Are guests usually invited by a formal invitation?

They are usually invited informally and orally by the person being baptized.

If not stated explicitly, should one assume that children are invited?

No.

If one can't attend, what should one do?

RSVP orally with regrets.

APPROPRIATE ATTIRE

Men: A jacket and tie or more casual attire, such as slacks and a shirt. No headcovering is required.

Women: A dress or a skirt and blouse or a pants suit or other casual attire. Halters and jeans are frowned upon. Clothing need not cover the arms and hems need not reach below the knees. Open-toed shoes and modest jewelry are permissible. No head covering is required.

There are no rules regarding colors of clothing.

GIFTS

Is a gift customarily expected?

No.

Should gifts be brought to the ceremony?

See above.

THE CEREMONY

Where will the ceremony take place?

In the main auditorium of the church.

When should guests arrive and where should they sit?

Arrive at the time for which the service has been called. Ushers will advise congregants and guests where to sit.

If arriving late, are there times when a guest should *not* enter the ceremony?

Do not enter during prayers.

Are there times when a guest should *not* leave the ceremony?

Do not leave during prayers.

Who are the major officiants, leaders or participants at the ceremony and what do they do?

- *The pastor,* who delivers a sermon.
- *The worship leader,* who leads musical worship.
- *The person to be baptized.*

What books are used?

No books are used during the baptism itself. During the rest of the worship service, a Bible is used. Several translations of the Old and New Testaments are used throughout the Church. Most commonly used is the New International Version of the King James translation of the Bible. Most churches no longer use a hymnal since the service emphasizes worship choruses.

To indicate the order of the ceremony:

Periodic announcements will be made by the pastor or worship leader.

Will a guest who is not a member of the International Church of the Foursquare Gospel be expected to do anything other than sit?

It is expected for guests to stand with the congregants. If it does not violate their religious beliefs, it is entirely optional for guests to kneel and sing with the congregants and to pray aloud with them.

Are there any parts of the ceremony in which a guest who is not a member of the International Church of the Foursquare Gospel should *not* participate?

If not a Christian, do not take communion, which is also known as the Lord's Supper.

If not disruptive to the ceremony, is it okay to:

- **Take pictures?** Yes.
- **Use a flash?** No.
- **Use a video camera?** Yes.
- **Use a tape recorder?** No.

Will contributions to the church be collected at the ceremony?

Contributions will not be collected at the baptism itself, but they will be collected during the rest of the worship service.

How much is customary to contribute?

Contributions are entirely optional. While the amount of the contribution is at the discretion of congregants or visitors, contributions between $1 and $5 are common.

AFTER THE CEREMONY

Is there usually a reception after the ceremony?

Yes, although no food or beverages will be served. The reception will usually be in either the church sanctuary or in the church's reception area.

Is there a traditional greeting for the family?

Just offer your congratulations.

Is there a traditional form of address for clergy who may be at the reception?

"Reverend."

Is it okay to leave early?

Yes.

Marriage Ceremony

The International Church of the Foursquare Gospel teaches that the family was the first institution ordained by God in the Garden of Eden. The basis for a family is marriage between a consenting adult male and female. Marriage, which is not to be entered into lightly, is said to be "until death do us part."

The marriage ceremony is a ceremony unto itself and may last 30 to 60 minutes.

BEFORE THE CEREMONY

Are guests usually invited by a formal invitation?

Yes.

If not stated explicitly, should one assume that children are invited?

No.

If one can't attend, what should one do?

RSVP by card or letter with regrets and send a gift.

178 · *How to Be a Perfect Stranger*

APPROPRIATE ATTIRE

Men: A jacket and tie. No head covering is required.

Women: A dress or a skirt and blouse. Clothing need not cover the arms and hems need not reach below the knees. Open-toed shoes and modest jewelry are permissible. No head covering is required.

There are no rules regarding colors of clothing.

GIFTS

Is a gift customarily expected?

Yes. Cash, savings bonds or small household items are frequently given.

Should gifts be brought to the ceremony?

Gifts may be either be brought to the ceremony or the reception afterward, or sent to the home of the newlyweds.

THE CEREMONY

Where will the ceremony take place?

In the auditorium of the church.

When should guests arrive and where should they sit?

Arrive shortly before the time for which the ceremony has been called. Ushers will usually advise guests about where to sit.

If arriving late, are there times when one should *not* enter the ceremony?

Do not enter during the processional or recessional of the wedding party.

Are there times when a guest should *not* leave the ceremony?

Do not leave during the processional or recessional of the wedding party.

Who are the major officiants, leaders or participants at the ceremony and what do they do?

◘ *The pastor,* who officiates.
◘ *The bride and groom and members of the wedding party.*

What books are used?

None.

To indicate the order of the ceremony:

A program will be distributed.

Will a guest who is not a member of the International Church of the Foursquare Gospel be expected to do anything other than sit?

Stand when other guests arise during the ceremony.

Are there any parts of the ceremony in which a guest who is not a member of the International Church of the Foursquare Gospel should *not* participate?

No.

If not disruptive to the ceremony, is it okay to:

- **Take pictures?** Yes.
- **Use a flash?** Yes.
- **Use a video camera?** Yes.
- **Use a tape recorder?** Yes.

Will contributions to the church be collected at the ceremony?

No.

AFTER THE CEREMONY

Is there usually a reception after the ceremony?

Yes. It may be in the same building where the wedding ceremony was held or in a catering hall. Receptions usually include light food, such as cake, mints, nuts and punch. There will be no alcoholic beverages or dancing, although there might be music. The reception may last 30 to 60 minutes.

Would it be considered impolite to neither eat nor drink?

No.

Is there a grace or benediction before eating or drinking?

Yes.

Is there a grace or benediction after eating or drinking?

No.

Is there a traditional greeting for the family?

Just offer your congratulations.

Is there a traditional form of address for clergy who may be at the reception?

"Reverend."

Is it okay to leave early?

Yes.

Funerals and Mourning

Members of the International Church of the Foursquare Gospel believe that all Christians who have died will one day rise from their graves and meet the Lord. Meanwhile, Christians who are still alive will be raptured (caught up with those who have risen from their graves) and will also be with the Lord. All who have thus joined with God will live forever.

An International Church of the Foursquare Gospel funeral usually begins with singing, Scripture reading or prayer. This is followed with hymns, prayer and worship to God and a sermon by the pastor.

A ceremony unto itself, the funeral service lasts about 30 to 60 minutes.

BEFORE THE CEREMONY

How soon after the death does the funeral usually take place?

Within two to three days.

What should someone who is not a member of the International Church of the Foursquare Gospel do upon hearing of the death of a member of that faith?

Telephone or visit the bereaved to offer condolences and sympathies and offer to assist in any way possible.

APPROPRIATE ATTIRE

Men: A jacket and tie. No head covering is required.

Women: A dress or a skirt and blouse. Clothing need not cover the arms and hems need not reach below the knees. Open-toed shoes and modest jewelry are permissible. No head covering is required.

Dark, somber colors for clothing are advised.

GIFTS

Is it appropriate to send flowers or make a contribution?

Flowers may be sent to the funeral home or church where the funeral service is held. Contributions may be sent to a memorial fund determined by the bereaved.

Is it appropriate to send food?

Yes. Send it to the home of the bereaved.

THE CEREMONY

Where will the ceremony take place?

At a funeral home.

When should guests arrive and where should they sit?

Arrive at the time for which the ceremony has been scheduled. Ushers usually advise guests where to sit.

If arriving late, are there times when a guest should *not* enter the ceremony?

No.

Will the bereaved family be present at the funeral home before the ceremony?

Possibly.

Is there a traditional greeting for the family?

Just offer your condolences.

Will there be an open casket?

Usually.

Is a guest expected to view the body?

This is optional.

What is appropriate behavior upon viewing the body?

Look into the casket while walking slowly past it, then take a seat in the room in the funeral parlor where the service will be held.

Who are the major officiants at the ceremony and what do they do?

◘ *The pastor,* who delivers a sermon.

What books are used?

None.

To indicate the order of the ceremony:

A program will be distributed and a display will indicate the order of prayers and hymns.

Will a guest who is not a member of the International Church of the Foursquare Gospel be expected to do anything other than sit?

Yes. It is expected for guests to stand with the congregants. If it does not violate their religious beliefs, it is entirely optional for guests to sing with the congregants and to pray aloud with them.

Are there any parts of the ceremony in which a guest who is not a member of the International Church of the Foursquare Gospel should *not* participate?

No.

If not disruptive to the ceremony, is it okay to:

- **Take pictures?** No.
- **Use a flash?** No.
- **Use a video camera?** No.
- **Use a tape recorder?** Yes.

Will contributions to the church be collected at the ceremony?

No.

THE INTERMENT

Should guests attend the interment?

Attendance is optional.

Whom should one ask for directions?

An usher or the funeral director or just follow the funeral procession.

What happens at the graveside?

There are prayers, songs and Scripture readings, and the casket is buried.

Do guests who are not members of the International Church of the Foursquare Gospel participate at the graveside ceremony?

No, they are simply present.

COMFORTING THE BEREAVED

Is it appropriate to visit the home of the bereaved after the funeral?

Yes, if one knows the family well. Visit briefly.

Will there be a religious service at the home of the bereaved?

No.

Will food be served?

Possibly, but not alcoholic beverages.

How soon after the funeral will a mourner usually return to a normal work schedule?

Two days to a week, depending upon the mourner's relationship to the deceased and individual preference. The Church has no set tradition.

How soon after the funeral will a mourner usually return to a normal social schedule?

This is entirely the choice of the bereaved, since the Church has no set tradition. It may be one or two weeks or more, and is often primarily determined by local cultural traditions and one's relationship to the deceased.

Are there mourning customs to which a friend who is not a member of the International Church of the Foursquare Gospel should be sensitive?

No.

Are there rituals for observing the anniversary of the death?

No.

V · HOME CELEBRATIONS

Not applicable to the International Church of the Foursquare Gospel.

Chapter 9 Contents

International Pentecostal Holiness Church

I · HISTORY AND BELIEFS

The International Pentecostal Holiness Church has its origins in the first Pentecostal denominations in the United States: The Pentecostal Holiness Church, the Fire-Baptized Holiness Church, and the Tabernacle Pentecostal Church. The first two churches merged in 1911; the last church joined them in 1915. In Canada, it is known as the Pentecostal Holiness Church of Canada.

The church emphasizes direct access to God, the Father; believes prayer can manifest miracles, especially divine healing; and is certain that the Holy Spirit may be evidenced during worship services by certain congregants speaking "in tongues," which are languages unknown to the speaker. The church also teaches the premillennial coming of Jesus Christ and that Jesus shed His blood for the complete cleansing of those who believe in Him from all indwelling sin.

Worldwide, the 12,802 churches of the International Pentecostal Holiness Church have 2.3 million members. The Church also has 155 missionaries in 80 countries.

The government of the Church gives individual churches a measure of denominational uniformity and local autonomy.

U.S. churches: 1,653
U.S. membership: 157,163
(*data from the* 1998 Yearbook of American and Canadian Churches)

For more information, contact:
The International Pentecostal Holiness Church
P.O. Box 12609
Oklahoma City, OK 73157
(405) 787-7110

Canadian churches: N/A
Canadian membership: 2,500
(data from the Pentecostal Holiness Church of Canada)

For more information, contact:
Pentecostal Holiness Church of Canada
16293 104th Avenue
Surrey, BC V4N 1Z7
(604) 583-5551

II · THE BASIC SERVICE

Worship in the International Pentecostal Holiness Church is marked by spontaneity and freedom of expression, and especially by exuberant prayer, music and Scripture reading, and "speaking in tongues." "Tongues" are used in three ways: praying, praising and giving messages from God by the Holy Spirit. "Praying in tongues" means that one is able to pray according to the will of God without the interference of one's natural desire. "Praising in tongues" lets the worshipper be free to express his or her love for God without the inhibitions of his natural language. This is the outward manifestation of the presence of the Holy Spirit.

Also, "messages in tongues" may be given during a service. These may be interpreted by the pastor or by another member of the church so they edify the entire congregation.

The worship service usually lasts slightly more than one hour.

APPROPRIATE ATTIRE

Men: A jacket and tie or more casual attire, such as slacks and an informal shirt. No head covering is required.

Women: A dress or a skirt and blouse or a pants suit. Shorts, halters, and revealing attire are never appropriate. Clothing need not cover the arms and hems need not reach below the knees. Open-toed shoes and modest jewelry are permissible. No head covering is required.

There are no rules regarding colors of clothing.

THE SANCTUARY

What are the major sections of the church?

- *The foyer,* where congregants and guests are welcomed by greeters or ushers upon arrival.
- *The auditorium,* where congregants and guests are seated for worship.
- *The platform or pulpit,* where the service leaders lead prayer or read Scriptures and preach; and where the music leader and choir sit during service.
- *The altar,* where communion is offered.

THE SERVICE

When should guests arrive and where should they sit?

Arrive shortly before the time for which the service has been called. Sit wherever you wish.

If arriving late, are there times when a guest should *not* enter the service?

Do not enter during prayers.

Are there times when a guest should *not* leave the service?

Do not leave during prayers.

Who are the major officiants, leaders or participants and what do they do?

- *The pastor,* who leads worship and delivers a sermon.
- *The minister of music,* who leads worship music.
- *The worship team,* who assist the minister of music.
- *The choir and soloists,* who present musical arrangements for the worshippers.

What are the major ritual objects of the service?

- *Communion trays,* which are used to serve communion to worshippers.
- *Anointing oil,* which is used during the laying on of hands during prayer. The pastors or elders place a drop of oil on their fingers and then touch it to the forehead of the person to whom they are ministering. This is an ancient symbol of being touched by the hand of God.

What books are used?

The Bible and a hymnal. The most common versions of the Bible used in the Church are the Authorized King James Version, the New King

James Version, the New International Version and the New American Standard Version. A variety of hymnals are used through the Church.

To indicate the order of the service:

A program will be distributed and periodic announcements will be made by the pastor or other worship leaders.

GUEST BEHAVIOR DURING THE SERVICE

Will a guest who is not a member of the International Pentecostal Holiness Church be expected to do anything other than sit?

No. It is optional for guests to stand, kneel, sing and read prayers aloud with congregants.

Are there any parts of the service in which a guest who is not a member of the International Pentecostal Holiness Church should *not* participate?

Guests who are not Christians do not receive communion since this is reserved strictly for believers in Christ.

If not disruptive to the service, is it okay to:

- **Take pictures?** Yes.
- **Use a flash?** Yes.
- **Use a video camera?** Yes.
- **Use a tape recorder?** Yes.

Will contributions to the church be collected at the service?

Yes, although guests are not expected to contribute.

How much is customary to contribute?

Contributions are entirely optional. While the amount of the contribution is entirely at the discretion of congregants or visitors, contributions between $1 and $5 are common.

AFTER THE SERVICE

Is there usually a reception after the service?

No.

Is there a traditional form of address for clergy whom a guest may meet?

"Pastor" or "Reverend."

GENERAL GUIDELINES AND ADVICE

None provided.

SPECIAL VOCABULARY

Key words or phrases which might be helpful for a visitor to know:

- *Salvation, Saved, Born Again:* Different terms for accepting Christ as one's Savior and His teaching as guiding principles.
- *Divine Healing:* Supernatural healing.
- *Holy Scriptures:* The inspired, inerrant, authoritative word of God.
- *Anointing with oil:* An ancient Christian practice in which the sick are anointed with oil in the name of the Lord. Prayers are also recited for their healing.
- *Foot washing:* Commemorates Christ's washing of his disciples' feet at the Last Supper. Individual churches determine the form and the frequency with which they will practice foot washing.
- *Lifting up of hands:* Holding up one's hands during prayer and praise in anticipation of receiving the presence and power of the Holy Spirit.
- *Sanctification:* Being cleansed of sin.

DOGMA AND IDEOLOGY

Members of the International Pentecostal Holiness Church believe:

- In the inspired authority of the Old and New Testaments.
- God is a trinity in unity, consisting of the Father, the Son and the Holy Ghost.
- Jesus Christ was born of a virgin birth, lived a sinless life, performed miracles, atoned for the sins of others on the cross, and was resurrected bodily to sit at the right hand of God, the Father.
- Regeneration by the Holy Ghost is absolutely essential for the salvation of the lost and sinful.
- Baptism in the Holy Spirit is evidenced by speaking in tongues.
- Atonement for one's sins provides for divine healing and is available to all those who truly believe in Christ.
- Jesus Christ will bodily return to resurrect the dead. Believers who are resurrected will return to life; sinners will be resurrected to damnation.

Some basic books to which a guest can refer to learn more about the International Pentecostal Holiness Church:

The International Pentecostal Holiness Church Manual, 1993-1997 (Franklin Springs, Ga.: Life Springs Resources, 1993).

A Brief History of the Pentecostal Holiness Church by A.D. Beacham Jr. (Franklin Springs, Ga.: Life Springs Resources, 1993).

The Holiness Pentecostal Movement in the United States by Vinson Synan (Grand Rapids, Mich.: William B. Eerdmans Publishing Co., Inc., 1971).

The Pentecostal Holiness Church by Joseph E. Campbell (Franklin Springs, Ga.: The Publishing House of the Pentecostal Holiness Church, 1951).

Dictionary of Pentecostal and Charismatic Movements by Stanley M. Burgess, Gary B. McGee and Patrick H. Alexander (Grand Rapids, Mich.: Zondervan Publishing House, 1988).

III · HOLY DAYS AND FESTIVALS

- *Christmas*, celebrated on December 25. Marks the birth of Jesus Christ. Church members and non-church members can greet each other with "Merry Christmas!"

- *Good Friday.* The date of observance varies, although it usually occurs in April and is always the Friday before Easter. Marks the crucifixion of Christ in Jerusalem. There is no traditional greeting for this holiday.

- *Easter.* The date of observance varies, but it usually occurs in April and always on the Sunday after the first full moon that occurs on or after the spring equinox of March 21. Commemorates the resurrection of Jesus Christ after His crucifixion. The traditional greeting is "Happy Easter!"

- *Pentecost.* Occurs 50 days after Easter because this is when the Holy Spirit (the spirit of Jesus) descended on His apostles. Celebrates the power of the Holy Spirit and its manifestation in the early Christian church. There is no traditional greeting for this holiday.

IV · LIFE CYCLE EVENTS

Birth Ceremony

This ceremony, which is called a dedication, is based on the biblical account of Jesus calling young children to Him and blessing them. The Church does not believe that the dedication constitutes salvation, but rather that it lets the child's parents publicly commit themselves to their intentions to raise the child in the teachings of Jesus.

The ceremony is generally a solemn occasion that stresses the importance of families rearing their children in the faith.

During the dedication, which is for infants or young children and is the same for males and females, the pastor asks the parents to pledge to live in such a way that, at an early age, their child will be a Christian. They respond with, "We do." Some pastors also charge the congregation to help the parents by role-modeling Christian living for the child.

The dedication ceremony usually lasts about three to five minutes. It is part of a larger service (usually a Sunday morning worship service) that lasts about 60 minutes.

BEFORE THE CEREMONY

Are guests usually invited by a formal invitation?

Guests are usually invited orally by the parents of the newborn.

If not stated explicitly, should one assume that children are invited?

Yes.

If one can't attend, what should one do?

RSVP orally with regrets.

APPROPRIATE ATTIRE

Men: A jacket and tie or more casual attire, such as slacks and an informal shirt. No head covering is required.

Women: A dress or a skirt and blouse or a pants suit. Shorts, halters, and revealing attire are never appropriate. Clothing need not cover the arms and hems need not reach below the knees. Open-toed shoes and modest jewelry are permissible. No head covering is required.

There are no rules regarding colors of clothing.

GIFTS

Is a gift customarily expected?

No.

Should gifts be brought to the ceremony?

See above.

THE CEREMONY

Where will the ceremony take place?

In the main sanctuary of the church.

When should guests arrive and where should they sit?

Arrive shortly before the time for which the ceremony has been called. Sit wherever you wish.

If arriving late, are there times when a guest should *not* enter the ceremony?

Do not enter during prayers.

Are there times when a guest should *not* leave the ceremony?

Do not leave during prayers.

Who are the major officiants, leaders or participants at the ceremony and what do they do?

- *The pastor,* who leads the prayer of dedication as well as comments about the child or the occasion.
- *The child.*
- *The child's parents,* who offer the child and themselves for dedication to God.
- *The child's grandparents and godparents,* who may stand with the parents to witness the ceremony.

What books are used?

No books are used during the dedication itself. During the rest of the worship service, a Bible and a hymnal are used. The most common versions of the Bible used in the Church are the Authorized King James Version, the New King James Version, the New International Version and the New American Standard Version. A variety of hymnals are used.

To indicate the order of the ceremony:

A program will be distributed and periodic announcements will be made by the pastor.

Will a guest who is not a member of the International Pentecostal Holiness Church be expected to do anything other than sit?

No. It is optional for guests to stand, kneel, sing and read prayers aloud with congregants.

Are there any parts of the ceremony in which a guest who is not a member of the International Pentecostal Holiness Church should *not* participate?

The dedication service is part of a Sunday worship service at which communion is offered. Guests who are not Christians do not receive communion since this is reserved strictly for believers in Christ.

If not disruptive to the ceremony, is it okay to:

- **Take pictures?** Yes.
- **Use a flash?** Yes.
- **Use a video camera?** Yes.
- **Use a tape recorder?** Yes.

Will contributions to the church be collected at the ceremony?

Contributions will not be collected at the dedication service, but they will be collected during the broader worship service of which the dedication is a part. Guests are not expected to contribute.

How much is customary to contribute?

Contributions are entirely optional. While the amount of the contribution is at the discretion of the congregants or visitors, contributions between $1 and $5 are common.

AFTER THE CEREMONY

Is there usually a reception after the ceremony?

No.

Is there a traditional greeting for the family?

"Congratulations."

Is there a traditional form of address for clergy whom a guest may meet?

"Minister" or "Reverend."

Initiation Ceremony

This ceremony, which is the same for males and females, is called a baptism. During it, children who have reached the "age of accountability," which is usually considered to be eight to 10 years of age (although children as young as five or six have been baptized), are fully immersed in the baptismal waters.

Baptism is necessary because all people are born in a sinful condition and it fills one with the purging, cleansing and zeal of the Holy Spirit, the empowering quality of God. Baptism is a public testimony of the death of the individual's sinful nature and of one's new birth in the spirit of Jesus. It endows believers with the power to witness and serve others; a dedication to the work of God; a more intense love for Jesus; and certain spiritual gifts. Baptism, which is performed once for any individual, can occur at any time during one's life.

The baptismal ceremony is usually part of a regular Sunday morning or evening church service. The baptism itself may last about 15 to 30 minutes, depending on the number of persons being baptized.

BEFORE THE CEREMONY

Are guests usually invited by a formal invitation?

They are usually invited informally and orally.

If not stated explicitly, should one assume that children are invited?

Yes.

If one can't attend, what should one do?

RSVP orally with regrets.

APPROPRIATE ATTIRE

Men: A jacket and tie or more casual attire, such as slacks and an informal shirt. No head covering is required.

Women: A dress or a skirt and blouse or a pants suit. Shorts, halters, and revealing attire are never appropriate. Clothing need not cover the arms and hems need not reach below the knees. Open-toed shoes and modest jewelry are permissible. No head covering is required.

There are no rules regarding colors of clothing.

GIFTS

Is a gift customarily expected?

No.

Should gifts be brought to the ceremony?

See above.

THE CEREMONY

Where will the ceremony take place?

In the main sanctuary of the church.

When should guests arrive and where should they sit?

Arrive shortly before the time for which the ceremony has been called. Sit wherever you wish.

If arriving late, are there times when a guest should *not* enter the ceremony?

Do not enter during prayers.

Are there times when a guest should *not* leave the ceremony?

Do not leave during prayers.

Who are the major officiants, leaders or participants at the ceremony and what do they do?

◘ *The pastor,* who performs the baptism.
◘ *The person being baptized.*

What books are used?

None, although a Bible and hymnal are used during the service which includes the baptism. The most common versions of the Bible used in the Church are the Authorized King James Version, the New King James Version, the New International Version and the New American Standard Version. A variety of hymnals are used.

To indicate the order of the ceremony:

A program will be distributed and periodic announcements will be made by the pastor.

Will a guest who is not a member of the International Pentecostal Holiness Church be expected to do anything other than sit?

No. It is optional for guests to stand, kneel, sing and read prayers aloud with congregants.

Are there any parts of the ceremony in which a guest who is not a member of the International Pentecostal Holiness Church should *not* participate?

Baptism is part of a Sunday worship service at which communion is offered. Guests who are not Christians do not receive communion since this is reserved strictly for believers in Christ.

If not disruptive to the ceremony, is it okay to:

◼ **Take pictures?** Yes.
◼ **Use a flash?** Yes.
◼ **Use a video camera?** Yes.
◼ **Use a tape recorder?** Yes.

Will contributions to the church be collected at the ceremony?

Contributions will not be collected at the baptism, but they will be collected during the broader worship service of which the baptism is only a part. Guests are not expected to contribute.

How much is customary to contribute?

Contributions are entirely optional. While the amount of the contribution is at the discretion of the congregants or visitors, contributions between $1 and $5 are common.

AFTER THE CEREMONY

Is there usually a reception after the ceremony?

No.

Is there a traditional greeting for the family?

"Congratulations."

Is there a traditional form of address for clergy whom a guest may meet?

"Minister" or "Reverend."

Marriage Ceremony

The International Pentecostal Holiness Church teaches that the family was the first institution ordained by God in the Garden of Eden. The basis for a family is marriage between two consenting adults. Marriage is said to be "until death do us part."

The marriage ceremony is a ceremony unto itself and may last 30 to 60 minutes.

BEFORE THE CEREMONY

Are guests usually invited by a formal invitation?

Yes.

If not stated explicitly, should one assume that children are invited?

Yes.

If one can't attend, what should one do?

RSVP by card or letter with regrets and send a gift.

APPROPRIATE ATTIRE

Men: A jacket and tie. No head covering is required.

Women: A dress or a skirt and blouse or a pants suit. Clothing need not cover the arms and hems need not reach below the knees. Open-toed shoes and modest jewelry are permissible. No head covering is required.

There are no rules regarding colors of clothing.

GIFTS

Is a gift customarily expected?

Yes. Cash or U.S. savings bonds valued at $20 to $50 or small household items are most frequently given, as are any items listed in the newlywed's gift registry.

Should gifts be brought to the ceremony?

Gifts may be brought to the ceremony or the reception afterward.

THE CEREMONY

Where will the ceremony take place?

In the sanctuary of the church.

When should guests arrive and where should they sit?

Arrive shortly before the time for which the ceremony has been called. Ushers will usually advise guests where to sit.

If arriving late, are there times when a guest should *not* enter the ceremony?

Do not enter during the processional or recessional of the wedding party.

Are there times when a guest should *not* leave the ceremony?

Do not leave during the processional or recessional of the wedding party.

Who are the major officiants, leaders or participants at the ceremony and what do they do?

◼ *The pastor,* who officiates.
◼ *The bride and groom and members of the wedding party.*
◼ *Musicians,* who provide special music.

What books are used?

None.

To indicate the order of the ceremony:

A program will be distributed and periodic announcements will be made by the minister.

Will a guest who is not a member of the International Pentecostal Holiness Church be expected to do anything other than sit?

No.

Are there any parts of the ceremony in which a guest who is not a member of the Pentecostal Church of God should *not* participate?

No.

If not disruptive to the ceremony, is it okay to:

◼ **Take pictures?** No.
◼ **Use a flash?** No.
◼ **Use a video camera?** No.
◼ **Use a tape recorder?** Yes.

Will contributions to the church be collected at the ceremony?

No.

AFTER THE CEREMONY

Is there usually a reception after the ceremony?

Usually. It may be in the same building where the wedding ceremony was held or in a catering hall or in a private room at a hotel or restaurant. Receptions usually include light food, such as cake, nuts, hors d'oeuvres and punch. There will be no alcoholic beverages or dancing, although there might be music. The reception may last 30 to 60 minutes.

Would it be considered impolite to neither eat nor drink?

No.

Is there a grace or benediction before eating or drinking?

No.

Is there a grace or benediction after eating or drinking?

No.

Is there a traditional greeting for the family?

Just offer your congratulations.

Is there a traditional form of address for clergy who may be at the reception?

"Pastor" or "Reverend."

Is it okay to leave early?

Yes.

Funerals and Mourning

Members of the International Pentecostal Holiness Church believe that all Christians who have died will one day rise from their graves and meet the Lord in the air. Meanwhile, Christians who are still alive will be raptured (or caught up with those who have risen from their graves) and will also be with the Lord. All who have thus joined with God will live forever.

A funeral usually includes singing, Scripture reading or prayer. This is followed with hymns, prayer and worship to God, and a sermon by the pastor.

A ceremony unto itself, the funeral service lasts about 30 to 60 minutes.

BEFORE THE CEREMONY

How soon after the death does the funeral usually take place?

Within two to three days.

What should someone who is not a member of the International Pentecostal Holiness Church do upon hearing of the death of a member of that faith?

Telephone, visit or write the bereaved to offer condolences and sympathies and offer to assist in any way possible.

APPROPRIATE ATTIRE

Men: A jacket and tie. No head covering is required.

Women: A dress or a skirt and blouse. Shorts, halters, jeans, T-shirts and revealing attire are never appropriate. Clothing need not cover the arms and hems need not reach below the knees. Open-toed shoes and modest jewelry are permissible. No head covering is required.

Dark, somber colors for clothing are advised.

GIFTS

Is it appropriate to send flowers or make a contribution?

Flowers may be sent to the funeral home or the church where the funeral service is held. Contributions may be sent to a memorial fund determined by the bereaved.

Is it appropriate to send food?

Yes. Send any food you deem appropriate to the home of the bereaved.

THE CEREMONY

Where will the ceremony take place?

Either in a church or a funeral home.

When should guests arrive and where should they sit?

Arrive at the time for which the ceremony has been scheduled. Ushers usually advise guests where to sit.

If arriving late, are there times when a guest should *not* enter the ceremony?

No.

Will the bereaved family be present at the church or funeral home before the ceremony?

Yes.

Is there a traditional greeting for the family?

Just offer your condolences.

Will there be an open casket?

Usually.

Is a guest expected to view the body?

This is optional.

What is appropriate behavior upon viewing the body?

Look into the casket while walking slowly past it, then take a seat in the church sanctuary or the room in the funeral parlor where the service will be held.

Who are the major officiants at the ceremony and what do they do?

- *The minister,* who delivers a brief sermon and tribute to the deceased.
- *Family members and close friends,* who deliver eulogies.
- *Musicians,* who sing one or two songs.

What books are used?

The Bible and sometimes a hymnal. The most common versions of the Bible used in the Church are the Authorized King James Version, the New King James Version, the New International Version and the New American Standard Version. A variety of hymnals are used.

To indicate the order of the ceremony:

A program is sometimes distributed.

Will a guest who is not a member of the International Pentecostal Holiness Church be expected to do anything other than sit?

No. It is entirely optional for guests of other faiths to stand and sing with congregants.

Are there any parts of the ceremony in which a guest who is not a member of the International Pentecostal Holiness Church should *not* participate?

No.

If not disruptive to the ceremony, is it okay to:

- **Take pictures?** Yes.
- **Use a flash?** Yes.
- **Use a video camera?** Yes.
- **Use a tape recorder?** Yes.

Will contributions to the church be collected at the ceremony?
No.

THE INTERMENT

Should guests attend the interment?
Attendance is optional.

Whom should one ask for directions?
The minister or funeral director.

What happens at the graveside?
There are prayers, songs and Scripture readings, and comments about the deceased may be made by the minister, family or close friends.

Do guests who are not members of International Pentecostal Holiness Church participate at the graveside ceremony?
No, they are simply present.

COMFORTING THE BEREAVED

Is it appropriate to visit the home of the bereaved after the funeral?
Yes, if one knows the family well. It is best to limit the visit to about 15 minutes.

Will there be a religious service at the home of the bereaved?
No.

Will food be served?
Possibly, but no alcoholic beverages.

How soon after the funeral will a mourner usually return to a normal work schedule?
A week or two, depending upon individual preference. The Church has no set tradition.

How soon after the funeral will a mourner usually return to a normal social schedule?

This is entirely the choice of the bereaved, since the Church has no set tradition. It may be one or two weeks or more, and is often primarily determined by local cultural traditions.

Are there mourning customs to which a friend who is not a member of the International Pentecostal Holiness Church should be sensitive?

No.

Are there rituals for observing the anniversary of the death?

No.

V · HOME CELEBRATIONS

The Housewarming or New Home Dedication

When does it occur?

Soon after the family has settled into its new home.

What is its significance?

To dedicate a new home to God.

What is the proper greeting to the celebrants?

Just offer your congratulations.

BEFORE THE CEREMONY

Are guests usually invited by a formal invitation?

Yes.

If not stated explicitly, should one assume children are invited?

No.

If one can't attend, what should one do?

RSVP with regrets and send a gift.

APPROPRIATE ATTIRE

Men: A jacket and tie or more casual attire, such as slacks and an informal shirt. No head covering is required.

Women: A dress or a skirt and blouse or a pants suit. Shorts, halters, and revealing attire are never appropriate. Clothing need not cover the arms and hems need not reach below the knees. Open-toed shoes and modest jewelry are permissible. No head covering is required.

There are no rules regarding colors of clothing.

GIFTS

Is a gift customarily expected?

Yes.

If one decides to give a gift, is a certain type of gift appropriate?

Give anything you wish that seems appropriate for a new home.

THE CEREMONY

The home dedication lasts about 15 to 30 minutes. It is customary to arrive early. The major officiate is the minister, who blesses the home and dedicates it to God. If arriving late, do not enter during prayers.

What are the major ritual objects of the ceremony?

None.

What books are used?

A Bible. The most common versions of the Bible used in the Church are the Authorized King James Version, the New King James Version, the New International Version and the New American Standard Version.

Will a guest who is not a member of the International Pentecostal Holiness Church be expected to do anything than sit?

No.

Are there any parts of the ceremony in which a guest who is not a member of the International Pentecostal Holiness Church should *not* participate?

No.

If not disruptive to the ceremony, is it okay to:
- **Take pictures?** Yes.
- **Use a flash?** Yes.
- **Use a video camera?** Yes.
- **Use a tape recorder?** Yes.

EATING AND DRINKING

Is a meal part of the celebration?

No, although light snacks may be served. If so, they will be served after the home dedication.

Will there be alcoholic beverages?

No.

Would it be considered impolite to neither eat nor drink?

No.

Is there a grace or benediction before eating or drinking?

Yes.

Is there a grace or benediction after eating or drinking?

No.

At the meal, will a guest be asked to say or do anything?

No.

Will there be:
- **Dancing?** No.
- **Music?** No.

GENERAL GUIDELINES AND ADVICE

None provided.

Chapter 10 Contents

10
Mennonite/Amish

I · HISTORY AND BELIEFS

There are nearly 20 organized groups of Mennonites in North America. They vary in life style and religious practice, but all originate from the same sixteenth century Anabaptist movement in Europe. The Anabaptist movement began when a small group of religious reformers claimed Protestant reformers were not sufficiently "radical." They also differed with mainstream Protestants on the timing of baptism. Protestants called for baptism of infants, while Anabaptists mandated that one should be baptized after reaching an "age of accountability," which usually begins with early adolescence and confers the ability to profess belief for one's self.

The name "Mennonite" is derived from that of the sixteenth century Dutch Anabaptist leader, Menno Simons. Originally a Roman Catholic priest, Simons became convinced of the falsity of traditional Catholic doctrine and practice of his time, but hesitated at breaking with the Church. He joined the Anabaptists, who were then being persecuted. Grateful for his leadership, the group later adopted a variation on his name.

Over the years, Mennonites have maintained cultural traditions and religious beliefs in differing ways. While this has led to the formation of various Mennonite groups, they hold certain beliefs in common. Among these are that one should emulate Jesus in everyday living and behavior; that the Bible is the inspired word of God; and that Jesus taught the way of peace. Mennonite faith cannot easily be labeled a liberal or a conservative Christian denomination. Rather, it is an alternative to mainstream religion, one that emphasizes evangelism, peace and justice, and that focuses on a holistic approach to Christ's way of personal salvation, while maintaining concern for the physical as well as the spiritual needs of others.

The one over-arching Mennonite belief that differs from all Christian denominations (except for the Society of Friends, or "Quakers," and the Church of the Brethren) is the Church's stand on war and violence. In principle, Mennonites have always been conscientious objectors to war, although individual members have opted for non-combatant roles and even military service. More recently, the broadest emphasis has been placed on "non-violence" so it includes such issues as abortion and capital punishment.

Mennonites began emigrating to North America from Switzerland in the mid-seventeenth century, spreading westward from Pennsylvania and concentrating on rural colonies where they practiced their faith and Swiss culture.

In a second spurt of Mennonite emigration in the late nineteenth century, Mennonites of Dutch, German and Swiss ancestry who had settled in the Ukraine fled Czarist efforts to conscript them into the Russian army. They settled primarily in the Midwestern areas of the United States and Canada. A third wave of emigration followed both world wars.

An emphasis on missionary work in this century has helped the Church develop so much into an international institution that now more than one-third of adult Mennonites are non-whites. Mennonites combine a keen sense of evangelism with a theology of relief and material aid to people in want. For 75 years, the Mennonite Central Committee, a relief agency operating around the world, has helped the needy and addressed issues of peace and justice.

The Amish, or the Amish-Mennonite, as they are more properly known, originated from a disagreement among European Mennonites regarding "shunning," a practice that had been adopted by the Dutch Mennonites in 1632. Shunning demanded avoiding a fellow Mennonite who had transgressed. In the late 17th century, a Swiss Mennonite, Jacob Ammann, became concerned over laxity in the Swiss and Alsatian Mennonite communities when a woman who had admitted speaking a falsehood was not shunned. Ammann also rejected a prevalent belief that the souls would be saved of those who were sincerely sympathetic to the Mennonite, but did not join the faith. And he urged simplicity and uniformity as a guard against pride. This included the admonition that men not trim their beards. Today, the Amish call for simplicity extends to not using motorized vehicles, partly because of concerns that they could take Amish too far from their own community.

The group that eventually coalesced around Ammann and his teachings called themselves "Amish" in his honor. The first Amish arrived in North America around 1727, but a congregation was not formed until 1749 in Berks County, Pennsylvania. By the mid-19th century, there were significant Amish communities in Lancaster and Chester counties in Pennsylvania and in Holmes County, Ohio, as well as in Waterloo County, Ontario, Canada.

The largest Mennonite and Amish denominations in the United States are the Mennonite Church, with 1,004 churches and almost 91,000 members; the Old Order Amish Church, which is widely known for its resistance to modern technology, has 898 churches and almost 81,000 members; and the General Conference Mennonite Church, with 270 churches and 36,685 members.

Smaller, more traditional denominations include the Beachy Amish Mennonite (138 churches; 8,399 members); the Fellowship of Evangelical Bible Churches (37 churches; 4,039 members); and the Reformed Mennonite Church (10 churches; 346 members).

The largest Mennonite and Amish denominations in Canada include the Conference of Mennonites in Canada–General Conference, Mennonite Church, with 223 churches and 33,123 members (including 8,145 members from the Mennonite Church); the General Conference of the Mennonite Brethren Churches–Canada, with 207 churches and 28,368 members; and various Russian Mennonite immigrant groups numbering 20,164 members.

Smaller, more traditional denominations include Old Order Mennonite (5,763 members); Beachy Amish and Old Order Amish (1,612 members); Mennonite Church (independent and unaffiliated groups, 2,187 members).

U.S. churches: 2,455
U.S. membership: 266,693
(data from the 1998 Yearbook of American and Canadian Churches*)*

For more information, contact:
The Beachy Amish Mennonite Church
Route 1 Box 176
Meyersdale, PA 15552
(814) 662-2483

The Mennonite Church
421 South Second Street
Suite 600
Elkhart, IN 46516
(219) 294-7131
mcgb@juno.com

The Old Order Amish Church
4324 SR 39
Millersburg, OH 44654
(216) 893-2883

The General Conference Mennonite Church
722 Main Street, P.O. Box 347
Newton, KS 67114
(316) 283-5100

The General Conference of Mennonite Brethren
4812 East Butler Avenue
Fresno, CA 93727
(209) 452-1713

Canadian churches: 3,126
Canadian membership: 91,217
(data compiled from Mennonite World Conference Directory, 1994; Mennonite
Year Book, 1997; *and* 1998 Yearbook of American and Canadian Churches)

For more information, contact:
Conference of Mennonites in Canada
600 Shaftesbury Boulevard
Winnipeg, MB R3P 0M4
(204) 888-6781

Canadian Conference of Mennonite Brethren Churches
#3 169 Riverton Avenue
Winnipeg, MB R2L 2E5
(204) 669-6575

Evangelical Mennonite Conference of Canada
Box 1268 440 Main Street
Steinbach, MB R0A 2A0
(204) 326-6401

Evangelical Mennonite Mission Conference
Box 52059 Niakwa Post Office
Winnipeg, MB R2M 5P9
(204) 253-7929

II · THE BASIC SERVICE

To Mennonites and Amish, worship is a time to pray, to praise God, to sing hymns and to read or listen to the word of God as read from the Bible. Worship is considered to be a "corporate event"—the coming together of a body of believers focused on Christ and living a Christ-like life each day. It is also a time for personal spiritual fulfillment.

The length of Sunday morning worship services varies. Beachy Amish services may last two and one-half hours, while General Conference Mennonite churches services last 30 to 60 minutes and General Conference of Mennonite Brethren services last slightly more than one hour.

APPROPRIATE ATTIRE

Men: Expected attire varies. In more conservative denominations, such as the Beachy Amish Mennonite, a suit jacket is worn, but without a tie. In other denominations, such as the General Conference Mennonite Church, casual attire is acceptable, but those attending the Church for the first time are advised to wear a jacket and tie. In the General Conference of Mennonite Brethren, a jacket and tie or slightly more casual attire is acceptable.

In no denomination is a head covering required.

Women: Expected attire varies. In more conservative denominations, such as the Beachy Amish Mennonite, women are expected to wear dresses that cover their arms and have hems that reach below their knees. Neither open-toed shoes nor modest jewelry are permissible. Church members cover their heads, but visitors are not expected to do so.

In less conservative denominations, such as the General Conference

Mennonite Church or the General Conference of Mennonite Brethren, women may wear dresses, a skirt and blouse or a pants suit or more casual attire, although those attending the Church for the first time are advised to dress somewhat conservatively. Clothing need not cover their arms nor hems reach below the knees. Open-toed shoes and modest jewelry are permissible. No head covering is required.

Dark, solid colors are advised for more conservative denominations, such as the Beachy Amish Mennonite. For the services of less conservative groups, there are no rules regarding colors of clothing.

THE SANCTUARY

What are the major sections of the church?

- *The sanctuary*, where the congregation gathers for worship.
- *The pulpit*, where lay and religious leaders speak to the congregation.
- *Choir loft or seats*, which may be either on the raised area in front of the congregation or in another location in the sanctuary.

THE SERVICE

When should guests arrive and where should they sit?

Arrive shortly before the time for which the service has been called. Beachy Amish Mennonite churches always start their services at 9:30 a.m. on Sunday mornings. Other denominations begin worship at various times, so the visitor should check the time in advance with the church or with a friend who is Mennonite.

In most Mennonite denominations, ushers will usually advise congregants and guests where to sit. Beachy Amish do not have ushers.

If arriving late, are there times when a guest should *not* enter the service?

Do not enter during Scripture readings or while prayers are being said. It may be best for tardy congregants and guests to enter while a hymn is being sung.

Are there times when a guest should *not* leave the service?

No.

Who are the major officiants, leaders or participants and what do they do?

- *Preachers or pastors*, who read Scripture, lead prayers, make announcements and deliver the sermon.

◼ *Musicians or song leaders,* who direct the choir or lead hymn singing.

◼ *Lay church members,* who have been asked in advance of the service to read Scripture or to sing.

What are the major ritual objects of the service?

◼ *The communion table,* from which communion is served.

◼ *A Bible,* which often lies open on the communion table.

What books are used?

In each denomination, various translations of the Bible are used. In the Mennonite Brethren Church, the most common versions are the New International Version and the New Revised Standard Version. More conservative denominations may use the King James Version.

Various hymnals are also used throughout the denominations. The Mennonite Church and the General Conference Mennonite Church use *Hymnal: A Worship Book* (Newton, Kans.: Faith and Life Press, 1992). The Mennonite Brethren Church uses *Worship Together* (Fresno, Ca.: The Board of Faith and Life, The General Conference of Mennonite Brethren Churches, 1995).

A church bulletin may also be used that includes prayers, responses or hymns.

To indicate the order of the service:

A program may be distributed or the pastor may make periodic announcements.

GUEST BEHAVIOR DURING THE SERVICE

Will a guest who is neither Mennonite nor Amish be expected to do anything other than sit?

In all but the most conservative Churches, a visitor would rarely do wrong by remaining seated when congregants stand or kneel, although the latter is rare in most congregations. However, if it does not violate their religious beliefs, the guest would be more in place by standing when others stand. Also, it is optional for guests to sing and read prayers aloud with the congregants.

Are there any parts of the service in which a guest who is neither Mennonite nor Amish should *not* participate?

Communion is not offered to guests who are not Christian.

If not disruptive to the service, is it okay to:

■ **Take pictures?** Not in more conservative denominations, such as the Beachy Amish Mennonite. Possibly (and only with prior permission of the pastor) in less conservative denominations, such as the General Conference Mennonite Church or the General Conference of Mennonite Brethren.

■ **Use a flash?** No.

■ **Use a video camera?** Not in more conservative denominations, such as the Beachy Amish Mennonite. Possibly (and only with prior permission of the pastor) in less conservative denominations, such as the General Conference Mennonite Church or the General Conference of Mennonite Brethren.

■ **Use a tape recorder?** Possibly (and only with prior permission of the pastor) in all Mennonite churches.

Will contributions to the church be collected at the service?

Collections will be taken in the churches of most Mennonite denominations, but not in those of the General Conference of Mennonite Brethren.

How much is customary to contribute?

Guests are not expected to contribute, but should they choose to do so, $1 to $4 is appropriate.

AFTER THE SERVICE

Is there usually a reception after the service?

Most denominations do not have a reception after the service, although some churches belonging to the General Conference Mennonite Church occasionally hold potluck meals on Sunday afternoons. No alcoholic beverages are served at these. Grace over the food is usually recited before the meal, which may last between 30 and 60 minutes.

Churches belonging to the General Conference of Mennonite Brethren usually have a "coffee time" after the service at which coffee and rolls are served. This may last about 30 minutes.

Is there a traditional form of address for clergy whom a guest may meet?

"Pastor."

Is it okay to leave early?

Yes.

GENERAL GUIDELINES AND ADVICE

Guests are always welcome and should feel free to ask church members or a pastor about the congregants' faith and religious practice.

SPECIAL VOCABULARY

Key words or phrases which might be helpful for a visitor to know:

- *Holy Communion:* A rite through which Mennonites and Amish believe they receive Christ's body and blood as assurance that God has forgiven their sins.
- *Lessons:* Readings from the Bible (or "Scripture"), including the Old Testament (the Hebrew scriptures, written before the birth of Jesus); the Epistles (generally from one of the letters of St. Paul or another New Testament writer); and the Gospel (a reading from Matthew, Mark, Luke or John, the "biographers" of Jesus).

DOGMA AND IDEOLOGY

Mennonites and Amish believe:

- Jesus Christ is central to worship and to everyday living, which should emulate Christ's example.
- The Bible is the inspired word of God.
- Church membership is voluntary, with adult baptism upon one declaring his or her faith.
- Jesus Christ taught the way of peace, and one should not serve in the military.

Basic books to which a guest can refer to learn more about Mennonites and Amish:

An Introduction to Mennonite History by Cornelius J. Dyck (Scottsdale, Pa.: Herald Press, 1993).

Smith's Story of the Mennonites by C. Henry Smith (Newton, Kans.: Faith and Life, 1981).

Building on the Rock by Walfred J. Fahrer (Scottsdale, Pa.: Herald Press, 1995).

Who Are the Mennonite Brethren? by Katie Wiebe (Hillsboro, Kans.: Kindred Press, 1984).

III · HOLY DAYS AND FESTIVALS

◘ *Christmas,* which always falls on December 25, celebrates the birth of Christ. Many General Conference Mennonite Church congregations observe Christmas Eve, which falls on December 24, with a worship service that may include singing, re-enactments of the Nativity scene in Bethlehem, and a reading of the Christmas story from the Bible. The traditional greeting is "Merry Christmas."

◘ *Ash Wednesday,* which occurs 40 days before Easter, commemorates the beginning of Lent, which is a season for preparation and penitence before Easter itself. There is no traditional greeting for this holiday.

◘ *Easter,* which always falls on the Sunday after the first full moon that occurs on or after the spring equinox of March 21. Commemorates the death and resurrection of Jesus. The traditional greeting is "Happy Easter."

◘ *Pentecost.* Occurs 50 days after Easter because this is when the Holy Ghost (the spirit of Jesus) descended on His followers. Celebrates the power of the Holy Spirit and its manifestation in the early Christian church. There is no traditional greeting for this holiday.

IV · LIFE CYCLE EVENTS

Birth Ceremony

Smaller, more conservative denominations (such as the Beachy Amish Mennonite) do not have a formal celebration for the birth of a child. Some larger Mennonite denominations, such as the General Conference Mennonite Church and the General Conference of Mennonite Brethren, have a "child consecration," which is held when a child is an infant or a toddler.

During the consecration, which is part of a regular Sunday worship service, the pastor blesses the child and his or her parents, and congregants respond to an oral invitation to help raise the child in a Christian environment. The ceremony itself lasts only two or three minutes.

BEFORE THE CEREMONY

Are guests usually invited by a formal invitation?

No. The consecration is usually announced at the previous Sunday's worship service.

If not stated explicitly, should one assume that children are invited?

Yes.

If one can't attend, what should one do?

Verbally give your best wishes to the new parents.

APPROPRIATE ATTIRE

Men: Expected attire varies. Generally in those denominations that have a child consecration, casual attire is acceptable, but those attending the Church for the first time are advised to wear a jacket and tie. No head covering is required regardless of a specific denomination's degree of conservatism.

Women: Expected attire varies. Generally in those denominations that have a child consecration, women may wear a dress, a skirt and blouse or a pants suit or more casual attire, although those attending the Church for the first time are advised to dress conservatively. Clothing need not cover their arms nor hems reach below the knees. Open-toed shoes and modest jewelry are permissible. No head covering is required.

Generally in those denominations that have a child consecration, there are no rules regarding colors of clothing.

GIFTS

Is a gift customarily expected?

No.

Should gifts be brought to the ceremony?

See above.

THE CEREMONY

Where will the ceremony take place?

In the church's sanctuary.

When should guests arrive and where should they sit?

Arrive shortly before the time for which the service has been called. Ushers will usually advise congregants and guests where to sit.

If arriving late, are there times when a guest should *not* enter the ceremony?

Do not enter during the invocation. It may be best for tardy congregants and guests to enter while a hymn is being sung.

Are there times when a guest should *not* leave the ceremony?

No.

Who are the major officiants, leaders or participants at the ceremony and what do they do?

- *The pastor,* who blesses the child and parents, and asks congregants to help raise the child in a Christian environment.
- *The child,* parents and occasionally siblings.

What books are used?

In each denomination, various translations of the Bible are used. In the Mennonite Brethren Church, the most common versions are the New International Version and the New Revised Standard Version. More conservative denominations may use the King James Version.

Various hymnals are also used throughout the denominations. The Mennonite Church and the General Conference Mennonite Church use *Hymnal: A Worship Book* (Newton, Kans.: Faith and Life Press, 1992). The Mennonite Brethren Church uses *Worship Together* (Fresno, Calif.: The Board of Faith and Life, The General Conference of Mennonite Brethren Churches, 1995).

A church bulletin may also be used that includes prayers, responses or hymns.

To indicate the order of the ceremony:

Ushers will distribute a program.

Will a guest who is neither Mennonite nor Amish be expected to do anything other than sit?

In all but the most conservative Churches, a visitor would rarely do wrong by remaining seated when congregants stand or kneel, although the latter is rare in most congregations. However, if it does not violate their religious beliefs, the guest would be more in place by standing when others stand. Also, it is optional for guests to sing and read prayers aloud with the congregants.

Are there any parts of the ceremony in which a guest who is neither Mennonite nor Amish should *not* participate?

Communion is not offered to guests who are not Christian.

If not disruptive to the ceremony, is it okay to:

■ **Take pictures?** Not in more conservative denominations, such as the Beachy Amish Mennonite. Possibly (and only with prior permission of the pastor) in less conservative denominations, such as the General Conference Mennonite Church or the General Conference of Mennonite Brethren.

■ **Use a flash?** No.

■ **Use a video camera?** Not in more conservative denominations, such as the Beachy Amish Mennonite. Possibly (and only with prior permission of the pastor) in less conservative denominations, such as the General Conference Mennonite Church or the General Conference of Mennonite Brethren.

■ **Use a tape recorder?** Possibly (and only with prior permission of the pastor) in all Mennonite churches.

Will contributions to the church be collected at the ceremony?

There will no collection at the child consecration itself, but there will be one during the worship service which includes the consecration in the churches of most Mennonite denominations, but not in those of the General Conference of Mennonite Brethren.

How much is customary to contribute?

Guests are not expected to contribute, but should they choose to do so, $1 to $4 is appropriate.

AFTER THE CEREMONY

Is there usually a reception after the ceremony?

No.

Is there a traditional greeting for the family?

"Congratulations."

Is there a traditional form of address for clergy whom a guest may meet?

"Pastor."

Initiation Ceremony

In most denominations, a baptism is held for males and females who are in their early adolescence. In the General Conference of Mennonite Brethren, baptism may occur anytime from the onset of early adolescence into adulthood.

During the ceremony, candidates express their commitment to Christ, and kneel while a pastor sprinkles or pours water on their heads. Candidates may be baptized either individually or, if an adolescent, with their Sunday School classmates. The baptism may be either a service unto itself or part of a Sunday worship service. The baptism may last 15 to 30 minutes.

BEFORE THE CEREMONY

Are guests usually invited by a formal invitation?

No. The baptismal candidate and/or his or her family may verbally invite friends and extended family.

If not stated explicitly, should one assume that children are invited?

Yes.

If one can't attend, what should one do?

Verbally RSVP with best wishes.

APPROPRIATE ATTIRE

Men: Expected attire varies with the denomination and with the setting of the baptism. If the baptism is performed outdoors, wear casual clothing (although jeans and T-shirts are frowned upon).

If the baptism is performed indoors by a more conservative denomination (such as the Beachy Amish Mennonite), a suit jacket is worn, but not a tie. If it is performed indoors as part of worship by other denominations (such as the General Conference Mennonite Church or the General Conference of Mennonite Brethren), casual attire appropriate for worship is acceptable, but those attending the Church for the first time are advised to dress conservatively in a jacket and tie.

In no denomination is a head covering required.

Women: Expected attire varies. If the baptism is performed outdoors, wear casual clothing (although jeans and T-shirts are frowned upon).

If the baptism is performed indoors by a more conservative denomination (such as the Beachy Amish Mennonite), women are expected to wear dresses that cover their arms and have hems that reach below their knees. Neither open-toed shoes nor modest jewelry are permissible. Church members cover their heads, but visitors are not expected to do so.

If the baptism is performed indoors as part of worship by other denominations (such as the General Conference Mennonite Church or the General Conference of Mennonite Brethren), women may wear dresses, a skirt and blouse or a pants suit or more casual attire, although those attending the Church for their first time are advised to dress conservatively. Clothing need not cover their arms nor hems reach below the knees. Open-toed shoes and modest jewelry are permissible. No head covering is required.

Dark, solid colors are advised for more conservative denominations, such as the Beachy Amish Mennonite. For less conservative denominations, there are no rules regarding colors of clothing.

GIFTS

Is a gift customarily expected?

No.

Should gifts be brought to the ceremony?

See above.

THE CEREMONY

Where will the ceremony take place?

Either outdoors or in the church's sanctuary.

When should guests arrive and where should they sit?

Arrive shortly before the time for which the worship or baptism service has been called. If the baptism is being held indoors, ushers will usually advise congregants and guests where to sit.

If arriving late, are there times when a guest should *not* enter the ceremony?

Do not enter while Scriptures are being read, prayers are being recited or during the invocation to worship. It may be best for tardy congregants and guests to enter while a hymn is being sung.

Are there times when a guest should *not* leave the ceremony?

No.

Who are the major officiants, leaders or participants at the ceremony and what do they do?

- *The pastor,* who baptizes the candidate.
- *The candidate.*

What books are used?

In each denomination, various translations of the Bible are used. In the Mennonite Brethren Church, the most common versions are the New International Version and the New Revised Standard Version. More conservative denominations may use the King James Version.

Various hymnals are also used throughout the denominations. The Mennonite Church and the General Conference Mennonite Church use *Hymnal: A Worship Book* (Newton, Kans.: Faith and Life Press, 1992). The Mennonite Brethren Church uses *Worship Together* (Fresno, Calif.: The Board of Faith and Life, The General Conference of Mennonite Brethren Churches, 1995).

To indicate the order of the ceremony:

A program will be distributed.

Will a guest who is neither Mennonite nor Amish be expected to do anything other than sit?

In all but the most conservative Churches, a visitor would rarely do wrong by remaining seated when congregants stand or kneel, although the latter is rare in most congregations. However, if it does not violate their religious beliefs, the guest would be more in place by standing when others stand. Also, it is optional for guests to sing and read prayers aloud with the congregants.

Are there any parts of the ceremony in which a guest who is neither Mennonite nor Amish should *not* participate?

No.

If not disruptive to the ceremony, is it okay to:

- **Take pictures?** Possibly (and only with prior permission of the pastor).
- **Use a flash?** Possibly (and only with prior permission of the pastor).
- **Use a video camera?** Possibly (and only with prior permission of the pastor).
- **Use a tape recorder?** Possibly (and only with prior permission of the pastor).

Will contributions to the church be collected at the ceremony?

There will no collection at the baptism itself, but there will be one if it is part of a Sunday worship service in the churches of most Mennonite denominations, but not in those of the General Conference of Mennonite Brethren.

How much is customary to contribute?

Guests are not expected to contribute, but should they choose to do so, $1 to $4 is appropriate.

AFTER THE CEREMONY

Is there usually a reception after the ceremony?

Yes, although no food is served. It is usually held in the same building or the same outdoor site as the baptismal ceremony. If held indoors, those who have just been baptized gather at the back of the sanctuary to be greeted by well-wishers. The reception may last about 30 minutes.

Is there a traditional greeting for the family?

No. Just offer your congratulations.

Is there a traditional form of address for clergy whom a guest may meet?

"Pastor."

Is it okay to leave early?

Yes.

Marriage Ceremony

Mennonites and Amish believe that marriage was instituted by God for companionship, procreation and the nurturing of children. Those who marry should share a common Christian commitment. Divorce constitutes a basic violation of God's will.

A Mennonite or Amish wedding is an act of worship in which the couple profess their love for and their commitment to each other before God and ask His blessing on their wedding. The same decorum exercised in any worship service should be exercised in the wedding service.

During the ceremony, the wedding party progresses in, then the pastor reads appropriate lessons from the Bible and asks the bride and groom about their commitment to one another. The pastor delivers a brief homily, weddings vows and rings are exchanged, and the couple are pronounced man and wife.

The wedding is often a ceremony unto itself but may be part of a broader worship service. It usually lasts about 30 to 60 minutes, although some may last more than one hour.

BEFORE THE CEREMONY

Are guests usually invited by a formal invitation?

Yes.

If not stated explicitly, should one assume that children are invited?

No.

If one can't attend, what should one do?

RSVP with regrets and send a gift. (Note: Gifts are not expected at weddings of the General Conference of Mennonite Brethren.)

APPROPRIATE ATTIRE

Men: In more conservative denominations, such as the Beachy Amish Mennonite, a suit jacket coat is worn, but without a tie. In other denominations, such as the General Conference Mennonite Church or the General Conference of Mennonite Brethren, a jacket and tie are worn. No head covering is required.

Women: In more conservative denominations, such as the Beachy Amish Mennonite, women are expected to wear dresses that cover their arms and have hems that reach below their knees. Neither open-toed shoes nor modest jewelry are permissible. Church members cover their heads, but visitors are not expected to do so.

In less conservative denominations, such as the General Conference Mennonite Church or the General Conference of Mennonite Brethren, women may wear a dress or a skirt and blouse. Clothing need not cover women's arms nor hems reach below the knees. Open-toed shoes and modest jewelry are permissible. No head covering is required.

Dark, solid colors are advised for more conservative denominations, such as the Beachy Amish Mennonite. For less conservative denominations, there are no rules regarding colors of clothing.

GIFTS

Is a gift customarily expected?

Gifts are not expected at weddings in the General Conference of Mennonite Brethren. They are generally expected at weddings of other Mennonite denominations. Items for setting up a household are appropriate.

Should gifts be brought to the ceremony?

Yes.

THE CEREMONY

Where will the ceremony take place?

In the main sanctuary of the church.

When should guests arrive and where should they sit?

Arrive shortly before the time for which the ceremony has been called. Ushers will advise guests where to sit.

If arriving late, are there times when a guest should *not* enter the ceremony?

Do not enter during the procession of the wedding party or while prayers are being recited.

Are there times when a guest should *not* leave the ceremony?

No.

Who are the major officiants, leaders or participants at the ceremony and what do they do?

- *The bishop or pastor* (depending on the denomination) who performs the wedding ceremony.
- *The bride and groom and their parents.*
- *Musicians and/or song leaders.*

What books are used?

In each denomination, various translations of the Bible are used. In the Mennonite Brethren Church, the most common versions are the New International Version and the New Revised Standard Version. More conservative denominations may use the King James Version.

Various hymnals are also used throughout the denominations. The Mennonite Church and the General Conference Mennonite Church use *Hymnal: A Worship Book* (Newton, Kans.: Faith and Life Press, 1992). The Mennonite Brethren Church uses *Worship Together* (Fresno, Calif.: The Board of Faith and Life, The General Conference of Mennonite Brethren Churches, 1995).

To indicate the order of the ceremony:

A program will be distributed.

Will a guest who is neither Mennonite nor Amish be expected to do anything other than sit?

Guests are expected to stand with congregants when they arise. If it does not violate their religious beliefs, it is optional for them to sing and read prayers aloud with the congregants.

Are there any parts of the ceremony in which a guest who is neither Mennonite nor Amish should *not* participate?

If the wedding is part of a broader worship service at which communion is offered, it is not given to guests who are not Christian.

If not disruptive to the ceremony, is it okay to:

- **Take pictures?** Not allowed in most denominations. Possibly (and only with prior permission of the pastor) in the General Conference of Mennonite Brethren.
- **Use a flash?** Not allowed in most denominations. Possibly (and only with prior permission of the pastor) in the General Conference of Mennonite Brethren.
- **Use a video camera?** Not allowed in most denominations. Possibly (and only with prior permission of the pastor) in the General Conference of Mennonite Brethren.
- **Use a tape recorder?** Not allowed in most denominations. Possibly (and only with prior permission of the pastor) in the General Conference of Mennonite Brethren.

Will contributions to the church be collected at the ceremony?

No.

AFTER THE CEREMONY

Is there usually a reception after the ceremony?

Yes. This is usually held in the same building as the wedding ceremony. Refreshments may range from sandwiches, nuts and beverages to a full meal. Almost always, cake and ice cream are served. There will be no alcoholic beverages. There will be no dancing, although musicians may play background music after weddings of some less conservative denominations (such as the General Conference Mennonite Church). The reception may last from 30 minutes to more than two hours.

Would it be considered impolite to neither eat nor drink?

No.

Is there a grace or benediction before eating or drinking?
Possibly.

Is there a grace or benediction after eating or drinking?
No.

Is there a traditional greeting for the family?
"Congratulations" or "Best wishes."

Is there a traditional form of address for clergy who may be at the reception?
"Pastor."

Is it okay to leave early?
Yes.

Funerals and Mourning

Mennonites and Amish regard death as part of God's plan. Those who die as believers will share in the resurrection and be with Christ forever. The righteous will inherit the Kingdom of God; the unrighteous shall suffer the anguish of eternal hell. At the resurrection, Christ will create a new heaven and a new earth in which righteousness will reign.

A funeral or memorial service in a Mennonite or Amish church celebrates the life of the deceased and their passing into eternal spiritual life after death.

The funeral service may last between 30 and 90 minutes.

BEFORE THE CEREMONY

How soon after the death does the funeral usually take place?
Two to three days.

What should a non-Mennonite or non-Amish do upon hearing of the death of a member of that faith?
In most denominations, one may telephone or visit the bereaved or send them a card or letter to express condolences and concern for the family. Depending on one's relationship with the bereaved, one may also personally visit them.

APPROPRIATE ATTIRE

Men: In more conservative denominations, such as the Beachy Amish Mennonite, a suit jacket is worn, but without a tie. In other denominations, such as the General Conference Mennonite Church or the General Conference of Mennonite Brethren, a suit or a jacket and tie are worn.

No Mennonite denomination requires a head covering.

Women: In more conservative denominations, such as the Beachy Amish Mennonite, women are expected to wear dresses that cover their arms and have hems that reach below their knees. Neither open-toed shoes nor modest jewelry are permissible. Church members cover their heads, but visitors are not expected to do so. No head covering is required.

In less conservative denominations, such as the General Conference Mennonite Church and the General Conference of Mennonite Brethren, women may wear a dress or a skirt and blouse. Clothing need not cover women's arms nor hems reach below the knees. Open-toed shoes and modest jewelry are permissible. No head covering is required.

Dark, somber, solid colors are advised for all denominations.

GIFTS

Is it appropriate to send flowers or make a contribution?

Do not send flowers to bereaved who belong to more conservative denominations, such as the Beachy Amish Mennonite Church. For funerals in other Mennonite denominations, flowers are appropriate. These may be sent to the home of the bereaved upon hearing of the death or to the church where the funeral will be held. Contributions may be made in memory of the deceased to a cause designated by the bereaved family.

Is it appropriate to send food?

Food may be sent to the home of the bereaved upon hearing of the death or after the funeral. It is recommended to send prepared foods that can be refrigerated until needed.

THE CEREMONY

Where will the ceremony take place?

Usually in the main sanctuary of the church; sometimes in a funeral home.

When should guests arrive and where should they sit?

Arrive shortly before the time for which the funeral has been called. Ushers will advise guests where to sit.

If arriving late, are there times when a guest should *not* enter the ceremony?

Do not enter while prayers are being recited.

Will the bereaved family be present at the church or funeral home before the ceremony?

No.

Is there a traditional greeting for the family?

Express your concern by using such phrases as "My condolences to you" or "I want to express my sympathy to you."

Will there be an open casket?

Often in some Mennonite or Amish denominations. Rarely in the General Conference of Mennonite Brethren.

Is a guest expected to view the body?

Usually.

What is appropriate behavior upon viewing the body?

Pause in front of the casket or walk slowly past it, then sit in the sanctuary where the funeral will be held.

Who are the major officiants at the ceremony and what do they do?

- *The pastor,* who presides.
- *The song leader and/or musicians,* who lead or provide music.

What books are used?

Various translations of the Bible are used. In the Mennonite Brethren Church, the most common versions are the New International Version and the New Revised Standard Version. More conservative denominations may use the King James Version.

In each denomination, various hymnals are used. The Mennonite Church and the General Conference Mennonite Church use *Hymnal: A Worship Book* (Newton, Kans.: Faith and Life Press, 1992). The Mennonite Brethren Church uses *Worship Together* (Fresno, Calif.: The Board of Faith and Life, The General Conference of Mennonite Brethren Churches, 1995).

To indicate the order of the ceremony:

A program may be provided. If not, periodic announcements will be made by the pastor.

Will a guest who is neither Mennonite nor Amish be expected to do anything other than sit?

Guests who do not belong to these Churches are expected to stand with congregants when they arise. If it does not violate their religious beliefs, it is optional for them to sing and read prayers aloud with the congregants.

Are there any parts of the ceremony in which a guest who is neither Mennonite nor Amish should *not* participate?

No.

If not disruptive to the ceremony, is it okay to:

- **Take pictures?** No.
- **Use a flash?** No.
- **Use a video camera?** No.
- **Use a tape recorder?** No.

Will contributions to the church be collected at the ceremony?

No.

THE INTERMENT

Should guests attend the interment?

This is entirely optional. Often, the interment is intended only for family and close friends, and sometimes only for family.

Whom should one ask for directions?

An usher.

What happens at the graveside?

The pastor recites some opening words and a brief sermon, Scripture is read, and the casket is lowered into the ground and covered.

Do guests who are neither Mennonite nor Amish participate at the graveside ceremony?

No, they are simply present.

COMFORTING THE BEREAVED

Is it appropriate to visit the home of the bereaved after the funeral?

Yes, for anywhere from five to 20 minutes. It is appropriate to inquire about how the family is doing during this time of grief. Unless one is a close friend or a family member, it is advised to avoid asking for details about the illness and the death of the deceased.

Will there be a religious service at the home of the bereaved?

No.

Will food be served?

Possibly, but no alcoholic beverages.

How soon after the funeral will a mourner usually return to a normal work schedule?

The Church has no set ritual, but it is common for bereaved to be absent from work for a few days to a whole week after the funeral.

How soon after the funeral will a mourner usually return to a normal social schedule?

The Church has no set ritual, but it is common for bereaved to abstain from socializing from a few days to a whole week after the funeral.

Are there mourning customs to which a friend who is neither Mennonite nor Amish should be sensitive?

No.

Are there rituals for observing the anniversary of the death?

Cards remembering the deceased are appreciated upon the one-year anniversary of the death.

V · HOME CELEBRATIONS

Not applicable to Mennonites or Amish.

Chapter 11 Contents

Native American/First Nations

Native American/First Nations religion does not exist as a single, readily identifiable faith. (In practice, few Native Peoples use the word "religion" to describe their traditional ceremonies and practices. The term is used here to help those outside the community relate in some way to the understandings and "the way of life" of aboriginal/indigenous peoples.) Indigenous Americans (whom United States law recognizes as American Indians and Alaska Natives) and First Nations peoples in Canada have diverse and rich religious traditions. Although it is impossible to generalize about the diverse ceremonial practices of Native Americans/First Nations peoples, some suggestions regarding respectful behavior at their religious ceremonies can be made based on the beliefs and values that are the foundation of their deeply spiritual worldviews.

Because these beliefs and values are intimately related to Native people's sense of the sacred, they directly influence what would count as respectful and appropriate behavior for those invited to attend most Native American/First Nations religious ceremonies. Since even those who are well-intentioned are often not aware of these beliefs and values, they may behave in ways that Native Peoples interpret as disrespectful toward their religious ceremonies and practices. Diverse religious traditions explain why those who have briefly visited—or actually lived—with Native Peoples report that they have encountered a people who are deeply connected to the sacred.

According to the 1990 United States census, American Indian

and Alaska Native population totals approximately 1.9 million. Although this is roughly one percent of the total population of the United States, the more than 500 nations of the Native Peoples represent approximately 90 percent of the ethnic diversity in the United States. Among Native Peoples, there are nine major language families with almost 200 distinct dialects. From a constitutional viewpoint, the First Americans are citizens of their own various nations as well as of the United States.

Many First Nations people in Canada do not consider themselves to be "American" nor, for that matter, citizens of Canada. They see themselves as people of First Nations communities such as "Whata First Nations," or "Shawanaga First Nations," or "Peepeekisis First Nations." "Indian" is a term specifically used by the government of Canada to define certain aboriginal people mentioned in the Indian Act of 1867 and excludes many people of aboriginal ancestry. There are 53 aboriginal languages in Canada, including Inuit and Metis languages.

If you consider the geographic and cultural diversity of the five largest tribal groups in the United States alone—the Cherokee in North Carolina and Oklahoma, the Navajo in Arizona and New Mexico, the Chippewa of the Northern and Great Lakes regions, the Sioux (which include the Lakota, Dakota and Nakota) spread across the Northern Plains, and the Choctaw in Mississippi and Oklahoma—you begin to grasp why it is impossible to generalize about the cultural practices and specifically, the religious ceremonies and practices of First Americans/First Nations peoples.

I · HISTORY AND BELIEFS

Over the last 500 years, Native Peoples have endured what they consider to be almost constant disrespect. Recognizing this unpleasant legacy will help those desiring to visit Native American religious ceremonies understand why many Native Peoples are wary about sharing the most important elements of their identity with those who do not share their faith.

In 1879, for instance, the Carlisle Indian Boarding School was created in Carlisle, Pennsylvania. This was the first of what would eventually be dozens of off-reservation boarding schools designed to "solve" the "Indian Problem." In the late 1870s, the federal government assumed that the "Indian Problem" could be eradicated by education built around creating institutions dedicated to the complete cultural assimilation of First American boys and girls and erasing their beliefs, values and culture. Similar policies were enacted by the federal government of Canada.

Not surprisingly, given the centrality of the sacred to Native culture and identity, completely eradicating their indigenous religious and spiritual traditions was deemed a prerequisite for successful "education." Christian clergy often ran these schools since "civilizing" these children meant converting them to Christianity.

Understanding just this small part of the history of Native Peoples when attending their religious events and ceremonies can help you appreciate the intrinsically communitarian and private nature of their religious practices.

Native American/First Nations religion is primarily about experience, not about theology or doctrine.

It is simultaneously a personal and a profoundly communal experience. The nearly universal rule among Native Peoples that explains this is that ceremonies, customs and various cultural traditions, which are all ways of exercising spirituality, are, at their core, *community* activities for community members. Religious experience is profoundly shaped by one's membership and involvement in a community and one's life at a specific geographic place in relation to the whole of Creation.

Native spirituality denies the dichotomies common to Western religions.

The Western dualisms of supernatural vs. natural, spiritual vs. earthly/worldly, sacred vs. profane and heaven vs. hell do not easily fit with Native spirituality. Unlike religious traditions that see life on earth filled primarily with evil, toil and suffering, Native spirituality perceives the world as deeply endowed with the sacred power of the Creator.

Native languages, oral traditions, symbols, ceremonial objects and ceremonial practices speak directly to the recognition that humans are surrounded by the spiritual power of the Creator. Traditional prayers and ceremonies embody the widely held belief that we are imbued with one small part of the spirit of our Creator.

For Native peoples, the entire natural world is full of the sacred.

Each living part of Creation, and especially the places important to each tribe or village, serve as but one entrance into the power of the sacred. With this recognition of the complexity of Creation and the Creator's power comes the obvious realization that humans are but one part of the natural world, and not necessarily a privileged part or even the only "persons" inhabiting the earth.

Consequently, the high degree of religious diversity among Native Peoples reflects another widely shared element in traditional Native religious practices.

Native religious activities are almost universally attached to specific places.

These sacred sites mark the appropriate place for the enactment of certain ceremonies and religious activities. Even Native Peoples who experienced painful removal and relocation from their indigenous homelands in the eighteenth and nineteenth centuries found sacred sites in places new to them where their religious traditions could be carried out.

Most Native sacred sites are not analogous to a church, a temple or a shrine, which are consecrated as sacred by humans and built from blueprints, plans and drawings. Instead, Native ceremonial sites are often located on the land where specific tribes identify their spiritual center.

The places Native Peoples identify as their respective homelands and the communities that exist there are at the center of their religious experience. At the most fundamental level, the rich spirituality of Native peoples is literally "grounded" in their experience of the natural world as the cathedral of their Creator.

Native religious traditions are profoundly holistic.

Native faiths or teachings often refer to Creation itself as a complex web of life or a sacred circle in which all aspects of the natural world connect to each other. Because of this, humanity, in most Native worldviews, does not hold a privileged place above the rest of Creation, but is understood to be only a small part of Creation.

In many Native worldviews, many "persons" other than humans inhabit the world. Native Peoples attribute the qualities of power, consciousness and volition generally identified with the Western view of personhood to many living things. Consequently, Native Peoples perceive the environment to be inhabited with four-legged "persons" that swim in the water or winged "persons" that fly. To the Native way of thinking, these "persons" are also part of the moral and political community. Most importantly, they are also part of the spiritual community. In Native thought, to recognize that the earth is sacred is also to acknowledge all the "members" of our many respective communities.

The holistic nature of Native worldviews and spirituality gives a centrality to the idea of balance in one's life and in the world. Living in a good, healthy, beautiful way requires one to recognize that growth and success are achieved by integrating psychological, physical and spiritual well-being.

Native religious traditions openly acknowledge the existence of unseen powers.

Forces and mysteries exist that First Peoples experience and recognize, but cannot see or fully understand or comprehend. These sacred powers are not mysteries that need to be solved, but exist because humanity cannot know and understand everything about Creation or the Creator.

Native religions have no tradition of proselytizing.

Spiritual leaders and wisdom keepers do not undertake missionary activities. Their dependence on experience and on understanding the diversity of the circle of life makes it perfectly acceptable—and, perhaps to them, inevitable—that people from different places will have different religions. Consequently, First Peoples were always confused by other people who insisted they be just like them. This appreciation for the biological and cultural diversity of Mother Earth and her children explains Native respect for people's different ways of honoring the Creator and Creation. It also explains why Native people are often wary of those so interested in their traditions when the Creator gave all human beings a knowledge of the sacred.

II · ETIQUETTE SUGGESTIONS

Invitations are rarely given to strangers or outsiders to attend Native religious ceremonies and observances. In fact, it is usually preferred that one be a stranger to Native religious practices unless an invitation has been extended to attend a particular ceremony.

This statement may seem harsh unless you remember that Native Peoples primarily view their ceremonies as personal experiences shaped by an essentially community-based ceremony or ritual. It is, therefore, improbable that you would arrive as an outsider at a Native religious ceremony. Indigenous custom and habit generally frown on outsiders, even polite ones, from attending what is First Peoples' most precious way of identifying themselves as a people. The personal and communal nature of religious experience, combined with the lack of any mission to convert others or share traditions with those from outside one's Native community, means that it is best for you to respectfully keep your distance, unless specifically invited by a Native person to attend a ceremony.

Once invited, you will find hosts who are warm and open and who will give you as much information as is required to respectfully observe a ceremony. In addition, you will discover that Native people are very forgiving of slight breaches of etiquette, especially since, given the nature of the ceremonies, there is little expectation that visitors have prior knowledge of what they are observing and the specific behavior expected of them.

GENERAL GUIDELINES AND ADVICE

Here are some general guidelines:

▪ Pay attention. Be quiet. Listen.

▪ Once a ceremony or service begins, refrain from asking questions.

▪ Forget your ego and self-consciousness. These have no place in Native religious ceremonies. As human beings, we are all simultaneously beautiful and pitiful. Elders often use the latter term as an expression of our humility in the presence of the sacred. It speaks to the First Peoples' acknowledgment that man is just one small part of Creation.

▪ Worship takes many forms.

▪ Inquire beforehand about how you should dress for a specific religious event since it may take place outside, given Native people's attachment to nature and sacred sites. Weather conditions and the climate in general should always be taken into consideration when choosing attire for a particular ceremony or ritual.

▪ Be prepared to sit and stand for long periods of time. Ceremonies often require both.

- Be prepared to stay awhile at the ceremony. Ceremonies take as long as they need to take. Do not look at your watch. Ceremonies may last more than a few hours; sometimes they continue for several days.
- Before the ceremony begins, inquire about the appropriateness of coming and going during the course of the ceremony.
- Generally, contributions are not collected at Native ceremonies. In many situations in Canada, it is customary to give tobacco to the leader of the ceremony. It indicates respect and that you have come in humility and in need of teaching and prayer.
- Do not worry about doing the "wrong thing." Native people are very forgiving of your unfamiliarity with their faith and spiritual rituals.
- The best forms of address to use for religious or tribal leaders are "Mr.", followed by that person's last name. Do not use any of the stereotypical terms that have been promulgated by entertainment media, such as "Chief" or "Medicine Man."
- Try to limit your questions to a very practical nature and focus them on your behavior. Many Native people find it rude to be asked about the meaning of everything that will be done at a ceremony, or all the sacred objects that will be used or the nature of symbolism invoked. In Native religious traditions, experience is the greatest teacher. Meaning may not easily lend itself to a verbal or theological explanation. Again, your host or hostess will generally give you as much information as he or she feels you need.

QUESTIONS TO ASK

Here are some questions you might ask your hosts:

- When should I arrive?
- Where should I sit?
- If arriving late, are there times when I should *not* enter the service or ceremony?
- Are there times when I should *not* leave the service or ceremony?
- Who are the major officiants, leaders or participants at a service or ceremony and what do they do?
- What are the major ritual objects of a service or ceremony?
- What books, if any, are used?
- Are any announcements given to tribal members and/or their guests to indicate the order of the service or ceremony?

240 · *How to Be a Perfect Stranger*

- Will a guest who is not a Native person be expected to do anything other than sit?
- Are there any parts of the service or ceremony in which someone who is not a Native person should *not* participate?
- If not disruptive to the service or ceremony, is it okay to:
  - Take pictures?
  - Use a flash?
  - Use a video camera?
  - Use a tape recorder?
- Is there usually a reception after the service or ceremony?
- Is there a traditional form of address for religious or tribal leaders?
- Is it okay to leave early?

SPECIAL VOCABULARY

A few key words or phrases which might be helpful for a visitor to know and which will help you appreciate the diversity of ceremonial practice:

- *Blessingway Ceremony:* A ceremonial chant that recounts the Navajo Creation story and that is usually recited over two nights. It is performed to maintain a positive or healthy environment and to prevent imbalance or disharmony.
- *Faith:* Native Peoples would not say that their spirituality is based on "faith," as that word is commonly used. Native spirituality is grounded in experiencing the sacred in the natural world.
- *Potlatch Ceremony:* A diverse, complex series of ceremonies practiced by the Native Peoples of the northwest coast of North America. Its central function is to maintain balance and harmony among one's community. It generally consists of a community feast during which the host, typically a family, presents gifts to guests and also reenacts their family's oral history from mythic times to the present.
- *Religion:* Traditionally, Native Peoples do not think of their spirituality as a religion embodied in formal doctrine or theology. Rather, they understand their spirituality as embodying a way of life. It is the very manner in which one lives. From a Native standpoint, religion might be thought of as the awareness of the sacred in our lives and the acknowledgment of it through ceremony, custom and habit.
- *The Sacred:* As opposed to a conception of god or deity, for which many Native languages have no specific word, "the sacred" broadly captures the experience of the divine in this world.

◼ *Sacred Circle:* A symbolic representation of many Native peoples' conception of the world and life. It captures ecological cycles of life and death and represents one's journey along the path of life.

◼ *Sacred Sites:* Sites that Native Peoples recognize as being imbued with a specific or special aspect of the sacred.

◼ *Stomp Dances:* A common style of dance with tribes originally from the Southeastern United States. The primary rhythm is provided by singing, the use of gourds rattled by men, and turtle shells that are filled with pebbles and tied to women's legs.

◼ *Sun Dance Ceremony:* The most important annual religious ceremony for about thirty Plains tribes. Its meaning varies somewhat from tribe to tribe, but it is basically a test of courage and a demonstration of personal sacrifice. During the three-day ceremony, men undergo "piercing." This means they are suspended from a sacred pole by skewers of wood inserted into their chests.

◼ *Sweat Lodge Ceremony:* A ceremony common to many Native peoples. Its functions and use vary from tribe to tribe, but it generally provides purification and healing and restores balance in one's life.

◼ *Wisdom Keepers:* Also known as Elders. Living repositories of Native traditional wisdom, ceremonial practices and customs. The title does not necessarily imply age, since it is earned through extensive training and practice.

Some basic books to which a guest can refer to learn more about Native American faiths:

God Is Red: A Native View of Religion by Vine Deloria, Jr. (Golden, Colo.: Fulcrum Publishing, 1994).

Handbook of American Indian Religious Freedom by Christopher Vecsey (New York: The Crossroad Publishing Co., 1991).

Native American Religions: North America, edited by Lawrence E. Sullivan (New York: Macmillan, 1989).

The Native American Sweat Lodge: History and Legends by Joseph Bruchac (Freedom, Calif.: The Crossing Press, 1993).

Native Religions of North America by Ake Hultkrantz (San Francisco: Harper & Row, 1987).

The Sacred: Ways of Knowledge, Sources of Life by Peggy V. Beck, Anna Lee Walters and Nia Francisco (Tsaile, Ariz.: Navajo Community College Press, 1992).

III. SEASONAL CEREMONIES

In addition to the life-cycle ceremonies noted below, Native American/First Nations religions also have seasonal ceremonies throughout the year. These are invariably tied to cycles of nature. Native Americans in the Southwest, for example, observe the Green Corn Ceremony. This marks the full ripening of the late corn crop, which is usually in July or August. The ceremony is essentially a purification and renewal ceremony. Renewal is represented through the ripening of the corn and the promise of another year's bounty. Purification occurs at three levels: Throughout all Creation; throughout society; and within each individual.

The Indigenous Peoples of the Southwest closely guard the details of the Green Corn Ceremony, which is not open to those from outside the local Native American community.

Another ceremony tied to the seasons is the Hopis' Soyalangw Ceremony. This highly secretive ceremony is held at the winter solstice and involves the highest Hopi priests. It marks the beginning of a new year and stresses the importance of renewal and the maintenance of balance throughout all Creation. It also emphasizes that each person understand his or her proper place within Creation.

Non-invited guests cannot witness a Soyalangw Ceremony since it is held inside a *kiva*, a ceremonial lodge. But public dances linked to the ceremony are held after the ritual is concluded. Visitors might see these were they to journey to a Hopi village. While the dances are related to the Soyalangw Ceremony, they are widely perceived as "social dances" and are enveloped by fewer restrictions and more informal protocol than other Hopi ceremonies.

In the Canadian context, there are many ceremonies that are sacred and secret. Anyone who is allowed to participate should do so with a quiet, humble, respectful attitude.

IV. LIFE CYCLE EVENTS

Birth Ceremonies

While Native American birth ceremonies vary widely, three specific tribal traditions show some similarities.

ZUNI

On the eighth day of its new life, a Zuni baby's head is washed by the women of the father's clan and the infant is "introduced" to the world at sunrise. Corn meal is placed in the infant's hand and more corn meal is sprinkled to the east to acknowledge the rising sun. The paternal grandmother offers what serves as both a prayer and an introduction for the new infant. In part, this prayer asks the sun father to help the infant start the road of life in a good way.

OMAHA

Traditionally, the Omaha Indians also "introduce" their infants to the universe on the eighth day of their new lives. In the Omaha religious tradition, the child benefits from being introduced to the entirety of Creation. This includes the natural elements and the "beings" on which fragile human life heavily depends. In this ceremony, a spiritual elder stands at the door of the dwelling where the newborn lives and asks all the parts and beings of Creation to take notice of the infant and to help make the infant's future path of life smooth.

NAVAJO

Among the Navajo, special care is taken of the child before birth. Expecting parents are instructed not to attend certain ceremonies and funerals for fear that harm could come to the unborn child. Before birth, a Blessingway Ceremony is often performed for the mother and soon-to-be-born infant. This ceremony includes one of the central ceremonial chants of the Navajo religious tradition. The Blessingway Ceremony and chant, which is performed over two nights and often referred to as a "no sleep chant," recounts the events of Navajo Creation and invokes the sense of harmony and balance that pervades Creation. This chant is often used to help people when there is a sense of imbalance in one's life or an illness. For an impending birth, this ceremony and chant are performed to ensure the health and safety of mother and child.

Among the Navajo, a rather unique celebration is held when an infant gives its first laugh. This jubilant celebration involves a "give-away" sponsored by the person who first saw or helped the infant laugh. In this celebration, a meal is usually given by the sponsor (on the reservation, a sheep may be butchered for this meal) to guests and simple, not necessarily extravagant gifts are given by the sponsor to each guest. The celebration marks the first time the infant is allowed to wear jewelry. In Navajo traditions, this celebration is crucial because it is believed the infant will grow up to be selfish if the "give-away" is not held.

Although each of these birth ceremonies slightly varies, they also have much in common. Each marks the proper start of the child down the path of life by ensuring that he or she is introduced to the sacred in a manner that will result in a healthy, harmonious and balanced life.

◾

Sharing a meal is a traditional part of each of these ceremonies. A polite guest will always stay and enjoy this meal with his hosts. The meal and the conversation and fellowship during it are expressions of the good relations with others that the infant will experience as he or she embarks on their own path in life. Most parents will accept gifts for their children at these ceremonies. It is advisable that such practical gifts as clothing or a blanket be presented, although toys are also appropriate.

However, in the case of the Navajo, as indicated above, pretty "materialistic" items would not be given to the child until after the infant laughs and a "give-away" is held.

At any Native Peoples ceremony that welcomes a newborn, the child's parents and grandparents can be greeted with "Congratulations."

Initiation Ceremonies

Although complex, strictly proscribed ceremonial practices once marked the onset of puberty for Native boys and girls, many of these ceremonies are no longer performed. Modern life and its schedules and routines implicitly discourage the observance of most of these elaborate ceremonies, which lasted over several days and, in some cases, several months.

The coming-of-age religious ceremonies that continue today are most often given for girls when they begin menstruation. These ceremonies often involve a young girl going into seclusion for several days during her first menstrual period and being instructed by her mother, grandmothers and aunts about the value and power of womanhood. While earlier Native religious traditions often allowed little or no interaction with the larger community during this sacred event in a young woman's life, today's tribes, notably the Navajo and Apache, that continue to ceremonially mark this event allow everyone to share in this coming-of-age ceremony. Among the Navajo and the Apache, these ceremonies last four days. While the young woman undergoes her instructions separate from the larger community, feasting and socializing occurs for those celebrating the event.

At any of these Native Peoples coming-of-age ceremonies, the child and his or her parents can be greeted with "Congratulations," plus a statement that reflects your pride in the young teen's achievement.

Marriage Ceremonies

As with each of the above circle of life ceremonies, one of the central functions of the marriage ceremony is to impress upon the participants (in this case, the bride and groom) the importance of the new stage of life they are entering. The marriage ceremony both celebrates the event and prepares the new husband and wife to begin their journey together in a good way.

Traditionally, marriage ceremonies have always been community celebrations, although they have also been modernized in some ways. As Nico Strange Owl-Raben explained in an article about her Cheyenne wedding in a 1991 issue of *Native Peoples* magazine,

I use the word "tradition" carefully. Tradition is not a stagnant thing. It is always changing and adapting. My wedding could not have been like my grandmother's. It was not possible. I have heard about the changes in my grandmother's generation and I have seen what happened in my mother's. Now my generation is experiencing change. My wedding incorporated tradition so that we could have a blend.

Consequently, contemporary Native wedding ceremonies often combine old and new ways. For instance, Ms. Strange Owl-Raben's Cheyenne wedding combined traditional Cheyenne attire, custom and symbolism with some modern societal conventions. The ceremony was held outside amid a semi-circle of tipis that had been erected in a Northern Rocky Mountain alpine meadow—a cathedral, of sorts, in Native worldviews. In keeping with Cheyenne tradition, the bride's wedding dress was made of buckskin by the bride's mother and maternal aunts. The groom, a non-Cheyenne, wore a business suit. The bride entered the ceremony riding a horse led by her father in a procession led by her mother. After a judge performed a civil marriage ceremony, a traditional Cheyenne ceremony that consisted of a simple blessing was offered by Richard Tall Bull, a Southern Cheyenne Wisdom Keeper or Elder.

The blessing was the center of the traditional Cheyenne ceremony. After completing the prayer, Mr. Tall Bull burned sacred cedar and fanned the smoke over the couple and then fanned it into the sky with a sacred eagle feather. This manner of offering prayers is widely shared by Native Peoples throughout North America. Cedar, sweet grass, sage and tobacco are often burned as sacraments when prayers are offered, and the eagle feather is an almost-universally shared sacred ceremonial item among Native Peoples. The power of the feather is closely associated with the power of the eagle, and the right to possess and use it is earned.

Another aspect of the traditional Cheyenne marriage ceremony is the strict traditions regarding relationships between the future wife and husband and their respective in-laws. In the Cheyenne tradition, the new husband should not interact with his new mother-in-law and her sisters (his wife's maternal aunts). By custom, they are to live as if they are "invisible" to each other. To a non-Native, this might appear rude. But in Cheyenne traditions, such conduct is deemed to be a way to ensure familial harmony.

Many Native Peoples have similar practices. Although it would be impolite for a guest to directly inquire about this behavior, careful observation will usually reveal whether the "invisibility" between certain persons is part of the customs of the Native Peoples you are visiting.

After the formal marriage ceremony, as in most religious faiths, a celebratory meal follows. Presents are welcomed by the newly married couple and are generally of a very practical nature, such as blankets, dishes, pots, pans and small household items. (In the case of Ms. Strange Owl-Raben's wedding, her mother gave the couple a traditional gift of a tipi, a dwelling that is central to living the Cheyenne way of life even today. Of course, the gift of a tipi would be fitting for plains tribes, but of little utility to any of the tribes of the Southwest or Southeast where tipis are not used.)

At a Native American/First Nations wedding ceremony, the bride and groom can be greeted with "Congratulations," plus a wish that they enjoy a happy and fruitful life together.

Funerals and Mourning

Many Native peoples believe that death is the beginning of another journey, into the next world. Since one's spirit often needs help to make this journey, strict rules often govern the behavior of the living relatives of the deceased to ensure their loved one a good start in his or her journey to the other world. Some Potawatomi continue their ancient tradition of setting a place for the spirit of the deceased person at a funeral feast, in order for the spirit of the deceased to partake of the "spirit" food.

Among the Yuchi, who are politically recognized as part of the Creek Nation of Oklahoma and number less than 1,000, Christian burial customs are occasionally interwoven with Yuchi traditions. These may include placing such items as a hunting rifle, a blanket, some tobacco and other personal items in an adult male's coffin before internment. This reflects the Yuchi belief that one's journey in an afterlife is not significantly different from our present life.

At a Native funeral, express your sympathy and empathy to the bereaved. While Native beliefs assert that death is not necessarily the termination of life, the bereaved still mourn the absence from this life of the one who has died.

Many tribes restrict what bereaved relatives can eat and/or what kind of activities they can engage in after the death of a loved one. This represents a sacrifice by the living for those who have moved on in the circle of life.

Chapter 12 Contents

12

Orthodox Churches

(Includes the Antiochian Orthodox Church; the Carpatho-Russian Orthodox Church; the Greek Orthodox Church; the Orthodox Church in North America (also known as the Russian Orthodox Church); the Romanian Orthodox Church; the Serbian Orthodox Church; and the Ukrainian Orthodox Church. An entire chapter was devoted to Greek Orthodoxy in the first volume of How to Be a Perfect Stranger *since it is the Orthodox denomination with the largest membership in the United States.)*

I · HISTORY AND BELIEFS

The Orthodox Church, or the eastern half of the Christian Church, was formed in 1054 A.D. In that year the Great Schism occurred, causing a complete breakdown in communication and relations between the Roman Catholic Church, based in Rome, and the Orthodox Church, based in Constantinople. When the patriarchs of the various Orthodox churches meet, they are presided over by the Patriarch of Constantinople (present-day Istanbul), who is considered to be the "first among equals."

The term "Orthodox" is used to reflect adherents' belief that they believe and worship God correctly. Essentially, Orthodox Christians consider their beliefs similar to those of other Christian traditions, but believe that the balance and integrity of the teachings of Jesus' 12 apostles have been preserved inviolate by their Church.

Orthodoxy holds that the eternal truths of God's saving revelation in Jesus Christ are preserved in the living tradition of the

249

Church under the guidance and inspiration of the Holy Spirit, which is the empowering spirit of God and the particular endowment of the Church. While the Holy Scriptures are the written testimony of God's revelation, Holy Tradition is the all-encompassing experience of the Church under the guidance and direction of the Holy Spirit.

Orthodox churches are hierarchical and self-governing. They are also called "Eastern," because they stem from countries that shared the Christian heritage of the eastern part of the Roman and Byzantine Empire. They completely agree on matters of faith, despite a diversity of culture, language and the lands in which they flowered before arriving in North America.

Orthodox churches in North America today include:

- The American Carpatho-Russian Orthodox Greek Catholic Church, a self-governing diocese formalized in 1938 whose founders came from present-day Slovakia.
- The Antiochian Orthodox Christian Archdiocese of North America, an Arabic-language church whose first parish in North America was founded in Brooklyn in 1895. The Church in Antioch traces its origins to the days of the apostles, Peter and Paul, and to the Syrian city of Antioch in which the Book of Acts says the followers of Jesus Christ were first called "Christians."
- The Greek Orthodox Archdiocese of America, which is under the jurisdiction of the Ecumenical Patriarchate of Constantinople in Istanbul.
- The Orthodox Church in America, which was given full, independent status by the Russian Orthodox Church in 1970. It is comprised of ethnic Russians, Bulgarians, Albanians and Romanians.
- The Romanian Orthodox Church in America, which was founded in 1929 and was granted ecclesiastical autonomy in 1950 from the church in Romania.
- The Serbian Orthodox Church in the U.S.A. and Canada, which was created in 1921 and whose patriarchal seat is in Belgrade, Yugoslavia.
- The Ukrainian Orthodox Church of America, which was organized in 1928; and the Ukrainian Orthodox Church of Canada, which was organized in 1918, and which is the largest Ukrainian Orthodox Church beyond the borders of the Ukraine.

U.S. churches:

Antiochian Orthodox: 16
Carpatho-Russian Orthodox: 78
Greek Orthodox: 532
Romanian Orthodox: 37
Russian Orthodox (also known as the Orthodox Church
in America, or the OCA): 600
Serbian Orthodox: 68
Ukrainian Orthodox: 27

U.S. membership:

Antiochian Orthodox: 50,000
Carpatho-Russian Orthodox: 12,541
Greek Orthodox: 2 million
Romanian Orthodox: 65,000
Russian Orthodox (also known as the Orthodox Church
in America, or the OCA): 2 million
Serbian Orthodox: 67,000
Ukrainian Orthodox: 5,000

*(data from the respective denominations and from
the* 1998 Yearbook of American and Canadian Churches)

For more information, contact:

The American Carpatho-Russian Orthodox Greek Catholic Church
312 Garfield Street
Johnstown, PA 15906
(814) 536-4207

The Antiochian Orthodox Christian Archdiocese of North America
358 Mountain Road
Englewood, NJ 07631
(201) 871-1355

The Greek Orthodox Archdiocese of America
8-10 East 79th Street
New York, NY 10021
(212) 570-3500

The Orthodox Church in America
P.O. Box 675
Syosset, NY 11791-0675
(516) 922-0550
info@oca.org
www.oca.org

The Romanian Orthodox Episcopate of America
P.O. Box 309
Grass Lake, MI 49240
(517) 522-4800
roeasolia@aol.com
www.roea.org

The Serbian Orthodox Church in the U.S.A. and Canada
St. Sava Monastery
P.O. Box 519
Libertyville, IL 60048
(847) 367-0698

The Ukrainian Orthodox Church of America
3 Davenport Avenue, Suite 2A
New Rochelle, NY 10805
(914) 636-7813

Canadian churches:
Antiochan Orthodox: 15
Greek Orthodox: 76
Romanian Orthodox: not available
Russian Orthodox (also known as the Orthodox Church in
America): 606
Serbian Orthodox: not available
Ukrainian Orthodox: 258

Canadian membership:
Antiochan Orthodox: 100,000
Greek Orthodox: 350,000
Romanian Orthodox: not available
Russian Orthodox (also known as the Orthodox Church
in America): 1,000,000
Serbian Orthodox: not available
Ukrainian Orthodox: 120,000
(*data from the* 1998 Yearbook of American and Canadian Churches)

For more information, contact:
Antiochan Orthodox Christian Archdiocese of North America
St. George's Orthodox Church
575, rue Jean Talon est, bur. 555
Montreal, PQ H2R 1T8

Greek Orthodox Diocese of Toronto (Canada)
86 Overlea
Toronto, ON M4H 1C6
(416) 429-5757

The Orthodox Church in America (Canada Section)
P.O. Box 179
Spencerville, ON K0E 1X0
(613) 925-5226

Romanian Orthodox
Descent of the Holy Ghost,
Romanian Orthodox Church
2895 Seminole Street
Windsor, ON N8Y 1Y1

Serbian Orthodox Church in the U.S.A. and Canada
Diocese of Canada
7470 McNiven Road, R.R. 3
Campbellville, ON L0P 1B0
(905) 878-0043

Ukrainian Orthodox Church of Canada
Office of the Consistory
9 Saint John's Avenue
Winnipeg, MB R2W 1G8
(204) 586-3093

II · THE BASIC SERVICE

In the Orthodox churches, the purpose of worship and theology is mystical union with God. The liturgy is not a private performance by a priest, since he cannot perform the liturgy alone, but a joint act of laity and clergy. The language of prayer alludes to the majesty and transcendence of God, while also conveying God's presence.

Distinctive to Orthodox services is the burning of incense by a priest or bishop. The rising smoke from the incense represents prayers being carried to heaven.

Eucharistic services take place every Sunday and every major feast day. They usually last from one and a half to two hours.

APPROPRIATE ATTIRE

Men: A jacket and tie. More casual clothing is permissible in the summer, although jeans are discouraged. No head covering is required.

Women: A dress or a skirt and blouse. Clothing should cover the arms and hems should reach below the knee. A head covering is not required. Open-toed shoes and modest jewelry may be worn. Shorts, tank tops and sneakers should not be worn.

There are no rules regarding colors of clothing.

THE SANCTUARY

What are the major sections of the church?

- *The vestibule*, or main entrance.
- *The nave*, where one worships and participates in the services.
- *The sanctuary*, the altar area where the priest or bishop stands.

THE SERVICE

When should guests arrive and where should they sit?

It is customary to arrive either early or at the time for which the service has been called. In most Orthodox churches, ushers will advise guests where to sit.

If arriving late, are there times when a guest should *not* enter the service?

Do not enter during scripture readings and priestly blessings.

Are there times when a guest should *not* leave the service?

No.

Who are the major officiants, leaders or participants and what do they do?

- *A bishop*, who is the chief celebrant.
- *A priest*, who may be the chief celebrant or the assistant to the bishop.
- *The deacon, sub-deacon and altar-server*, all of whom assist the bishop or priest.
- *Acolytes*, altar boys who assist the adult officiants.

What are the major ritual objects of the service?

- *Icons*, two-dimensional artistic images of saints or of events in the life of Christ.
- *A gold-covered book containing the four Gospels from the New Testament.*
- *Censer*, an incense holder with bells. Smoke from the incense represents prayers being carried to heaven.
- *Chalice*, a gold cup. Held by a priest or bishop and contains the Holy Eucharist, the bread and wine, which, after being consecrated by the

Holy Spirit through the bishop or priest, become mystically changed into the body and blood of Christ.

What books are used?

The American Carpatho-Russian Orthodox Diocese uses *The Divine Liturgy of St. John Chrysostom* (Johnstown, Pa.: American Carpatho-Russian Orthodox Diocese, 1988); and the *Come to Me Prayer Book* (Johnstown, Pa.: American Carpatho-Russian Orthodox Diocese, 1986).

The Antiochian Orthodox Church uses *The Service Book* (Englewood, N.J.: Antiochian Archdiocese, 1987); *The Orthodox Study Bible* (Nashville, Tenn.: Thomas Nelson Publishers, 1993); *The Hymnal for Congregational Singing* (Englewood, N.J.: Antiochian Archdiocese, 1996); and *The Liturgikon* (Englewood, N.J.: Antiochian Archdiocese, 1994).

The Romanian Orthodox Episcopate of America uses *Holy Liturgy for Orthodox Christians* (Grass Lake, Mich.: Romanian Orthodox Episcopate of America, 1975) and *Union Liturgical Responses* (Grass Lake, Mich.: Romanian Orthodox Episcopate of America, 1977).

The Orthodox Church in America uses *Divine Liturgy* (New York: The Orthodox Church in America, 1967).

Several books may be used in the Greek Orthodox, Serbian Orthodox and Ukrainian Orthodox Churches, such as *The Divine Liturgy of St. John Chrysostom* (Brookline, Ma.: Holy Cross Orthodox Press, 1985).

To indicate the order of the service:

A program will be distributed or, most often, guests follow a liturgy service book that is in the pews.

GUEST BEHAVIOR DURING THE SERVICE

Will a guest who is not a member of an Orthodox church be expected to do anything other than sit?

Yes. Stand when the congregants rise. Kneeling with them is appropriate only if it does not violate a visitor's own religious beliefs. Otherwise, visitors may sit when congregants kneel. Reading prayers aloud and singing with the congregants are optional.

Are there any parts of the service in which a guest who is not a member of an Orthodox church should *not* participate?

Do not participate in holy communion. This is the high point of the service. It occurs after a priest or bishop advances toward the congregation from the altar, holds up the chalice and says, "With fear of God, with faith and with love, draw near." Congregants then go forward to receive communion.

If not disruptive to the service, is it okay to:

- **Take pictures?** Yes, but only with prior permission of a church official.
- **Use a flash?** Yes, but only with prior permission of a church official.
- **Use a video camera?** Yes, but only with prior permission of a church official.
- **Use a tape recorder?** Yes, but only with prior permission of a church official.

Will contributions to the church be collected at the service?

Yes. Trays are passed through the congregation at the end of the service.

How much is customary to contribute?

Contributions are entirely optional. While the amount of the contribution is at the discretion of congregants or visitors and the various Orthodox churches do not feel comfortable recommending specific amounts to guests, contributions between $1 and $5 are common.

AFTER THE SERVICE

Is there usually a reception after the service?

A 30- to 60-minute reception is usually held in a room or hall adjoining the church. Light food, such as coffee and pastry, is ordinarily served. No alcoholic beverages are served at this reception in Orthodox churches (although alcohol may be served on special occasions at receptions or banquets). In the Orthodox Church in America, also known as the Russian Orthodox Church, there will be a prayer of blessing before eating or drinking.

Is there a traditional form of address for clergy who may be at the reception?

"Father."

Is it okay to leave early?

Yes.

GENERAL GUIDELINES AND ADVICE

Many Orthodox churches have books or pamphlets in each pew that explain the service and that follow it, word for word. Also, since about 50 percent of each Orthodox service is in English, guests who are not Orthodox should not anticipate a service which is predominantly in another language.

SPECIAL VOCABULARY

Key words or phrases which might be helpful for a visitor to know:

- *Theotokos* ("Thee-oh-TOH-kohs"): "Mother of God."
- *Prokimenon* ("Proh-KEE-min-non"): "Offertory."
- *Proskomen* ("PROS-koh-men"): "Let us attend."
- *Dynamis* ("THEE-nah-mees"): "With greater power."

DOGMA AND IDEOLOGY

Members of Orthodox churches believe:

- In the Holy Trinity (The Father, the Son and the Holy Spirit).
- That after consecration, the Eucharist, the ritual meal of bread and wine that occurs during the service, is the body and blood of Christ. This is in contrast to some Christian denominations that consider the Eucharist to be symbolic.
- That the final authority for the Church is not vested in the Pope.

Some basic books to which a guest can refer to learn more about Orthodox churches:

The Liturgikon, by the Antiochian Archdiocese (Englewood, N.J.: Antiochian Archdiocese, 1994).

Orthodox Christian Catechism, 2 vols., edited by Duane Pederson (Hollywood, Calif.: Orthodox Christian Prison Ministry, 1996).

The Orthodox Church, four vols., by Thomas Hopko (Crestwood, N.Y.: St. Vladimir Seminary Press, 1976).

The Orthodox Church, by Timothy Ware (London, England: Penguin Books, 1993).

The Greek Orthodox Church, by Bishop Kalistos Ware (New York: Penguin Books, 1980).

III · HOLY DAYS AND FESTIVALS

■ *Elevation of the Cross.* Observed on September 14. Marks the finding of the true cross by the Empress Helena, the mother of Emperor Constantine, in the fourth century. This is a strict fast day. There is no traditional greeting for this holiday.

■ *Nativity of Christ,* a one-week celebration that begins December 25. Marks the birth of Jesus Christ. Orthodox church members traditionally greet each other with "Christ is born!" The response is, "Glorify Him!" Non-Orthodox can greet church members with "Merry Christmas!"

■ *Theophany of Our Lord,* a one-week celebration beginning January 6. Marks the baptism of Jesus Christ. Church members traditionally greet each other with "Glory to Jesus Christ!" The response is "Glory Forever!" Non-Orthodox can greet members with a smile and a handshake.

■ *Annunciation,* March 25. Marks the conception of Jesus Christ within the Virgin Mary. There are no traditional greetings for this holiday. Although this holiday usually occurs during Lent, a 40-day fast during which one abstains from eating fish, meat and dairy products, church members may eat fish on this one day.

■ *Palm Sunday.* Date of observance varies, although it usually occurs in April and is always the Sunday before Easter. Marks the entrance of Jesus Christ into Jerusalem. Although Palm Sunday occurs during Lent, a 40-day fast during which one abstains from eating fish, meat and dairy products, members of Orthodox churches may eat fish on this day.

■ *Easter,* also called Pascha ("PAS-ka"). Date of observance varies, but it usually occurs in April. Observes the resurrection of Jesus Christ after His crucifixion. The traditional greeting among church members is "Christ is risen!" The response to this is "Truly He is risen!" Those who do not belong to the Orthodox church can greet church members with "Happy Easter."

IV · LIFE CYCLE EVENTS

Birth Ceremony

The ceremony marking the birth of a child is the same for a male and a female infant. It marks initiation into the Church, forgiveness of sins and the beginning of the Christian life. Through baptism, one dies with Christ so he or she may rise with Christ.

The Antiochian Orthodox Church refers to this service as "Churching."

The baptism service incorporates Chrismation (known in other Christian denominations as confirmation), Baptism and First Communion. During the baptism, the child is fully immersed three times in a baptismal font, and then anointed (or "chrismated") with oil on the forehead, chest, hands, neck, back and feet. The communion emphasizes the fullness of participation in the sacramental life of the church. During it, the child is given the body and blood of Jesus Christ, which is known as the Eucharist, and which is bread and wine which have been consecrated by the Holy Spirit at a divine liturgy conducted by a priest or bishop.

In the Antiochian Orthodox Church, the ceremony may be celebrated as part of the Sunday Divine Liturgy. In most Orthodox churches, Baptism/Chrismation is a ceremony unto itself.

BEFORE THE CEREMONY

Are guests usually invited by a formal invitation?

Yes, usually either by a written invitation or over the telephone.

If not stated explicitly, should one assume that children are invited?

Yes.

If one can't attend, what should one do?

Telephone your regrets to the family, send a gift and visit the family soon after the ceremony.

APPROPRIATE ATTIRE

Men: A jacket and tie. More casual clothing is permissible in the summer, although jeans are discouraged. No head covering is required.

Women: A dress or a skirt and blouse. Clothing should cover the arms and hems should reach below the knee. A head covering is not required. Open-toed shoes and modest jewelry may be worn. Shorts, tank tops and sneakers should not be worn.

There are no rules regarding colors of clothing.

GIFTS

Is a gift customarily expected?

Yes. If one chooses to give a gift, either cash or baby clothes are appropriate.

Should gifts be brought to the ceremony?

Yes.

THE CEREMONY

Where will the ceremony take place?

Most often in the main vestibule of the parents' house of worship.

When should guests arrive and where should they sit?

Arrive early. Usually those present stand during the ceremony since it does not take place in the main sanctuary.

If arriving late, are there times when a guest should *not* enter the ceremony?

Do not enter during scripture readings and priestly blessings.

Are there times when a guest should *not* leave the ceremony?

No.

Who are the major officiants, leaders or participants at the ceremony and what do they do?

- *A bishop,* who is the chief celebrant.
- *A priest,* who may be the chief celebrant or the assistant to the bishop, and who baptizes and confirms the child.
- *The deacon, sub-deacon and altar server,* all of whom assist the bishop or priest.

What books are used?

The American Carpatho-Russian Church and the Antiochian Orthodox Church use *The Service Book* (Englewood, N.J.: Antiochian Archdiocese, 1987); *The Orthodox Study Bible* (Nashville, Tenn.: Thomas Nelson Publishers, 1993); *The Hymnal for Congregational Singing* (Englewood, N.J.: Antiochian Archdiocese, 1996).

The Romanian Orthodox Episcopate of America uses *Holy Baptism* (Grass Lake, Mich.: Romanian Orthodox Episcopate of America, 1993).

The Orthodox Church in America uses the *Baptismal Service Book* (New York: The Orthodox Church in America, 1967).

Several books may be used in the Greek Orthodox, Serbian Orthodox and Ukrainian Orthodox Churches, such as *The Divine Liturgy of St. John Chrysostom* (Brookline, Ma.: Holy Cross Orthodox Press, 1985).

To indicate the order of the ceremony:

A program may be distributed.

Will a guest who is not a member of an Orthodox church be expected to do anything other than stand with those present?

No. Reading prayers aloud and singing with the congregants are optional. If the Baptism/Chrismation is part of the Sunday Divine Liturgy (as it may be in the Antiochian Orthodox Church), then guests may kneel with congregants only if it does not violate their own religious beliefs. Otherwise, visitors may sit when congregants kneel. Guests are expected to stand with the congregants.

Are there any parts of the ceremony in which a guest who is not a member of an Orthodox church should *not* participate?

If the Baptism/Chrismation is part of the Sunday Divine Liturgy, when holy communion is offered, then those who are not Orthodox should not participate. This is the high point of the service and occurs after a priest or bishop advances toward the congregation from the altar, holds up the chalice and says, "With fear of God, with faith and with love, draw near." Congregants then go forward to receive communion.

If not disruptive to the ceremony, is it okay to:

- **Take pictures?** Yes, but only with prior permission of a church official.
- **Use a flash?** Yes, but only with prior permission of a church official.
- **Use a video camera?** Yes, but only with prior permission of a church official.
- **Use a tape recorder?** Yes, but only with prior permission of a church official.

Will contributions to the church be collected at the ceremony?

No, unless the Baptism/Chrismation is part of the Sunday Divine Liturgy. Then, trays are passed through the congregation at the end of the service.

How much is customary to contribute?

Contributions are entirely optional. While the amount of the contribution is at the discretion of congregants or visitors and the various Orthodox churches do not feel comfortable recommending specific amounts to guests, contributions between $1 and $5 are common.

AFTER THE CEREMONY

Is there usually a reception after the ceremony?

Yes. This may last from 30 minutes to two hours and may be held in the same building as the ceremony, at the parents' home or at a catering hall. A meal will be served, often accompanied by alcoholic beverages.

Would it be considered impolite to neither eat nor drink?

No.

Is there a grace or benediction before eating or drinking?

Yes. An invocation is recited to bless the food.

Is there a grace or benediction after eating or drinking?

Yes.

Is there a traditional greeting for the family?

Guests who are not members of an Orthodox church can just offer their congratulations. Parents who belong to the Antiochian Orthodox Church are often greeted with the phrase, "A blessed Churching" or "A blessed baptism," although the traditional greeting for all occasions in the Church is "Mabbrook" ("MAB-brook"), which means "Blessings." For other Orthodox churches, there is no traditional greeting.

Is there a traditional form of address for clergy who may be at the reception?

Yes. It is "Father."

Is it okay to leave early?

Yes.

Initiation Ceremony

In most Orthodox churches, baptism around the age of one-to-three months serves as one's initiation into the church. But in the Antiochian Orthodox Church, a 15-30 minute ceremony is done with pre-adolescents in an individual ceremony (not with a class of others).

BEFORE THE CEREMONY

Are guests usually invited by a formal invitation?

Yes.

If not stated explicitly, should one assume that children are invited?

Yes in most Orthodox churches.

If one can't attend, what should one do?

Telephone your regrets to the family and send a gift to the child. Visit the family at another time.

APPROPRIATE ATTIRE

Men: A jacket and tie. More casual clothing is permissible in the summer, although jeans are discouraged. No head covering is required.

Women: A dress or a skirt and blouse. Clothing should cover the arms and hems should reach below the knee. A head covering is not required. Open-toed shoes and modest jewelry may be worn. Shorts, tank tops and sneakers should not be worn.

There are no rules regarding colors of clothing.

GIFTS

Is a gift customarily expected?

Yes. Either cash or clothes are appropriate.

Should gifts be brought to the ceremony?

Yes.

THE CEREMONY

Where will the ceremony take place?

In the baptismal area of the family's house of worship.

When should guests arrive and where should they sit?

Arrive early. An usher will advise guests where to sit.

If arriving late, are there times when a guest should *not* enter the ceremony?

Do not enter during scripture readings and priestly blessings.

Are there times when a guest should *not* leave the ceremony?

No.

Who are the major officiants, leaders or participants at the ceremony and what do they do?

- *A bishop,* who is the chief celebrant.
- *A priest,* who may be the chief celebrant or the assistant to the bishop.
- *The deacon, sub-deacon and altar server,* all of whom assist the bishop or priest.

What books are used?

The Service Book (Englewood, N.J.: Antiochian Archdiocese, 1987); *The Orthodox Study Bible* (Nashville, Tenn.: Thomas Nelson Publishers, 1993); and *The Hymnal for Congregational Singing* (Englewood, N.J.: Antiochian Archdiocese, 1996).

To indicate the order of the ceremony:

A program will be distributed to congregants and guests.

Will a guest who is not a member of an Orthodox church be expected to do anything other than sit?

Stand when the congregants arise. Kneeling with them is appropriate only if it does not violate a visitor's own religious beliefs. Otherwise, visitors may sit when congregants kneel. Reading prayers aloud and singing with the congregants are optional.

Are there any parts of the ceremony in which a guest who is not a member of an Orthodox church should *not* participate?

Yes. Holy communion. This is the high point of the ceremony. It occurs after a priest or bishop advances toward the congregation from the altar, holds up the chalice and says, "With fear of God, with faith and with love, draw ye near." Congregants then go forward to receive communion.

If not disruptive to the ceremony, is it okay to:

- **Take pictures?** Yes, but only with prior permission of a church official.
- **Use a flash?** Yes, but only with prior permission of a church official.

▪ **Use a video camera?** Yes, but only with prior permission of a church official.

▪ **Use a tape recorder?** Yes, but only with prior permission of a church official.

Will contributions to the church be collected at the ceremony?

Yes. Trays are passed through the congregation at the end of the ceremony.

How much is customary to contribute?

Contributions are entirely optional. While the amount of the contribution is at the discretion of congregants or visitors and the various Orthodox churches do not feel comfortable recommending specific amounts to guests, contributions between $1 and $5 are common.

AFTER THE CEREMONY

Is there usually a reception after the ceremony?

Members of the church often hold a reception after the ceremony. This may last from 30 minutes to two hours and may be held in the same building as the ceremony, at a catering hall or at the parents' home. A meal will be served, often accompanied by alcoholic beverages.

Would it be considered impolite to neither eat nor drink?

No.

Is there a grace or benediction before eating or drinking?

Yes. An invocation is recited to bless the food.

Is there a grace or benediction after eating or drinking?

Yes.

Is there a traditional greeting for the family?

Just offer your congratulations. A traditional greeting for all occasions in the Antiochian Orthodox Church is "Mabbrook" ("MAB-brook"), which means "Blessings."

Is there a traditional form of address for clergy who may be at the reception?

"Father."

Is it okay to leave early?

Yes.

Marriage Ceremony

To Orthodox Christians, marriage is a sacrament of union between man and woman, who enter it to be mutually complemented and to propagate the human race. In the Orthodox churches, rings are blessed and the bride and groom each wear crowns during the ceremony to symbolize sacrifices made in marriage, the priestly nature of marriage and the fact that the bride and groom are now heads of their creation. The 45- to 60-minute marriage ceremony is a ceremony unto itself and not part of a larger service.

BEFORE THE CEREMONY

Are guests usually invited by a formal invitation?

Yes.

If not stated explicitly, should one assume that children are invited?

No.

If one can't attend, what should one do?

RSVP with regrets and send a gift.

APPROPRIATE ATTIRE

Men: A jacket and tie. No head covering is required.

Women: A dress or a skirt and blouse. Clothing should cover the arms and hems should reach below the knee. A head covering is not required. Open-toed shoes and modest jewelry may be worn

There are no rules regarding colors of clothing.

GIFTS

Is a gift customarily expected?

Yes. Customarily, this may be cash or household goods.

Should gifts be brought to the ceremony?

Bring the gift to the ceremony or the reception or send it to the home of the newlyweds.

THE CEREMONY

Where will the ceremony take place?

In the main sanctuary of the church chosen by the celebrants and their family.

When should guests arrive and where should they sit?

It is customary to arrive either early or at the time for which the ceremony has been called. Ushers will advise guests on where to sit.

If arriving late, are there times when a guest should *not* enter the ceremony?

Do not enter during scripture readings and priestly blessings.

Are there times when a guest should *not* leave the ceremony?

No.

Who are the major officiants, leaders or participants at the ceremony and what do they do?

- *A bishop,* who is the chief celebrant.
- *A priest,* who may be the chief celebrant or the assistant to the bishop.
- *The deacon, sub-deacon and altar server,* all of whom assist the bishop or priest.
- *The bride and groom.*

What books are used?

In most Orthodox churches, only officiating bishops and priests use a text at a marriage ceremony.

To indicate the order of the ceremony:

A program will be distributed to congregants and guests.

Will a guest who is not a member of an Orthodox church be expected to do anything other than sit?

Stand when the congregants arise. Kneeling with them is appropriate only if it does not violate a visitor's own religious beliefs. Otherwise, visitors may sit when congregants kneel. Reading prayers aloud and singing with the congregants are optional.

Are there any parts of the ceremony in which a guest who is not a member of an Orthodox church should *not* participate?

No.

If not disruptive to the ceremony, is it okay to:

▪ **Take pictures?** Yes, but only with prior permission of a church official.

▪ **Use a flash?** Yes, but only with prior permission of a church official.

▪ **Use a video camera?** Yes, but only with prior permission of a church official.

▪ **Use a tape recorder?** Yes, but only with prior permission of a church official.

Will contributions to the church be collected at the ceremony?
No.

AFTER THE CEREMONY

Is there usually a reception after the ceremony?

Yes. This may last from one to four hours and may be held in the same building as the ceremony, at a catering hall or at the bride's parents' home. A meal will be served, often accompanied by alcoholic beverages.

Would it be considered impolite to neither eat nor drink?
No.

Is there a grace or benediction before eating or drinking?
Yes.

Is there a grace or benediction after eating or drinking?
No.

Is there a traditional greeting for the family?

In the Antiochian Orthodox Church, the traditional greeting for all occasions is "Mabbrook" ("MAB-brook"), which means "Blessings."
In the Romanian Orthodox Church, the traditional greeting is "La multi ani!" ("Lah MOOLTZ AH-nee"), which means "Many years!"
In other Orthodox churches, "Congratulations" is appropriate.

Is there a traditional form of address for clergy who may be at the reception?
"Father."

Is it okay to leave early?
Yes.

Funerals and Mourning

Orthodox churches believe that death is the separation of the soul (the spiritual dimension of each human being) from the body (the physical dimension of each human being). Upon death, we immediately begin to experience a foretaste of heaven and hell. This experience, known as the partial judgment, is based on the general character of our lives regarding behavior, character and communion with God.

At some unknown time in the future, the churches teach, Jesus Christ will return and inaugurate a new era in which His kingdom shall be established. The final judgment will then occur. In our resurrected existence, we will either live eternally in heaven in communion with God, or eternally in hell and out of communion with God.

The 30- to 60-minute funeral ceremony is not part of a larger service, although in the American Carpatho-Russian Church, the Eucharistic liturgy (essentially the Sunday morning worship service) is often celebrated in addition to the funeral service. This is done at the discretion of the bereaved family and may cause the entire ceremony to last up to 90 minutes.

BEFORE THE CEREMONY

How soon after the death does the funeral usually take place?

Usually within two to three days.

What should a non-Orthodox do upon hearing of the death of a member of that faith?

It is appropriate to visit or telephone the bereaved at their home before the funeral to express condolences and recall the life of the deceased. When visiting a bereaved family before the service, a traditional greeting to a member of the Antiochian Orthodox Church is "May his [or her] memory be eternal."

APPROPRIATE ATTIRE

Men: A jacket and tie. No head covering is required.

Women: A dress or a skirt and blouse. Clothing should cover the arms and hems should reach below the knee. A head covering is not required. Open-toed shoes and modest jewelry may be worn.

Somber, dark colors are recommended for both men and women.

GIFTS

Is it appropriate to send flowers or make a contribution?

It is appropriate to send flowers to the funeral home before the funeral. It is also appropriate to make a contribution in the memory of the deceased to either his or her church or to a fund or charity designated by the family of the deceased.

Is it appropriate to send food?

Yes. This is ordinarily sent to the home of the bereaved upon either initially hearing about the death or after the funeral.

THE CEREMONY

Where will the ceremony take place?

Either at a funeral home or at the house of the worship of the deceased.

When should guests arrive and where should they sit?

Arrive early or at the time for which the ceremony has been called. Ushers will advise guests where to sit.

If arriving late, are there times when a guest should *not* enter the ceremony?

No.

Will the bereaved family be present at the church or funeral home before the ceremony?

Yes.

Is there a traditional greeting for the family?

In the Antiochian Orthodox church, a traditional greeting is "May God give you the strength to bear your loss." In other Orthodox churches, express your condolences.

Will there be an open casket?

Yes.

Is a guest expected to view the body?

This is optional.

What is appropriate behavior upon viewing the body?

Stand briefly in front of the casket and offer a silent prayer. A Christian might also cross himself or herself and kiss the cross or icon resting on the casket.

Who are the major officiants at the ceremony and what do they do?

◗ *A bishop,* who is the chief celebrant.
◗ *A priest,* who may be the chief celebrant or the assistant to the bishop.
◗ *The deacon, sub-deacon and altar server,* all of whom assist the bishop or priest.

What books are used?

In most Orthodox churches, only officiating bishops and priests use a text at a funeral ceremony.

To indicate the order of the ceremony:

A program will be distributed.

Will a guest who is not a member of an Orthodox church be expected to do anything other than sit?

Stand when the congregants arise. Kneeling with them is appropriate only if it does not violate a visitor's own religious beliefs. Otherwise, visitors may sit when congregants kneel. Reading prayers aloud and singing with the congregants are optional.

Are there any parts of the ceremony in which a guest who is not a member of an Orthodox church should *not* participate?

No, unless the Eucharistic liturgy is celebrated. In that case, guests who are not Orthodox do not partake in holy communion. This is the high point of the ceremony. It occurs after a priest or bishop advances toward the congregation from the altar, holds up the chalice and says, "With fear of God, with faith and with love, draw ye near." Congregants then go forward to receive communion.

If not disruptive to the ceremony, is it okay to:

◗ **Take pictures?** No.
◗ **Use a flash?** No.
◗ **Use a video camera?** No.
◗ **Use a tape recorder?** No.

Will contributions to the church be collected at the ceremony?

No.

THE INTERMENT

Should guests attend the interment?

This is entirely optional.

Whom should one ask for directions?

Ask the funeral director or a family member.

What happens at the graveside?

There will be a brief prayer ceremony, followed by the officiating priest or bishop usually putting soil on top of the casket so it forms the shape of a cross, and then each person present placing one flower on the casket or spreading soil on the casket. The flowers usually come from those sent to the church for the funeral and then conveyed to the cemetery with the casket. There will be no cremation since this is not permitted in Orthodox churches.

Do guests who are not members of an Orthodox church participate at the graveside ceremony?

No. They are simply present.

COMFORTING THE BEREAVED

Is it appropriate to visit the home of the bereaved after the funeral?

Yes. The tradition in the Orthodox Church in America is to briefly visit the bereaved the same day as the funeral. Religious objects that a visitor may see at such a visit are icons, two-dimensional artistic images of saints; a lighted candle; and burning incense.

Will there be a religious service at the home of the bereaved?

No.

Will food be served?

A Meal of Mercy is often given in the church hall, a restaurant or the home of the deceased shortly after the burial. At the homes of members of the Antiochian Orthodox Church, usually coffee, pastries and/or fruit are served.

How soon after the funeral will a mourner usually return to a normal work schedule?

The bereaved usually stays home from work for one week.

How soon after the funeral will a mourner usually return to a normal social schedule?

The bereaved usually avoids social gatherings for two months. In some cases, especially that of widows, the bereaved may avoid such occasions for a full year after the loss of the deceased.

Are there mourning customs to which a friend who is not a member of an Orthodox church should be sensitive?

Mourners usually avoid social gatherings for the first 40 days after the death. They may also wear only black clothing during this same period.

Are there rituals for observing the anniversary of the death?

A memorial service is held on the Sunday closest to the 40th day after the death. Subsequent memorial services are held on the annual anniversary of the death.

V · HOME CELEBRATIONS

The Home Blessing

When does it occur?

Either on January 6, the Epiphany, which is the traditional date for having one's home blessed annually, or shortly after moving into a new home.

What is its significance?

Holy water, which is sprinkled in each room, is used to sanctify the home, just as Jesus' baptism sanctified the waters of the River Jordan and all creation.

What is the proper greeting to the celebrants?

"Congratulations" or "May God grant you many years!"

BEFORE THE CEREMONY

Are guests usually invited by a formal invitation?

Either by telephone or a written invitation.

If not stated explicitly, should one assume children are invited?

No.

If one can't attend, what should one do?

Telephone the celebrants with your regrets.

APPROPRIATE ATTIRE

Men: A jacket and tie or more casual clothing (except jeans) are appropriate. A head covering is not required.

Women: A dress or a skirt and blouse or a pants suit. It is not required to wear clothing that covers the arms or hems that extend below the knees or to cover one's head. Open-toed shoes and modest jewelry may be worn. A head covering is not required.

There are no rules regarding colors of clothing.

GIFTS

Is a gift customarily expected?

This is entirely optional.

If one decides to give a gift, is a certain type of gift appropriate?

The usual sort of housewarming gift, which should be brought to the house when you arrive.

THE CEREMONY

The home blessing ceremony lasts between 15 and 30 minutes. The major officiant is the priest, who blesses the home.

What are the major ritual objects of the ceremony?

- *The cross,* which represents Christ's victory over death through His resurrection.
- *Water,* which is a vehicle for sanctification.
- *A basil flower,* which is used to sprinkle water in the air in the configuration of a cross in each room throughout the house as the priest recites blessings.
- *A candle,* which symbolizes that Christ is the Light of the world.

What books are used?

Prayerbooks may be distributed.

Will a guest who is not a member of an Orthodox church be expected to do anything other than sit?

Stand when the celebrants rise.

Are there any parts of the ceremony in which a guest who is not a member of an Orthodox church should *not* participate?

No.

If not disruptive to the ceremony, is it okay to:

- **Take pictures?** Yes.

- **Use a flash?** Yes.
- **Use a video camera?** Yes.
- **Use a tape recorder?** Yes.

EATING AND DRINKING

Is a meal part of the celebration?

Possibly. If so, it is served after the ceremony.

Will there be alcoholic beverages?

Possibly.

Would it be considered impolite to neither eat nor drink?

No.

Is there a grace or benediction before eating or drinking?

Yes. An invocation is recited to bless the food.

Is there a grace or benediction after eating or drinking?

No.

At the meal, will a guest be asked to say or do anything?

No.

Will there be:

- **Dancing?** No.
- **Music?** No.

GENERAL GUIDELINES AND ADVICE

None provided.

Chapter 13 Contents

13

Pentecostal Church of God

I · HISTORY AND BELIEFS

The Pentecostal Church of God was founded in Chicago in 1919 by a group of participants in the then-current Pentecostal revival movement in the United States. Many people involved in the movement spontaneously spoke "in tongues" (or in a language unknown to those speaking it) and claims were made of divine healing that saved lives. Since many of these experiences were associated with the coming of the Holy Spirit (the empowering quality of God) on the Day of Pentecost, participants in the revival were called Pentecostals.

The group that met in Chicago was convinced that a formal Pentecostal church was necessary because many smaller, new, independent Pentecostal houses of worship had become the targets of small-time crooks and con-men. They deemed their fledgling Pentecostal Church of God to be indispensable for the Pentecostal revival to continue to thrive.

Pentecostals tenaciously believe in their direct access to God, the Father, and believe prayer can manifest miracles. Worship services are demonstrative and energetic and are often marked by congregants speaking "in tongues." These are languages unknown to the speaker. Such speaking is interpreted as meaning that one is the recipient of the Holy Spirit. Alcohol and tobacco are prohibited to church members.

The Pentecostal Church of God has a combination of representative and congregational forms of government. While local churches are self-governing and elect their own ministers and local leaders, they are also expected to harmoniously function with the Church's district and general organization. The bylaws of local churches cannot conflict with the Church's district or general bylaws. Each minister is accountable to his or her District Board in matters of faith and conduct.

The Church's biennial General Convention is its highest legislative body. Policy is made and governed by the Church's General Executive Board.

The Church's World Missions Department has ministers in 42 countries and maintains schools in most of these nations, as well. In addition, the Church's Indian Mission Department makes outreach to Native Americans.

Although the Pentecostal Church of God is not present within Canada, the broader Pentecostal tradition is well-represented by the Pentecostal Assemblies of Canada and the Pentecostal Assemblies of Newfoundland, which have a combined total of 1,257 churches, 234,000 members and offices in Mississauga, Ontario, and St. John's, Newfoundland, respectively.

U.S. churches: 1,230
U.S. membership: 111,900
(*data from the* 1998 Yearbook of American and Canadian Churches)

For more information, contact:
The Pentecostal Church of God
4901 Pennsylvania
P.O. Box 850
Joplin, MO 64802
(417) 624-7050
peg@clandjop.com

II · THE BASIC SERVICE

Worship in the Pentecostal Church of God is marked by spontaneity and freedom of expression, and especially by exuberant prayer, music and Scripture reading, and "speaking in tongues." "Tongues" are used in three ways: praying, praising and giving messages from God through the Holy Spirit. "Praying in tongues" means that one is able to pray according to the will of God without the interference of one's natural desire. "Praising in tongues" lets the worshipper be free to express his or her love for God without the inhibitions of their natural language. This is the outward manifestation of the presence of the Holy Spirit.

Also, "messages in tongues" may be given during a service. According to Scripture, these "messages" should be interpreted by one who has the gift to make such an interpretation so they can edify the entire congregation.

The Lord's Supper (which certain other Christian denominations call "communion") may be offered at a worship service. The frequency of its observance by an individual church is at the discretion of each congregation.

Most churches have services Sunday morning and evening and Wednesday night. The Sunday morning service and the Wednesday night service may last between 60 and 90 minutes. The Sunday evening service may last for two to three hours.

APPROPRIATE ATTIRE

Men: A jacket and tie, or more casual attire, such as slacks and an informal shirt. No head covering is required.

Women: A dress or a skirt and blouse or other casual attire. Halters and shorts are frowned upon. Clothing need not cover the arms and hems need not reach below the knees. Open-toed shoes and modest jewelry are permissible. No head covering is required.

There are no rules regarding colors of clothing.

THE SANCTUARY

What are the major sections of the church?

- *The foyer*, where congregants and guests are greeted upon arrival by ushers or greeters.
- *The auditorium*, where congregants and guests are seated.
- *The platform or pulpit*, where the service leaders lead prayer, sing, read scriptures and preach.

THE SERVICE

When should guests arrive and where should they sit?

Arrive shortly before the time for which the service has been called. Sit wherever you wish.

If arriving late, are there times when a guest should *not* enter the service?

Do not enter during prayers.

Are there times when a guest should *not* leave the service?

Do not leave during prayers.

Who are the major officiants, leaders or participants and what do they do?

- *The minister,* who is in charge of the service and delivers a sermon.
- *The worship leader,* who leads singing and worship.
- *Associates,* who make announcements and help the worship leader.

What are the major ritual objects of the service?

There are none. Most churches have little, if any, adornment and usually lack statues and stained glass windows. The cross is the most commonly displayed symbol.

What books are used?

Several translations of the Old and New Testaments are used throughout the Church. The most commonly used is the King James translation. The most commonly used hymnals are *Messenger Hymns* (Joplin, Mo.: Messenger Publishing House, 1971) and *Messenger Melodies* (Joplin, Mo.: Messenger Publishing House, 1987).

Also, an overhead projector may be used to project the words of choruses to songs being sung by congregants.

To indicate the order of the service:

Programs may be distributed or periodic announcements may be made by the minister.

GUEST BEHAVIOR DURING THE SERVICE

Will a guest who is not a member of the Pentecostal Church of God be expected to do anything other than sit?

It is expected for guests to stand with the congregants. It is entirely optional for guests to sing with the congregants. Kneeling is seldom done during a service, although individual congregants may kneel at the end of the service in front of the altar. This is done entirely at their volition. Should there be kneeling during the service, guests may remain seated.

Are there any parts of the service in which a guest who is not a member of the Pentecostal Church of God should *not* participate?

Non-Christians should not participate in the Lord's Supper, which is a memorial to the death and resurrection of Jesus Christ. It is intended only for believers in Christ.

If not disruptive to the service, is it okay to:

- **Take pictures?** Yes, but only with prior permission of the minister.
- **Use a flash?** Rarely is this allowed—and only with prior permission of the minister—since it may distract from the service.
- **Use a video camera?** Rarely is this allowed, and only with prior permission of the minister.
- **Use a tape recorder?** Yes.

Will contributions to the church be collected at the service?

Yes.

How much is customary to contribute?

If one chooses to give, a contribution between $1 and $5 is appropriate, although any contribution is appreciated.

AFTER THE SERVICE

Is there usually a reception after the service?

No.

Is there a traditional form of address for clergy whom a guest may meet?

"Pastor," "Minister" or "Brother."

GENERAL GUIDELINES AND ADVICE

None provided.

SPECIAL VOCABULARY

Key words or phrases which might be helpful for a visitor to know:

- *Anointing with oil:* An ancient Christian practice in which the sick are anointed with oil in the name of the Lord. This may be done either at the beside of an ill person or at a Wednesday or Sunday worship service when the sick are asked to come forward to be anointed.

▪ *Foot washing:* Commemorates Christ's washing of his disciples' feet at the Last Supper. Individual churches determine the form and the frequency with which they will practice foot washing. For the ritual, men and women are in separate rooms and each gender washes the feet of other members of the same gender. Depending on their church's tradition, they may wash the feet of just one individual or of all those present. Many churches never have a foot washing service.

▪ *Lifting up of hands:* Holding up one's hands during prayer and praise in anticipation of receiving the presence and power of the Holy Spirit.

▪ *The rapture:* The "catching away" of believers by the Lord upon the return of Jesus Christ.

▪ *Regeneration:* When a person has fully accepted Jesus Christ as their Savior. Also known as "Born Again."

▪ *Salvation:* The time when one's sins are forgiven by God and one enters into a genuine relationship with the divine.

▪ *Sanctification:* Pentecostal doctrine in which holiness is considered to be a progressive work of God's grace beginning with regeneration.

DOGMA AND IDEOLOGY

Members of the Pentecostal Church of God believe:

▪ The Old and New Testaments are the inspired Word of God.

▪ God is a trinity in unity, consisting of the Father, the Son and the Holy Spirit (which is also known as the Holy Ghost).

▪ Jesus Christ was born of a virgin birth, lived a sinless life, performed miracles, atoned for the sins of others on the cross and was resurrected bodily to be at the right hand of God, the Father.

▪ Regeneration by the Holy Spirit is absolutely essential for the salvation of the lost and sinful.

▪ Baptism by water is through immersion, is a direct commandment of the Lord and is only for believers. Baptism symbolizes one's identification with Christ's death, burial and resurrection.

▪ Atoning for one's sins provides for divine healing.

▪ The Lord's Supper is a commandment of Christ, and is a memorial to His death and resurrection. It is for believers in Christ only.

▪ Jesus Christ will bodily return to reign on earth for one thousand years and, according to Church literature, "to resurrect the dead and to catch away the living saints to meet him in the air." This is often referred to as "the rapture." Teachings on the rapture are found in I Thessalonians (4:16-17). At the rapture, only believers in Christ will be resurrected to eternal life. The resurrection of sinners will occur seven years later, when they will face eternal damnation.

■ It is "unwise" to teach that Christ will return at a certain time or date.

Basic books to which a guest can refer to learn more about the Pentecostal Church of God:

Basic Bible Truth, by Aaron M. Wilson (Joplin, Mo.: Messenger Publishing House, 1987).

Dictionary of Pentecostal and Charismatic Movements, by Stanley M. Burgess, Gary B. McGee and Patrick H. Alexander (Grand Rapids, Mich.: Zondervan Publishing House, 1988).

III · HOLY DAYS AND FESTIVALS

■ *Christmas,* celebrated on December 25. Marks the birth of Jesus Christ. Church members and non-church members can greet each other with "Merry Christmas!"

■ *Good Friday.* The date of observance varies, although it usually occurs in April and is always the Friday before Easter. Marks the crucifixion of Christ in Jerusalem. There is no traditional greeting for this holiday.

■ *Easter.* The date of observance varies, but it usually occurs in April and is always on the Sunday after the first full moon that occurs on or after the spring equinox of March 21. Commemorates the resurrection of Jesus Christ after His crucifixion. The traditional greeting is "Happy Easter!"

■ *Pentecost.* Occurs 50 days after Easter because this is when the Holy Spirit descended on Christ's apostles. Celebrates the power of the Holy Spirit and its manifestation in the early Christian church. There is no traditional greeting for this holiday.

IV · LIFE CYCLE EVENTS

Birth Ceremony

This ceremony, which is called a dedication, is based on the biblical account of Jesus calling young children to Him and blessing them. The Church does not believe that the dedication constitutes salvation, but rather that it lets the child's parents publicly commit themselves to their intention to raise the child in the teachings of Jesus.

During the dedication, which is for infants or young children, the minister asks the parents to pledge to live in such a way that, at an early age, their child will be a Christian. They respond with, "We do." Some ministers also charge the congregation to help the parents by role-modeling Christian living for the child.

The dedication, which is the same for males and females, usually lasts about three to five minutes. It is part of a larger service (usually a Sunday morning worship service) that lasts about 60 to 90 minutes.

BEFORE THE CEREMONY

Are guests usually invited by a formal invitation?

No.

If not stated explicitly, should one assume that children are invited?

Yes.

If one can't attend, what should one do?

RSVP orally with regrets.

APPROPRIATE ATTIRE

Men: A jacket and tie or more casual attire, such as slacks and an informal shirt. No head covering is required.

Women: A dress or a skirt and blouse or other casual attire. Halters and shorts are frowned upon. Clothing need not cover the arms and hems need not reach below the knees. Open-toed shoes and modest jewelry are permissible. No head covering is required.

There are no rules regarding colors of clothing.

GIFTS

Is a gift customarily expected?

No.

Should gifts be brought to the ceremony?

See above.

THE CEREMONY

Where will the ceremony take place?

In the main auditorium of the church.

When should guests arrive and where should they sit?

Arrive shortly before the time for which the ceremony has been called. Sit wherever you wish.

If arriving late, are there times when a guest should *not* enter the ceremony?

Do not enter during prayers.

Are there times when a guest should *not* leave the ceremony?

Do not leave during prayers.

Who are the major officiants, leaders or participants at the ceremony and what do they do?

- *The minister,* who leads the prayer of dedication and makes comments about the infant.
- *The child's parents.*
- *The child.*

What books are used?

A Bible and a hymnal are used. Several translations of the Old and New Testaments are used throughout the Church. The most commonly used is the King James translation. The most commonly used hymnals are *Messenger Hymns* (Joplin, Mo.: Messenger Publishing House, 1971) and *Messenger Melodies* (Joplin, Mo.: Messenger Publishing House, 1987).

Also, an overhead projector may be used to project the words of choruses to songs being sung by congregants.

To indicate the order of the ceremony:

Periodic announcements will be made by the minister.

Will a guest who is not a member of the Pentecostal Church of God be expected to do anything other than sit?

It is expected for guests to stand with the congregants. It is entirely optional for guests to sing with the congregants. Kneeling is seldom done during a service, although individual congregants may kneel at the end of the service in front of the altar. This is done entirely at their volition. Should there be kneeling during the service, guests may remain seated.

Are there any parts of the ceremony in which a guest who is not a member of the Pentecostal Church of God should *not* participate?

Non-Christians should not participate in the Lord's Supper, which is a memorial to the death and resurrection of Jesus Christ. It is intended only for believers in Christ.

If not disruptive to the ceremony, is it okay to:

◘ **Take pictures?** Yes, but only with prior permission of the minister.

◘ **Use a flash?** Rarely is this allowed—and only with prior permission of the minister—since it may distract from the ceremony.

◘ **Use a video camera?** Rarely is this allowed, and only with prior permission of the minister.

◘ **Use a tape recorder?** Yes.

Will contributions to the church be collected at the ceremony?

Contributions will not be collected at the Dedication itself, but they will be collected during the rest of the worship service.

How much is customary to contribute?

If one chooses to give, a contribution between $1 and $5 is appropriate, however any contribution is appreciated.

AFTER THE CEREMONY

Is there usually a reception after the ceremony?

No.

Is there a traditional greeting for the family?

"Congratulations."

Is there a traditional form of address for clergy whom a guest may meet?

"Minister," "Pastor" or "Brother."

Initiation Ceremony

This ceremony, which is the same for males and females, is called a baptism. During it, those who have accepted Christ as their savior are fully immersed in the baptismal waters.

Baptism is necessary because all people are born in a sinful condition. It is considered to be an outward expression of an inward spiritual work, and a public testimony of the death of the individual's sinful nature and of one's new birth in the spirit of Jesus. It endows believers with the power to witness and serve others; a dedication to the work of God; a more intense love for Jesus; and certain spiritual gifts. Baptism, which is performed once for any individual, can occur at any time during one's life. It always occurs after one has accepted Jesus Christ as their Savior and after one has reached the age of accountability and knows right from wrong.

The baptismal ceremony is usually part of a regular Sunday morning or evening church service. The baptism itself may last about 15 to 30 minutes, depending on the number of persons being baptized.

BEFORE THE CEREMONY

Are guests usually invited by a formal invitation?

They are usually invited informally and orally.

If not stated explicitly, should one assume that children are invited?

Yes.

If one can't attend, what should one do?

RSVP orally with regrets.

APPROPRIATE ATTIRE

Men: A jacket and tie or more casual attire, such as slacks and an informal shirt. No head covering is required.

Women: A dress or a skirt and blouse or other casual attire. Halters and shorts are frowned upon. Clothing need not cover the arms and hems need not reach below the knees. Open-toed shoes and modest jewelry are permissible. No head covering is required.

There are no rules regarding colors of clothing.

GIFTS

Is a gift customarily expected?

No.

Should gifts be brought to the ceremony?

See above.

THE CEREMONY

Where will the ceremony take place?

In the main auditorium of the church.

When should guests arrive and where should they sit?

Arrive shortly before the time for which the service has been called. Sit wherever you wish.

If arriving late, are there times when a guest should *not* enter the ceremony?

Do not enter during prayers.

Are there times when a guest should *not* leave the ceremony?

Do not leave during prayers.

Who are the major officiants, leaders or participants at the ceremony and what do they do?

◪ *The minister,* who performs the baptism.

What books are used?

A Bible and a hymnal are used. Several translations of the Old and New Testaments are used throughout the Church. The most commonly used is the King James translation. The most commonly used hymnals are *Messenger Hymns* (Joplin, Mo.: Messenger Publishing House, 1971) and *Messenger Melodies* (Joplin, Mo.: Messenger Publishing House, 1987).

Also, an overhead projector may be used to project the words of choruses to songs being sung by congregants.

To indicate the order of the ceremony:

Periodic announcements may be made by the minister or whoever is leading the ceremony.

Will a guest who is not a member of the Pentecostal Church of God be expected to do anything other than sit?

It is expected for guests to stand with the congregants. It is entirely optional for guests to sing with the congregants. Kneeling is seldom done during the ceremony, although individual congregants may kneel at the end of the service directly in front of the altar. This is done entirely at their volition. Should there be kneeling during the service, guests may remain seated.

Are there any parts of the ceremony in which a guest who is not a member of the Pentecostal Church of God should *not* participate?

Non-Christians should not participate in the Lord's Supper, which is a memorial to the death and resurrection of Jesus Christ. It is intended only for believers in Christ.

If not disruptive to the ceremony, is it okay to:

◘ **Take pictures?** Yes, but only with prior permission of the minister.

◘ **Use a flash?** Yes, but only with prior permission of the minister.

◘ **Use a video camera?** Yes, but only with prior permission of the minister.

◘ **Use a tape recorder?** Yes.

Will contributions to the church be collected at the ceremony?

Contributions will not be collected at the baptism itself, but they will be collected during the rest of the worship service.

How much is customary to contribute?

If one chooses to give, a contribution between $1 and $5 is appropriate, however, any contribution is appreciated.

AFTER THE CEREMONY

Is there usually a reception after the ceremony?

No.

Is there a traditional greeting for the family?

"Congratulations."

Is there a traditional form of address for clergy whom a guest may meet after the ceremony?

"Minister," "Pastor" or "Brother."

Marriage Ceremony

The Pentecostal Church of God teaches that the family was the first institution ordained by God in the Garden of Eden. The basis for a family is marriage between a man and a woman. Marriage, which is not to be entered into lightly, is said to be "until death do us part."

The marriage ceremony is a ceremony unto itself and may last 30 to 60 minutes.

BEFORE THE CEREMONY

Are guests usually invited by a formal invitation?

Yes.

If not stated explicitly, should one assume that children are invited?

Yes.

If one can't attend, what should one do?

RSVP by card or letter with regrets and send a gift.

APPROPRIATE ATTIRE

Men: A jacket and tie or more casual attire, but not jeans or T-shirts. No head covering is required.

Women: A dress or a skirt and blouse. Clothing need not cover the arms and hems need not reach below the knees. Open-toed shoes and modest jewelry are permissible. No head covering is required.

There are no rules regarding colors of clothing.

GIFTS

Is a gift customarily expected?

Yes. Cash, savings bonds or small household items are most frequently given.

Should gifts be brought to the ceremony?

Gifts may either be brought to the ceremony or the reception afterward, or sent to the home of the newlyweds.

THE CEREMONY

Where will the ceremony take place?

In the sanctuary of the church.

When should guests arrive and where should they sit?

Arrive shortly before the time for which the ceremony has been called. Ushers will usually advise guests where to sit. Usually, the groom's family and friends sit on one side of the aisle and the bride's family and friends on the other.

If arriving late, are there times when a guest should *not* enter the ceremony?

Do not enter during the processional or recessional of the wedding party.

Are there times when a guest should *not* leave the ceremony?

Do not leave during the processional or recessional of the wedding party.

Who are the major officiants, leaders or participants at the ceremony and what do they do?

◘ *The minister,* who officiates.
◘ *The bride and groom and members of the wedding party.*

What books are used?

No books are used by the guests.

To indicate the order of the ceremony:

A program is sometimes distributed. If not, periodic announcements are made by the minister.

Will a guest who is not a member of the Pentecostal Church of God be expected to do anything other than sit?

Guests of other faiths are expected to stand when other guests arise during the ceremony.

Are there any parts of the ceremony in which a guest who is not a member of the Pentecostal Church of God should *not* participate?

No.

If not disruptive to the ceremony, is it okay to:

◘ **Take pictures?** Yes, but only with prior permission of the minister.
◘ **Use a flash?** Yes, but only with prior permission of the minister.
◘ **Use a video camera?** Yes, but only with prior permission of the minister.
◘ **Use a tape recorder?** Yes.

Will contributions to the church be collected at the ceremony?

No.

AFTER THE CEREMONY

Is there usually a reception after the ceremony?

Yes. It may be in the same building where the wedding ceremony was held or in a catering hall. Receptions usually include light food, such as finger foods, cake, mints, nuts and punch. There will be no alcoholic beverages or dancing, although there might be music. The reception may last 30 to 60 minutes.

Would it be considered impolite to neither eat nor drink?

No.

Is there a grace or benediction before eating or drinking?

No.

Is there a grace or benediction after eating or drinking?

No.

Is there a traditional greeting for the family?

Just offer your congratulations.

Is there a traditional form of address for clergy who may be at the reception?

"Pastor," "Minister" or "Brother."

Is it okay to leave early?

Yes.

Funerals and Mourning

Members of the Pentecostal Church of God believe that all Christians who have died will one day rise from their graves and meet the Lord "in the air." Meanwhile, Christians who are still alive will be caught up with those who have risen from their graves and will also be with the Lord. All who have thus joined with God will live forever.

A Pentecostal Church of God funeral usually begins with singing, Scripture reading or prayer. This is followed with hymns, prayer and worship to God, and a sermon and eulogy by the minister.

A ceremony unto itself, the funeral ceremony lasts about 30 to 60 minutes.

BEFORE THE CEREMONY

How soon after the death does the funeral usually take place?

Within two to three days.

What should someone who is not a member of the Pentecostal Church of God do upon hearing of the death of a member of that faith?

Telephone or visit the bereaved to offer condolences and sympathies and offer to assist in any way possible.

APPROPRIATE ATTIRE

Men: A jacket and tie. No head covering is required.

Women: A dress or a skirt and blouse. Clothing need not cover the arms and hems need not reach below the knees. Open-toed shoes and modest jewelry are permissible. No head covering is required.

Dark, somber colors for clothing are advised.

GIFTS

Is it appropriate to send flowers or make a contribution?

Flowers may be sent to the funeral home or church where the funeral ceremony is held. Contributions may be sent to a memorial fund determined by the bereaved.

Is it appropriate to send food?

Yes. Send or take it yourself to the home of the bereaved.

THE CEREMONY

Where will the ceremony take place?

Either in a church or a funeral home.

When should guests arrive and where should they sit?

Arrive at the time for which the ceremony has been scheduled. Ushers usually advise guests where to sit.

If arriving late, are there times when a guest should *not* enter the ceremony?

No.

Will the bereaved family be present at the church or funeral home before the ceremony?

Yes.

Is there a traditional greeting for the family?

Just offer your condolences.

Will there be an open casket?

Possibly. This varies with local custom.

Is a guest expected to view the body?

This is optional.

What is appropriate behavior upon viewing the body?

Look into the casket while walking slowly past it, then follow the instructions of the funeral director.

294 · *How to Be a Perfect Stranger*

Who are the major officiants at the ceremony and what do they do?

◪ *The minister,* who delivers a brief sermon and tribute to the deceased.

◪ *Musicians,* who sing two or three songs.

What books are used?

No books are used by mourners or guests.

To indicate the order of the ceremony:

Either a program will be distributed or the minister will make the necessary announcements.

Will a guest who is not a member of the Pentecostal Church of God be expected to do anything other than sit?

Guests of other faiths are expected to stand when other guests arise during the ceremony. While there is usually no kneeling during a funeral ceremony, if there is kneeling, guests of other faiths may remain seated.

Are there any parts of the ceremony in which a guest who is not a member of the Pentecostal Church of God should *not* participate?

No.

If not disruptive to the ceremony, is it okay to:

◪ **Take pictures?** No.

◪ **Use a flash?** No.

◪ **Use a video camera?** No.

◪ **Use a tape recorder?** Yes.

Will contributions to the church be collected at the ceremony?

No.

THE INTERMENT

Should guests attend the interment?

Attendance is optional.

Whom should one ask for directions?

An usher or the funeral director or just follow the funeral procession.

What happens at the graveside?

There is usually a prayer and Scripture readings, and sometimes a song. The casket is committed to the ground.

Do guests who are not members of the Pentecostal Church of God participate at the graveside ceremony?

No, they are simply present.

COMFORTING THE BEREAVED

Is it appropriate to visit the home of the bereaved after the funeral?

Yes, if one knows the family well.

Will there be a religious service at the home of the bereaved?

No.

Will food be served?

Possibly, but no alcoholic beverages.

How soon after the funeral will a mourner usually return to a normal work schedule?

A few days, depending upon individual preference. The Church has no set tradition.

How soon after the funeral will a mourner usually return to a normal social schedule?

This is entirely the choice of the bereaved, since the Church has no set tradition. It is often determined by local cultural traditions.

Are there mourning customs to which a friend who is not a member of the Pentecostal Church of God should be sensitive?

No.

Are there rituals for observing the anniversary of the death?

No.

V · HOME CELEBRATIONS

Not applicable to the Pentecostal Church of God.

Chapter 14 Contents

14

Reformed Church in America/Canada

I · HISTORY AND BELIEFS

The Reformed Church began in the 1500s in Europe when groups of Christians who were opposed to any authority or practice that they believed could not be supported by a careful study of the Bible set themselves apart from the established Roman Church of the time. These Reformers adhered to the basic teachings of the early Christian church, but they also wrote new teachings, such as the Heidelberg Catechism, which was first published in 1563 and is still a standard that guides the life and religious witness of the Reformed Church in America.

The tone of the Heidelberg Catechism is mild, gentle and devotional, and celebrates the comfort that one can derive in life and in death from Jesus Christ. The Reformed Church in America requires every minister to cover the contents of the Heidelberg Catechism once every four years in his or her preaching.

The Reform movement's first church in America was the Reformed Dutch Church, which was founded in 1628 in New Amsterdam (now New York City). Not until 1764 was there a Reformed Church in the British colonies that used the English language. Starting with the American Revolution, the Dutch influence in the Church waned as the number of congregants of Scottish, German and English extraction increased. Finally, in 1867, the Church changed its name to the Reformed Church in America.

The Canadian branch of the denomination, which consists of 41 churches, is called the Reformed Church in Canada. (The Reform tradition is also represented in Canada by the Christian Reformed Church of North America, which has 244 churches, a membership of 47,000 and offices in Burlington, Ontario.)

Each of the Reformed Church's local congregations is governed by a "consistory," which is comprised of the church's pastor and elected elders and deacons. Each church belongs to a "classis," which oversees the congregations within its particular jurisdiction. Each classis sends representatives to its regional synod, of which there are seven in the United States and one in Canada. It also sends representatives to the General Synod, which meets annually to set direction and policy for the Church as a whole.

The Church now supports missionaries on five continents. While the Church has been making concerted outreach to non-whites in the United States in recent years, its membership is still predominantly people with an Anglo-Saxon heritage: 95 percent of Church members are Caucasian; four percent are African-American; and two percent are Asian, Native American or Hispanic.

U.S. and Canadian churches: 950
U.S. and Canadian membership: 310,603
(*data from the* 1998 Yearbook of American and Canadian Churches)

For more information, contact:
The Reformed Church in America
475 Riverside Drive
New York, NY 10115
(212) 870-2841
rcags475@aol.com
www.rca.org

II · THE BASIC SERVICE

Worship in the Reformed Church strongly emphasizes the Church's belief that the officiating minister is not an intermediary between congregants and God and that he or she does not offer worship for the congregation. Because of that, worship in the Church offers fixed formulas for the Sunday service because, as a Reformed minister has written, "it would rather trust the wisdom of the church in its long history than the erratic cleverness of any one person."

But the Church also offers individual ministers and churches a measure of freedom: For ordinary Sunday services, full and complete models for worship are provided. A church may—or may not—use them, but they serve as guides for what ought to be used.

Sunday morning worship generally has three components:

◘ The Approach to God, in which congregants confess that they are not worthy to be in God's presence and so seek forgiveness in Jesus Christ.

◘ The Word of God, in which congregants hear the Word as found in the Scriptures, preaching and the sacraments.

◘ The Response to God's Word, in which congregants offers prayers and gratitude for God's work in the world.

Sunday worship also includes the Lord's Supper, which is also known as Holy Communion. Reformed Church congregations believe that Christ is spiritually present at communion.

The service usually lasts about one hour.

APPROPRIATE ATTIRE

Men: A jacket and tie would never be out of place, although many congregations welcome more casual attire if chosen with discretion and taste as appropriate for a worship service. No head covering is required.

Women: A dress or a skirt and blouse or a pant suit, although many congregations welcome more casual attire if chosen with discretion and taste as appropriate for a worship service. Clothing need not cover the arms and hems need not reach below the knees. Open-toed shoes and modest jewelry are permissible. No head covering is required.

There are no rules regarding colors of clothing.

THE SANCTUARY

What are the major sections of the church?

◘ *The narthex or foyer,* where worshippers are greeted.

◘ *The sanctuary,* where congregants and guests sit.

◘ *The chancel,* a raised section at the front of the sanctuary for a communion table, a pulpit and a lectern and where ministers and other worship leaders sit.

THE SERVICE

When should guests arrive and where should they sit?

Arrive about five to ten minutes before the scheduled start of the service. In many churches, ushers will advise guests where to sit.

If arriving late, are there times when a guest should *not* enter the service?

Do not enter while prayers are being recited, during the reading of Scriptures or during the sermon.

Are there times when a guest should *not* leave the service?

Do not leave while prayers are being recited, during the reading of Scriptures or during the sermon. If possible, do not leave except for an emergency.

Who are the major officiants, leaders or participants and what do they do?

- *The pastor,* who is the primary leader of the service. He or she preaches a sermon and presides over the communion and baptism.
- *Lay leaders,* who may greet congregants and guests, make announcements about church activities and lead prayers.

What are the major ritual objects of the service?

- *Candles,* which remind worshippers of God's illuminating presence.
- *Bread and wine or grape juice,* which are served to worshippers during the Lord's Supper, which is also known as communion. Most Reformed Church congregations believe that Christ is spiritually present at communion. Unlike certain other Christian churches, they do not believe that the bread and wine or grape juice are transubstantiated into the actual body and blood of Christ.
- *A Bible,* which is on the lectern or pulpit and which worship leaders read during the service.
- *The baptismal font,* which contains water used during services that include baptisms.
- *A cross,* which reminds worshippers of the suffering, death and resurrection of Christ. The cross does not have on it the "body" of Christ since its emphasis is on His resurrection.

What books are used?

The most commonly used of several Protestant Bibles is the New Revised Standard Version. The Reformed Church in America does not recommend a particular edition of this Bible. Many hymnals are used in the Reformed Church. The most recent hymnal published by the Church is *Rejoice in the Lord,* edited by Erik Routley (Grand Rapids, Mich.: William B. Eerdmans Publishing Co., 1985).

To indicate the order of the service:

A program will be distributed and the pastor or lay leader will make periodic announcements.

GUEST BEHAVIOR DURING THE SERVICE

Will a guest who is not a member of the Reformed Church be expected to do anything other than sit?

Guests are expected to join congregants when they stand during the service. It is entirely optional for them to read prayers aloud and sing with the congregation. In most congregations that belong to the Reformed Church, congregants do not kneel. In those churches where kneeling occurs, it is optional for guests to join in. Those guests who do not kneel should remain seated.

Are there any parts of the service in which a guest who is not a member of the Reformed Church should *not* participate?

Non-Christian guests should not participate in communion and in the Confession of Faith, which is the Apostle's Creed recited during communion.

If not disruptive to the service, is it okay to:

◘ **Take pictures?** No.
◘ **Use a flash?** No.
◘ **Use a video camera?** No.
◘ **Use a tape recorder?** No.

Will contributions to the church be collected at the service?

Yes. Ushers pass offering plates through the congregation during the service.

How much is customary to contribute?

It is entirely optional for guests to contribute. If they choose to do so, contributions between $1 and $20 are appropriate.

AFTER THE SERVICE

Is there usually a reception after the service?

Yes. Most churches serve such light foods as coffee, tea, juice and pastry. No alcoholic beverages will be served. If a meal is served, which is not a frequent occurrence, grace may be said before eating. The reception may be in the church's narthex or fellowship hall and may last about 30 minutes.

Is there a traditional form of address for clergy who may be at the reception?

"Pastor" or "Reverend."

Is it okay to leave early?

Yes.

GENERAL GUIDELINES AND ADVICE

Take your cues from those around you. Do not remain standing when congregants have re-seated themselves. Refrain from talking during services. Most churches offer a nursery or child care for young children.

SPECIAL VOCABULARY

Key words or phrases which might be helpful for a visitor to know:

- *"And also with you."* The proper response if someone says, "The peace of God be with you."

DOGMA AND IDEOLOGY

Members of the Reformed Church believe:

- In the Trinitarian concept of the Divinity. This consists of the Father, the Son (Jesus) and the Holy Spirit (the empowering spirit of God).
- Each person who believes and trusts in Jesus has their sins forgiven, is endowed with "courage in the struggle for justice and peace," and is granted "eternal life in Your realm which has no end."
- The Bible is the Word of God and the final authority for faith and practice.
- God is at work in all walks of life and in all activities of each person. Hence, the Church does not hesitate to call government, business or

any other authority to responsibility to the Lord.
- Each person is called by God to service in the Church and to service in the community in whatever vocation he or she may have.

A basic pamphlet to which a guest can refer to learn more about the Reformed Church:

Our Reformed Church by Howard G. Hageman (New York: Reformed Church Press, 1993). This may be obtained from The RCA Distribution Center, 4500 60th Street S.E., Grand Rapids, MI 49512; tel. (800) 968-7221.

III · HOLY DAYS AND FESTIVALS

- *Advent.* Occurs four weeks before Christmas. The purpose is to begin preparing for Christmas and to focus on Christ. There is no traditional greeting for this holiday.
- *Christmas.* Occurs on the evening of December 24 and the day of December 25. Marks the birth and the incarnation of God as a man. The traditional greeting is "Merry Christmas."
- *Lent.* Begins on Ash Wednesday, which occurs six weeks before Easter. The purpose is to prepare for Easter and to reflect upon Christ. There is no traditional greeting for Lent. Between Lent and Easter, abstention from entertainment is encouraged, as is increased giving to the poor. Often, there are midweek worship services. A few members of the Reformed Church engage in a moderate fast (abstaining from certain foods) during Lent.
- *Easter.* Always falls on the Sunday after the first full moon that occurs on or after March 21. Celebrates the Resurrection of Jesus Christ. The traditional greeting is "Happy Easter!" In worship services, the Pastor may greet congregants with, "He is risen!" Congregants respond with "He is risen, indeed!"
- *Pentecost Sunday.* The seventh Sunday after Easter. Celebrates the coming of the Holy Spirit, which is the empowering spirit of God in human life. This is often considered the birth of the Christian church. There is no traditional greeting for this holiday.

IV · LIFE CYCLE EVENTS

Birth Ceremony

The baptism ceremony is the same for males and females. Baptism can actually occur anytime from birth onward through adulthood. The ceremony is usually integrated into a regular church service and may last about 15 minutes.

In the Reformed Church, baptism is administered only once. Baptism initiates an individual into the Church and bestows God's grace upon that person. During the ceremony, the pastor pours or sprinkles water over the person's head. Another method of baptism that is used occasionally is "immersion," in which the person being baptized is lowered into the water and raised up again.

Baptism is almost always part of a larger Sunday morning service. The baptism itself may last about 15 minutes, while the entire service may last about one hour.

BEFORE THE CEREMONY

Are guests usually invited by a formal invitation?

Invitations are usually oral.

If not stated explicitly, should one assume that children are invited?

Yes.

If one can't attend, what should one do?

RSVP with regrets. Gifts are not expected.

APPROPRIATE ATTIRE

Men: A jacket and tie would never be out of place, although many congregations welcome more casual attire if chosen with discretion and taste as appropriate for a worship service. No head covering is required.

Women: A dress or a skirt and blouse or a pant suit, although many congregations welcome more casual attire if chosen with discretion and taste as appropriate for a worship service. Clothing need not cover the arms and hems need not reach below the knees. Open-toed shoes and modest jewelry are permissible. No head covering is required.

There are no rules regarding colors of clothing.

GIFTS

Is a gift customarily expected?

No.

Should gifts be brought to the ceremony?

See above.

THE CEREMONY

Where will the ceremony take place?

Almost always in the church's main sanctuary. Only occasionally does a baptism occur at the parents' home or outdoors.

When should guests arrive and where should they sit?

Arrive about five to ten minutes before the scheduled start of the service. In many churches, ushers will advise guests where to sit.

If arriving late, are there times when a guest should *not* enter the ceremony?

Do not enter while prayers are being recited, during the reading of Scriptures or during the sermon.

Are there times when a guest should *not* leave the ceremony?

Do not leave while prayers are being recited, during the reading of Scriptures, or during the sermon. If possible, do not leave except for an emergency.

Who are the major officiants, leaders or participants at the ceremony and what do they do?

- *The pastor,* who is the primary leader of the service and presides over the baptism.
- *The child being baptized.*
- *The child's parents,* who present the child and pledge to raise him or her in Christ's faith.
- *The congregation,* which welcomes the person being baptized into the community of faith.

What books are used?

The most commonly used of several Protestant Bibles is the New Revised Standard Version. The Reformed Church in America does not recommend a particular edition of this Bible. Many hymnals are used in the Reformed Church. The most recent hymnal published by the Church is *Rejoice in the Lord*, edited by Erik Routley (Grand Rapids, Mich.: William B. Eerdmans Publishing Co., 1985).

To indicate the order of the ceremony:

A program will be distributed and the pastor will make periodic announcements.

Will a guest who is not a member of the Reformed Church be expected to do anything other than sit?

Upon request of the family of the person being baptized, a guest may be asked to stand at the front of the sanctuary as a sponsor, a family member or a friend. If so, consult the family or the pastor for instructions. Ordinarily, guests are expected to join congregants when they stand during the service. It is entirely optional for them to read prayers aloud and sing with the congregation. In most congregations that belong to the Reformed Church, congregants do not kneel. In those churches where kneeling occurs, it is optional for guests to join in. Those guests who do not kneel should remain seated.

Are there any parts of the ceremony in which a guest who is not a member of the Reformed Church should *not* participate?

Non-members should not participate with congregants when they recite the "vows of the congregation," in which they pledge to help guide the person being baptized to lead a Christian life.

If not disruptive to the ceremony, is it okay to:

- **Take pictures?** No.
- **Use a flash?** No.
- **Use a video camera?** No.
- **Use a tape recorder?** No.

Will contributions to the church be collected at the ceremony?

Yes. Ushers pass offering plates through the congregation during the service.

How much is customary to contribute?

It is entirely optional for guests to contribute. If they choose to do so, contributions between $1 and $20 are appropriate.

AFTER THE CEREMONY

Is there usually a reception after the ceremony?

No.

Is there a traditional greeting for the family?

No. Just offer your congratulations.

Is there a traditional form of address for clergy whom a guest may meet?

"Pastor" or "Reverend."

Initiation Ceremony

Confirmation is celebrated for teenagers who were baptized as infants. It offers a teen who was baptized the opportunity to publicly assent to the baptismal promises and celebrates the affirmation of baptism in the life of the individual. One is usually confirmed with other teens who have been in the same confirmation class.

The confirmation is usually part of the regular Sunday worship service. It may last about 15 minutes, although the entire service may last about an hour.

BEFORE THE CEREMONY

Are guests usually invited by a formal invitation?

Invitations are usually issued orally.

If not stated explicitly, should one assume that children are invited?

Yes.

If one can't attend, what should one do?

RSVP with regrets. Gifts are not expected.

APPROPRIATE ATTIRE

Men: A jacket and tie would never be out of place, although many congregations welcome more casual attire if chosen with discretion and taste as appropriate for a worship service. No head covering is required.

Women: A dress or a skirt and blouse or a pant suit, although many congregations welcome more casual attire if chosen with discretion and taste as appropriate for a worship service. Clothing need not cover the arms and hems need not reach below the knees. Open-toed shoes and modest jewelry are permissible. No head covering is required.

There are no rules regarding colors of clothing.

GIFTS

Is a gift customarily expected?
No.

Should gifts be brought to the ceremony?
See above.

THE CEREMONY

Where will the ceremony take place?
In the church's main sanctuary.

When should guests arrive and where should they sit?
Arrive about five to ten minutes before the scheduled start of the service. In many churches, ushers will advise guests where to sit.

If arriving late, are there times when a guest should *not* enter the ceremony?
Do not enter while prayers are being recited, during the reading of Scriptures or during the sermon.

Are there times when a guest should *not* leave the ceremony?
Do not leave while prayers are being recited, during the reading of Scriptures or during the sermon. If possible, do not leave except for an emergency.

Who are the major officiants, leaders or participants at the ceremony and what do they do?
- *The confirmand(s),* the person(s) being confirmed.
- *The pastor,* who is the primary leader of the service. He or she preaches a sermon and presides over the communion and baptism.

What books are used?
The most commonly used of several Protestant Bibles is the New Revised Standard Version. The Reformed Church in America does not recommend a particular edition of this Bible. Many hymnals are used in the Reformed Church. The most recent hymnal published by the

Church is *Rejoice in the Lord*, edited by Erik Routley (Grand Rapids, Mich.: William B. Eerdmans Publishing Co., 1985).

To indicate the order of the ceremony:

A program will be distributed and the pastor will make periodic announcements.

Will a guest who is not a member of the Reformed Church be expected to do anything other than sit?

If the family or the confirmand has specifically asked you to join them while standing in front of the congregation, then do so. Ordinarily, guests are expected to join congregants when they stand during the service. It is entirely optional for them to read prayers aloud and sing with the congregation. In most churches belonging to the Reformed Church, congregants do not kneel. In those churches where kneeling occurs, it is optional for guests to join in. Those guests who do not kneel should remain seated.

Are there any parts of the ceremony in which a guest who is not a member of the Reformed Church should *not* participate?

No.

If not disruptive to the ceremony, is it okay to:

- **Take pictures?** No.
- **Use a flash?** No.
- **Use a video camera?** No.
- **Use a tape recorder?** No.

Will contributions to the church be collected at the ceremony?

Yes. Ushers pass offering plates through the congregation during the service.

How much is customary to contribute?

It is entirely optional for guests to contribute. If they choose to do so, contributions between $1 and $20 are appropriate.

AFTER THE CEREMONY

Is there usually a reception after the ceremony?

No, but there may be a receiving line in the church at which guests are congregants are greeted.

Is there a traditional greeting for the family?

No. Just offer your congratulations.

Is there a traditional form of address for clergy whom a guest may meet?

"Pastor" or "Reverend."

Marriage Ceremony

The Reformed Church teaches that the essence of marriage is a covenanted commitment that has its foundation in the faithfulness of God's love. The Church does not consider a wedding to be a sacrament, although the marital relationship is considered to be sacred.

The marriage ceremony is the occasion on which two people unite as husband and wife in the mutual exchange of marriage vows and wedding rings. The presiding official represents the Church and gives the marriage the Church's blessing. The congregation joins in affirming the marriage and in offering support and thanksgiving for the new family.

Usually, the wedding is a ceremony unto itself. Only rarely is it part of a regular Sunday worship service. It may last about 30 minutes.

BEFORE THE CEREMONY

Are guests usually invited by a formal invitation?

Yes.

If not stated explicitly, should one assume that children are invited?

Yes, although this may not apply to infants or toddlers.

If one can't attend, what should one do?

RSVP with regrets and send a gift.

APPROPRIATE ATTIRE

Men: A jacket and tie. No head covering is required.

Women: A dress or a skirt and blouse. Clothing need not cover the arms and hems need not reach below the knees. Open-toed shoes and modest jewelry are permissible. No head covering is required.

There are no rules regarding colors of clothing.

GIFTS

Is a gift customarily expected?

Yes. Cash or household items (such as sheets, kitchenware or small appliances) are appropriate.

Should gifts be brought to the ceremony?

Gifts may be brought to the ceremony or to the reception that follows the ceremony. They may also be sent to the home of the newlyweds.

THE CEREMONY

Where will the ceremony take place?

In the church's main sanctuary.

When should guests arrive and where should they sit?

Arrive shortly before the time for which the wedding has been scheduled. Usually, ushers will advise guests where to sit.

If arriving late, are there times when a guest should *not* enter the ceremony?

Do not enter during the processional or recessional of the wedding party or during the recitation of wedding vows. Follow the ushers' guidance for entering the ceremony.

Are there times when a guest should *not* leave the ceremony?

Do not leave during the processional or recessional of the wedding party or during the recitation of wedding vows. Follow the ushers' guidance for leaving the ceremony.

Who are the major officiants, leaders or participants at the ceremony and what do they do?

- *The pastor,* who presides over the ceremony.
- *The bride and groom and members of the wedding party.*

What books are used?

The most commonly used of several Protestant Bibles is the New Revised Standard Version. The Reformed Church in America does not recommend a particular edition of this Bible. Many hymnals are used in the Reformed Church. The most recent hymnal published by the Church is *Rejoice in the Lord,* edited by Erik Routley (Grand Rapids, Mich.: William B. Eerdmans Publishing Co., 1985).

To indicate the order of the ceremony:

The pastor will make periodic announcements.

Will a guest who is not a member of the Reformed Church be expected to do anything other than sit?

Guests are expected to join congregants when they stand during the ceremony.

Are there any parts of the ceremony in which a guest who is not a member of the Reformed Church should *not* participate?

No.

If not disruptive to the ceremony, is it okay to:

▣ **Take pictures?** No.
▣ **Use a flash?** No.
▣ **Use a video camera?** No.
▣ **Use a tape recorder?** No.

Will contributions to the church be collected at the ceremony?

No.

AFTER THE CEREMONY

Is there usually a reception after the ceremony?

Yes. It may be in a catering hall, a restaurant or a church reception hall, or at a home. There is usually a reception line and frequently a full meal is served. If the reception is not in the church, there may be alcoholic beverages and/or music and dancing. The presence of alcoholic beverages depends on family practice and choice. The reception may last one to two hours.

Would it be considered impolite to neither eat nor drink?

No.

Is there a grace or benediction before eating or drinking?

Grace may be said if a full meal is served.

Is there a grace or benediction after eating or drinking?

No.

Is there a traditional greeting for the family?

Just offer your congratulations.

Is there a traditional form of address for clergy who may be at the reception?

"Pastor" or "Reverend."

Is it okay to leave early?

Yes.

Funerals and Mourning

A funeral service is a time of comfort and hope for the bereaved. The hope of Church members is summarized by Jesus' words from John 11:25-26, "I am the resurrection and the life, says the Lord; whoever believes in Me though he die, yet shall he live; and whoever lives and believes in Me shall never die."

The Reformed Church believes that to be absent from the body is to be present with the Lord.

The funeral is a service unto itself. It lasts about 20 to 30 minutes.

BEFORE THE CEREMONY

How soon after the death does the funeral usually take place?

Two to three days.

What should someone who is not a member of the Reformed Church do upon hearing of the death of a member of that faith?

Telephone or visit the bereaved family or send a card to the bereaved to express your condolences.

APPROPRIATE ATTIRE

Men: A jacket and tie. No head covering is required.

Women: A dress or a skirt and blouse. Clothing need not cover the arms and hems need not reach below the knees. Open-toed shoes and modest jewelry are permissible. No head covering is required.

Dark, somber colors of clothing are advised. Bright, flashy tones are strongly discouraged.

GIFTS

Is it appropriate to send flowers or make a contribution?

Flowers may be sent to the home of the bereaved upon hearing of the death or after the funeral, or they may be sent to the church or funeral home where the funeral ceremony will be held. Contributions to a church or organization designated by the family may be made after the funeral.

Is it appropriate to send food?

Yes. This may be sent to the home of the bereaved.

THE CEREMONY

Where will the ceremony take place?

Either in a church or a funeral home.

When should guests arrive and where should they sit?

Arrive a few minutes before the time for which the ceremony has been scheduled. Sit wherever you wish, unless a specially marked section has been reserved for immediate family.

If arriving late, are there times when a guest should *not* enter the ceremony?

Do not enter during prayers, the sermon or the eulogy. Follow ushers' guidance about entering the ceremony.

Will the bereaved family be present at the church or funeral home before the ceremony?

Sometimes.

Is there a traditional greeting for the family?

No. Just offer your condolences.

Will there be an open casket?

Rarely. This depends on local customs and the preference of the family. "Viewing" time is sometimes scheduled in the days or hours before the funeral. "Viewing" may also be offered during or at the end of the funeral service itself.

Is a guest expected to view the body?

This is entirely optional. If there is a "viewing" at the funeral and you do not wish to participate, excuse yourself from the line that forms to pass the casket. If you happen to be in the line that passes the casket and you do not wish to view the body, simply avert your eyes.

What is appropriate behavior upon viewing the body?

View it silently and somberly. Do not touch it or place any flowers or memorabilia in the casket.

Who are the major officiants at the ceremony and what do they do?

- *A pastor,* who officiates and delivers the sermon.
- *Possibly a family member or a close friend,* who may also deliver a eulogy.

What books are used?

No books are used by the bereaved or guests.

To indicate the order of the ceremony:

Usually a program will be distributed; sometimes the pastor will make periodic announcements.

Will a guest who is not a member of the Reformed Church be expected to do anything other than sit?

No. It is entirely optional for guests to read prayers aloud or to sing, stand or kneel when those present do so. In most funerals officiated by the Reformed Church, congregants do not kneel. In those churches where kneeling occurs, those guests who do not kneel should remain seated.

Are there any parts of the ceremony in which a guest who is not a member of the Reformed Church should *not* participate?

No.

If not disruptive to the ceremony, is it okay to:

- **Take pictures?** No.
- **Use a flash?** No.
- **Use a video camera?** No.
- **Use a tape recorder?** No.

Will contributions to the church be collected at the ceremony?

No.

THE INTERMENT

Should guests attend the interment?

This is entirely optional and is usually at the discretion of the guest, unless the minister announces at the funeral ceremony that the interment is only for family members.

Whom should one ask for directions?

The funeral director.

What happens at the graveside?

Scriptures are read, prayers are recited and the casket is placed in the ground.

Do guests who are not members of the Reformed Church participate at the graveside ceremony?

No, they are simply present.

COMFORTING THE BEREAVED

Is it appropriate to visit the home of the bereaved after the funeral?

Often, there is a reception at the church or home of the bereaved after the funeral. If not, visiting a few days after the funeral is appropriate. It is recommended that the length of the visit be fairly brief, such as 15 to 20 minutes.

Will there be a religious service at the home of the bereaved?

Seldom is this done.

Will food be served?

No.

How soon after the funeral will a mourner usually return to a normal social schedule?

The Reformed Church does not specify the number of days that one should formally be in mourning. Local, ethnic and cultural customs are more relevant that any particular religious tradition of the Church.

Are there mourning customs to which a friend who is not a member of the Reformed Church should be sensitive?

No. Local, ethnic and cultural customs are more relevant that any particular religious tradition of the Church.

Are there rituals for observing the anniversary of the death?

No. Local, ethnic and cultural customs are more relevant that any particular religious tradition of the Church.

V · HOME CELEBRATIONS

Not applicable for the Reformed Church.

Chapter 15 Contents

15

Sikh

I · HISTORY AND BELIEFS

The Sikh faith originated in India in the late 15th century through the life and teachings of Guru Nanak (1469–1539 C.E.), the first Sikh guru. At a time of great religious conflict, he taught that all creation is a part of the One Creator. After Guru Nanak's life, he passed his "light" on successively to nine other gurus who further evolved his teachings. Each guru denounced India's caste system and the oppression of anyone based on class, creed, color or sex.

The 10th and last human guru, Guru Gobind Singh, initiated his followers as the *Khalsa*, which means "the Pure Ones." He instructed the *Khalsa* not to cut their hair (since doing so would tamper with God's image, in which they were created); to dress in white Sikh attire called *bana*, which consists of turbans and dress-like garments called *kurtas* and leggings called *churidars*; to be monogamous; and to live righteously. Before dying in 1708, Guru Gobind Singh "gave" the guruship to the Sikh scriptures known as the *Siri Guru Granth Sahib*. These scriptures were compiled by the fifth guru, Arjan Dev, and contain sacred writings by some Sikh gurus and several Hindu and Moslem saints. Since then, Sikhs have bowed before the *Siri Guru Granth Sahib*, consulted it as their only guru and treated it with reverence.

Today, there are 20 million Sikhs throughout the world.

U.S. temples/*gurdwaras*: 260
U.S. membership: 305,000
(1996 data from Sikh Dharma International)

For more information, contact:
Sikh Dharma International
P.O. Box 351149
Los Angeles, CA 90035
(310) 552-3416
or
Sikh Dharma International
Route 2, Box 132-D
Española, NM 87532
(505) 753-9438

Canadian temples/*gurdwaras:* 100
Canadian membership: 300,000
(data from Sikh Society of Alberta, Edmonton, Alberta)

For more information, contact:
Gurdwara
SRI Guru Singh Sabha
4504 Millwoods Road South
Edmonton, AB T6L 6Y8
(403) 462-7454

II · THE BASIC SERVICE

A Sikh service takes place in a *gurdwara*, which literally means "Gate to the Guru" and is an environment that has been especially readied for uplifting one's consciousness. The service may take place in someone's home, in a rented hall or in a special place built for the purpose. The main focus of any Sikh *gurdwara* is the *Siri Guru Granth Sahib*, a compilation of sacred writings that is covered in cloth and is usually at the front of the room. Sikhs bow to the *Siri Guru Granth Sahib*, which symbolizes the Infinite Word of God, as an act of humility and to acknowledge that an Infinite Power pervades all.

Everyone attending the *gurdwara* sits on the floor as an act of humility, equality and respect. They also sit in a cross-legged position, which is conducive to meditation. If helpful to their comfort, guests do not have to sit with their legs crossed.

The Sikh service consists of *kirtan* (songs of praise to God), an *ardas* (community prayer lead by any one person) and a *hukam* (the "Guru's Command"), which is read from the *Siri Guru Granth Sahib*. The *hukam*, which is a portion of the *Siri Guru Granth Sahib* chosen randomly by the reader, is first read in the original Gurmukhi language and then translated to English (or the main language of the congregation).

Often, guest speakers address the *sangat*, or congregation, on spiritual topics. Many *sangats* hold services every Sunday morning that last more than two hours. Other *sangats* may hold services that last about 30 minutes early every morning and sometimes every evening as well.

APPROPRIATE ATTIRE

Men: A jacket and tie or more casual, modest clothing. Shoes are always removed before entering the *gurdwara*, and the head must always be covered while in the *gurdwara*. Guests may wear any hat, cap or scarf that covers the top of the head.

Women: A modest dress, skirt and blouse, or pants suit. It is best if the legs are covered enough so one can comfortably sit cross-legged. Shoes are always removed before entering the *gurdwara*, and the head must always be covered with a scarf, hat or veil that covers the top of the head while in the *gurdwara*. Modest jewelry is permissible.

There are no rules regarding colors of clothing.

THE SANCTUARY

What are the major sections of the *gurdwara*?

Gurdwaras can range from a room or house converted for the purpose of worship to magnificent buildings inlaid with gold and marble. However, many *gurdwaras* have the following sections:

- *The entry room*, which has shelves where shoes can be left before entering the main room. Often, the entry room has bowls or sinks for washing one's hands and feet since one should purify one's self before being in the presence of the *Siri Guru Granth Sahib*.

  If there is no entry room, shoes should be left outside the *gurdwara*.
- *The main room*, where congregants sit on the covered floor in this area. In some *gurdwaras*, the men sit on the left and the women sit on the right.
- *The front or central area*, where the Sikh scriptures, the *Siri Guru Granth Sahib*, presides under a canopy and is elevated above the con-

gregation. To the right or left of the *Siri Guru Granth Sahib* is an area for *kirtanis*, musicians who lead congregants in song.

THE SERVICE

When should guests arrive and where should they sit?

Because of the length of the ordinary worship service, it is not required to arrive at the time designated for the start of worship. Guests should sit anywhere in the main area with the men on the left and women on the right, although this may not apply in some *gurdwaras*. Everyone, including guests, must always face the *Siri Guru Granth Sahib*, which is at the front (or central location) of the room.

Before entering the *gurdwara*, remove your shoes and cover your head. It is optional to wash your hands and feet. If desired, the guest may offer money or a gift, such as flowers or fruit, to the *Siri Guru Granth Sahib* and then bow before it. Money may be placed in a box with a slot on it or on an offering plate. Either will be in front of the *Siri Guru Granth Sahib*. Other gifts may be placed in front of the *Siri Guru Granth Sahib*.

Next, guests should sit on the floor facing the front. The feet of all present face away from the *Siri Guru Granth Sahib* as a sign of respect. It is important to refrain from eating, drinking or unnecessary conversation in the *gurdwara*.

If arriving late, are there times when a guest should *not* enter the service?

It is best to enter during the *kirtan*, or songs. Do not enter during the *ardas*, or community prayer, when everyone is standing.

Are there times when a guest should *not* leave the service?

A guest may leave at any time. However, it is recommended not to leave during the *ardas* (community prayer) or *hukam*, the reading from the *Siri Guru Granth Sahib*. It may be advisable for guests to sit near the door if they plan on leaving the service early.

Who are the major officiants, leaders or participants and what do they do?

- *The Granthi or Giani Ji*, who reads the *hukam* from the *Siri Guru Granth Sahib*.
- *Attendants*, several people who sit behind the *Siri Guru Granth Sahib* and attend to it by frequently waving a long-handled brush made of

long horse hair called a *chori sahib* above the *Siri Guru Granth Sahib*, or take out or put away the scriptures. The attendants also serve *prasad*, or sweet pudding, at the end of the service; read the *hukam* translation in English; and assist in the *gurdwara* as needed. Many people from the *sangat*, the congregation, participate in these functions.

◾ *Kirtanis*, musicians who lead the *sangat* in *kirtan*, songs of praise to God.

◾ *The master of ceremonies*, the person announcing guest speakers and the order of the service. This role is often fulfilled by the *gurdwara* secretary or *granthi* or *Giani Ji*.

What are the major ritual objects of the service?

◾ *The manji sahib*, the "bed" or platform for the *Siri Guru Granth Sahib*. It is covered by ornate cloths called *"ramalas."*

◾ *The chandoa*, the canopy hanging over the *Siri Guru Granth Sahib*.

◾ *The adi shakti or khanda*, a symbol shaped like a circle surrounded by two swords and cut through by one double-edged sword. It symbolizes the primal, creative energy of the universe. The sword cutting through the circle represents the breaking of the cycle of birth and death.

◾ *The kirpan*, a special knife used to bless *langar* ("sacred food") and *prasad* (sweet pudding) during the *ardas* (community prayer).

◾ *The chori sahib*, a long-handled brush made of long horse hair. It is identical to brushes used in ancient India that were waved over royalty to show their state of sovereignty. It is waved over the *Siri Guru Granth Sahib* to symbolize its sovereignty, to purify the energy around it, and to show its status as a living guru.

What books are used?

Booklets of sheets (containing transliteration and translation of the *kirtan* [songs of praise to God] to be sung) may be available, depending on the *gurdwara*. Efforts should be made not to put them on the floor. Since Sikhs respect the written word of God, anything containing it should not be stepped upon or marred in any way.

   If these booklets are available, they are often found at the front of the *gurdwara*.

To indicate the order of the service:

There may be a written program and/or the master of ceremonies may make periodic announcements.

GUEST BEHAVIOR DURING THE SERVICE

Will a guest who is not a Sikh be expected to do anything other than sit?

A guest will be expected to stand and sit at the same time as everyone else. It is entirely optional for the guest to sing or bow to the *Siri Guru Granth Sahib*. Guests are expected to accept *prasad* (sweet pudding) which is considered a blessing from the *Siri Guru Granth Sahib*.

Customarily, *prasad* is placed into one's hands, which are placed together with the palms up. One does not have to be a Sikh to eat the *prasad*.

Are there any parts of the service in which a guest who is not a Sikh should *not* participate?

Only Sikhs will be asked to serve *prasad*, read from the *Siri Guru Granth Sahib*, do the *ardas* (prayer) and to serve in any way needed. A guest will not be expected to perform any of these functions. Other than this, a guest may participate in every part of the service as desired.

If not disruptive to the service, is it okay to:

- **Take pictures?** Yes, but only if intended solely for personal use.
- **Use a flash?** Yes, but only if intended solely for personal use.
- **Use a video camera?** Yes, but only if intended solely for personal use.
- **Use a tape recorder?** Yes, but only if intended solely for personal use.

Will contributions to the *gurdwara* be collected at the service?

Donations collected at each service help fund the *langar* (the food provided after the service), *prasad* (sweet pudding) and the general maintenance and administration of the *gurdwara*. No collection plate is passed through the congregation. Instead, money, flowers or fruit may be offered to the *Siri Guru Granth Sahib*. Money may be placed in a box with a slot on it or on an offering plate. Either will be in front of the *Siri Guru Granth Sahib*. Other gifts may be placed in front of the *Siri Guru Granth Sahib*.

How much is customary to contribute?

The customary contribution is $1 to $5.

AFTER THE SERVICE

Is there usually a reception after the service?

Langar, or sacred food, is served after (and sometimes during) each service. It is available to all. *Langar* may be served in the *gurdwara* itself, outside, or in a special hall built for the purpose.

Also, a vegetarian meal is provided and often consists of East Indian cuisine. Since alcohol is prohibited to Sikhs, it will not be served. Guests with dietary restrictions may politely decline food. It is not considered impolite if they decline the offered food for this reason. Smoking is also strictly prohibited within the precincts and no one should have tobacco or cigarettes on his or her person. The reception may last anywhere from half an hour to several hours.

Is there a traditional form of address for clergy who may be at the reception?

"Granthi" and then their first name, or *"Giani Ji."*

Is it okay to leave early?

Yes.

GENERAL GUIDELINES AND ADVICE

Many *gurdwaras* do not designate specific people to help guests, but feel free to ask any Sikh to help you or to explain any part of the service you may not understand.

Remember to always face the *Siri Guru Granth Sahib* and to have your head covered throughout the service. Also, shoes are never worn within the *gurdwara*, even when a service is not taking place.

SPECIAL VOCABULARY

Key words or phrases which might be helpful for a visitor to know:

- *Siri Guru Granth Sahib* ("See-ree GOO-roo GRANTH SAH-heeb"): Scriptures compiled by the fifth Sikh guru, Arjan Dev, and which contain sacred writings by some Sikh gurus and several Hindu and Moslem saints. Sikhs bow before the *Siri Guru Granth Sahib*, consult it as their only guru, and treat it with reverence.
- *Prasad* ("prah-SAHD"): The sweet pudding served toward the end of the service. It consists of water, honey, wheat flour and clarified but-

ter. *Prasad* is considered to be a blessing from the *Siri Guru Granth Sahib* that everyone can eat.

- *Ardas* ("AHR-das"): Community prayer led by one person in the *gurdwara* service. Blessings for special occasions or events may be requested during the *ardas*.
- *Sangat* ("SAHN-gaht"): The congregation of Sikhs and guests who come together for a worship service.
- *Langar* ("LAHN-gahr"): The vegetarian meal prepared in a prayerful environment and served as an offering after or throughout the worship service to the *sangat*, including guests.
- *Sat Nam* ("SAHT NAHM"): A common phrase and greeting among Sikhs which means "True Name" and acknowledges the God in all.
- *Wahe Guruji ka khalsa, Wahe Guru ji ki fateh* ("WAH-beh GOO-ROO-ji kah KAHL-sah, WAH-heh GOO-ROO-ji kee FAH-teh"): A common greeting or phrase that means "The Pure Ones belong to God. Victory be to God!"

DOGMA AND IDEOLOGY

Sikhs believe:

- While one God pervades everyone and everything, there are many ways to worship God. Thus, Sikhs respect all religions without trying to "convert" others to Sikhism.
- The body is a temple that can serve the spirit. The body should be treated respectfully by not eating meat or eggs, or using alcohol, tobacco or drugs. Yoga and meditation can balance the body, mind and spirit.
- Women may fully participate in all *gurdwara* services and in any positions of leadership and ministry.
- The *Siri Guru Granth Sahib* is the only guru in a Sikh's life. It is written in Gurmukhi, the language of the 10 Sikh gurus. By reciting these words of the gurus, Sikhs believe they can achieve the same consciousness as did the gurus. Sikhs will never bow to any man or woman, only to the *Siri Guru Granth Sahib*.

Some basic books to which a guest can refer to learn more about Sikhism:

The Sikh Religion, 6 vols., by Arthur Macauliffe (Española, N. Mex.: Golden Temple Enterprises, 1990).

Philosophy and Faith of Sikhism by K.S. Duggal (Honesdale, Pa.: Himalayan Publishers, 1973).

Victory and Virtue Ceremonies and Code of Conduct of Sikh Dharma by Bhai Sahiba Dr. Inderjit Kaur (Española, N. Mex.: Golden Temple Enterprises, 1995).

Kundalini Yoga: The Flow of Eternal Power by Shakti Parwha Kaur Khalsa (Española, N. Mex.: Ancient Healing Ways, 1996).

III · HOLY DAYS AND FESTIVALS

Sikhs used to observe a lunar calendar, so the dates for holidays could not be accurately correlated to the solar calendar in use in the West. They now observe a solar calendar, so dates for holidays are fixed.

The birthdays of the 10 Sikh gurus are celebrated throughout the year:

- *Guru Gobind Singh* ("GOH-beend SING"): Celebrated January 5.
- *Guru Har Rai* ("hahr rye"): Celebrated January 31.
- *Guru Teg Bahadur* ("TEHG BAH-hah-door"): Celebrated April 18.
- *Guru Angad* ("Ahn-GAHD"): Celebrated April 18.
- *Guru Arjan* ("AHR-jahn"): Celebrated May 2.
- *Guru Amar Das* ("Ah-MAR DAHS"): Celebrated May 23.
- *Guru Hargobind* ("Hahr-GOH-beend"): Celebrated July 5.
- *Guru Har Krishnan* ("HAHR KRISH-nan"): Celebrated July 23.
- *Guru Ram Das* ("rahm dahs"): Celebrated October 9.
- *Guru Nanak* ("Nah-NAHK"): Celebrated November 23.

There are no traditional greetings for the above holidays.

Other important religious celebrations include:

- *Bhaisaki* ("BHAY-soo-ki"): When the *Khalsa* (the Pure Ones) was formed in 1699. This usually occurs in the middle of April. There is no traditional greeting for this holiday.
- *Guru Gaddi Day* ("GOO-ROO GAHD-dee"): Commemorates the *Siri Guru Granth Sahib* proclamation as the Living Guru. This usually occurs in November. There is no traditional greeting for this holiday.

To obtain a list of the exact days on which these holidays fall, consult with a Sikh center in your area.

Sikhs also observe the 6th of each month as a Holy Day. This day commemorates the attack by the Indian government on June 6, 1984, on the Akal Takhat in Amritsar in northern India. The government had mistakenly assumed that armed rebels were inside the Akal Takhat, a fortress that represents the temporal authority of the Sikhs. The Akal Takhat is adjacent to the Golden Temple, which houses the spiritual authority of the Sikhs. The two shrines are considered the holiest sites for Sikhs throughout the world.

These celebrations take place through the same *gurdwara* service as described earlier. Behavior and expectations for guests at these celebrations are the same as for the typical Sikh service.

IV · LIFE CYCLE EVENTS

Birth Ceremony

Among many Sikhs, it is traditional to name a newborn child by taking a *hukam* from the *Siri Guru Granth Sahib* and picking a name that begins with the first letter of the *hukam*. But this is not done in a religious ceremony. In the Sikh faith, there is no birth ceremony *per se*.

Initiation Ceremony

The *amrit* ceremony is a baptism that one chooses to undergo when he or she is ready to commit completely to the Sikh way of life. *Amrit* is given to anyone (usually an adult) who desires this commitment. It is usually administered to a group.

The ceremony focuses on the preparation of the *"amrit"* (holy water) by five "example Sikhs" called *Panj Piare*, or "Beloved Ones." An "example Sikh" is someone who best lives by the instructions and the example set by Guru Gobind Singh.

The *"amrit"* is then poured on the top of the head of those who have requested to be baptized, then splashed in their face. At the end of the ceremony, all participants and guests drink whatever water remains.

The ceremony incorporates many elements of a normal *gurdwara*, but adds baptism by water (not by immersion) and instructions for living as a Sikh that are given to the newly baptized by the five *Panj Piare*.

The *amrit* ceremony is given a few times each year between 4:00 and 6:00 a.m. Since the ceremony is primarily for those giving or receiving the baptism, special permission and instruction on conduct should be obtained from the head *granthi* for one to attend the ceremony as a guest.

BEFORE THE CEREMONY

Are guests usually invited by a formal invitation?

Outside guests are not usually invited to the ceremony. Permission for them to attend must first be obtained by the person undergoing the *amrit* ceremony from the head *granthi*. Once permission has been granted, guests are invited informally, usually by telephone.

If not stated explicitly, should one assume that children are invited?

No.

If one can't attend, what should one do?

Politely decline with a note or a telephone call.

APPROPRIATE ATTIRE

Men: A jacket and tie or more casual, modest clothing. Shoes are always removed before entering the *gurdwara*, and the head must always be covered while in the *gurdwara*. Guests may wear any hat, cap, or scarf that covers the top of the head.

Women: A modest dress, skirt and blouse, or pants suit. It is best if the legs are covered enough so one can comfortably sit cross-legged. Shoes are always removed before entering the *gurdwara*, and the head must always be covered with a scarf, hat or veil which covers the top of the head while in the *gurdwara*. Modest jewelry is permissible.

There are no rules regarding colors of clothing.

GIFTS

Is a gift customarily expected?

No.

Should gifts be brought to the ceremony?

See above.

THE CEREMONY

Where will the ceremony take place?

In the main room of the *gurdwara*.

When should guests arrive and where should they sit?

Guests should arrive before the time when the ceremony will begin since no one is allowed to enter after it starts. Guests should sit where they instructed to do so by the five *Panj Piare* who administer the ceremony.

Upon entering the *gurdwara*, remove your shoes and cover your head. It is optional to wash your hands and feet. If desired, the guest may offer money or a gift, such as flowers or fruit, to the *Siri Guru Granth Sahib* and then bow before it. Money may be placed in a box with a slot on it or on an offering plate. Either will be in front of the *Siri Guru Granth Sahib*. Other gifts may be placed in front of the *Siri Guru Granth Sahib*.

Next, guests should sit on the floor facing the front. The feet of all present should face away from the *Siri Guru Granth Sahib* as a sign of respect. It is important to refrain from eating, drinking or unnecessary conversation in the *gurdwara*.

If arriving late, are there times when a guest should *not* enter the ceremony?

No one is allowed to enter after the ceremony starts.

Are there times when a guest should *not* leave the ceremony?

Once entering the *amrit* ceremony, one may not leave until the ceremony has concluded so the commitment and concentration of participants is not disturbed.

Who are the major officiants, leaders or participants at the ceremony and what do they do?

- *The Panj Piare* ("Panj Pee-AR-ay"): Five Sikhs who constantly repeat a chant, administer the *amrit* and instruct those being baptized in their duties as Sikhs.
- *Granthi* ("GRAHN-thee") *or Giani Ji:* The person reading the *hukam* from the *Siri Guru Granth Sahib*.
- *Attendants:* Several people who serve *prasad* (sweet pudding) at the end of the ceremony, who read the *hukam* translation in English, and who assist in the *gurdwara*. Many people from the *sangat*, the congregation, participate in these functions.
- *Kirtanis:* Musicians who lead the *sangat* in *kirtan*, songs of praise to God.

◙ *The master of ceremonies:* The person announcing any guest speakers and the order of the service. This role is often fulfilled by the *gurdwara* secretary or *granthi* or *Giani Ji*.

What books are used?

Booklets of sheets (containing transliteration and translation of the *kirtan* (songs of praise to God) to be sung) may be available, depending on the *gurdwara*. Efforts should be made not to put them on the floor. Since Sikhs respect the written word of God, anything containing it should not be stepped upon or marred in any way.

If these booklets are available, they are often found at the front of the *gurdwara*.

To indicate the order of the ceremony:

There may be a written program and/or the master of ceremonies may make periodic announcements.

Will a guest who is not a Sikh be expected to do anything other than sit?

A guest will be expected to stand and sit at the same time as everyone else. It is entirely optional for the guest to sing or bow to the *Siri Guru Granth Sahib*. Guests are expected to accept *prasad* (sweet pudding) which is considered a blessing from the *Siri Guru Granth Sahib*. Customarily, *prasad* is placed into one's hands, which are placed together with the palms up. One does not have to be a Sikh to eat the *prasad*.

Are there any parts of the ceremony in which a guest who is not a Sikh should *not* participate?

Only Sikhs will be asked to serve *prasad*, read from the *Siri Guru Granth Sahib* and serve in any way needed.

If not disruptive to the ceremony, is it okay to:

◙ **Take pictures?** Only with prior permission of the head *granthi* and if intended solely for personal use.
◙ **Use a flash?** Only with prior permission of the head *granthi* and if intended solely for personal use.
◙ **Use a video camera?** Only with prior permission of the head *granthi* and if intended solely for personal use.
◙ **Use a tape recorder?** Only with prior permission of the head *granthi* and if intended solely for personal use.

Will contributions to the *gurdwara* be collected at the ceremony?

Donations collected at each service help fund the *langar* (the food provided after the service), *prasad* and the general maintenance and administration of the *gurdwara*. No collection plate is passed through the congregation. Instead, money or flowers may be offered to the *Siri Guru Granth Sahib* if one chooses to bow to it, which is optional. Money may be placed in a box with a slot on it or on an offering plate. Either will be in front of the *Siri Guru Granth Sahib*. Other gifts may be placed in front of the *Siri Guru Granth Sahib*.

How much is customary to contribute?

The customary contribution is $1 to $5.

AFTER THE CEREMONY

Is there usually a reception after the ceremony?

Langar, or sacred food, may be served after (and sometimes during) the ceremony. It is available to all. *Langar* may be served inside or outside the *gurdwara* or in a special hall built for the purpose.

Also, a vegetarian meal is provided and often consists of East Indian cuisine. Since alcohol is prohibited to Sikhs, it will not be served. The reception may last from 30 minutes to several hours.

Would it be considered impolite to neither eat nor drink?

No.

Is there a grace or benediction before eating or drinking?

No.

Is there a grace or benediction after eating or drinking?

No.

Is there a traditional greeting for the family?

The traditional greeting for newly baptized Sikhs is *"Wahe Guruji ka khalsa, Wahe Guru ji ki fateh"* ("WAH-beh GOO-ROO-ji kah KAHL-sah, WAH-heh GOO-ROO-ji kee FAH-teh"), which means "The Pure Ones belong to God. Victory be to God!"

Is there a traditional form of address for clergy who may be at the reception?

"*Granthi*" and then their first name, or "*Giani Ji.*"

Is it okay to leave early?

Yes.

Marriage Ceremony

A couple is considered to come together in a Sikh marriage to help each other on the spiritual path. The merging of two identities that takes place in a marriage is an earthly symbol for the more infinite merger between the soul and God.

A wedding can take place as part of the regular *gurdwara* service, but it may be a service unto itself. One or more couples may be married at the same time. A minister addresses the *sangat* (the congregation), then explains to the couple the Sikh concept of marriage and commitment. The bride and groom will be called to sit in front of the *Siri Guru Granth Sahib*. The *kirtanis* (musicians) will be seated on one side and the minister on the other side at the front of the *gurdwara*.

A short prayer called an *ardas* is recited to bless the wedding. Only immediate family and the wedding couple stand at this time. A *hukam*, or "Guru's command," for the wedding is then read from the *Siri Guru Granth Sahib*. Next, a special shawl is placed on the shoulder of the groom and in the hands of the bride. The shawl links the couple throughout the wedding ceremony.

The couple is considered to be married when they have circled the *Siri Guru Granth Sahib* four times after reciting four "marriage rounds," which are special verses from the *Siri Guru Granth Sahib*, in Gurmukhi and then in English (or the primary language of the *sangat*, the congregation). The rounds are then sung by the *kirtanis*. These marriage rounds were written by the fourth Sikh guru for his own wedding in the 16th century. They include special instructions for married life. During these rounds, family and close friends (including non-Sikh guests) may be invited to stand around the *Siri Guru Granth Sahib* to show their support for the couple whom they also encircle. In some *gurdwaras*, as the couple finishes the last round, the congregation may shower the couple with flower petals to show joy and congratulations. At this point, the couple is officially considered to be married and the minister may then make a legal pronouncement of marriage.

The first act of the newly married couple is to feed each other fruit. This illustrates their commitment to nourish and support each other.

If the wedding ceremony is part of a full worship service, the couple and their family and friends now rejoin the *sangat* and the service proceeds as usual.

The wedding itself usually lasts about one hour.

BEFORE THE CEREMONY

Are guests usually invited by a formal invitation?

Possibly, but not always. Sikh weddings are open to everyone.

If not stated explicitly, should one assume that children are invited?

Yes.

If one can't attend, what should one do?

Respond in writing or call, and send a gift if you desire to do so.

APPROPRIATE ATTIRE

Men: A jacket and tie or more casual, modest clothing. Shoes are always removed before entering the *gurdwara*, and the head must always be covered while in the *gurdwara*. Guests may wear any hat, cap, or scarf that covers the top of the head.

Women: A modest dress, skirt and blouse, or pants suit. It is best if the legs are covered enough so one can comfortably sit cross-legged. Shoes are always removed before entering the *gurdwara*, and the head must always be covered with a scarf, hat or veil which covers the top of the head while in the *gurdwara*. Modest jewelry is permissible.

There are no rules regarding colors of clothing.

GIFTS

Is a gift customarily expected?

There is no Sikh tradition dictating gift giving for weddings. If one wishes to present a gift, appropriate gifts may include household items (such as sheets, kitchenware or small appliances), a special, inspirational gift or money.

Should gifts be brought to the ceremony?

Gifts may either be left in the entry room or brought to a later reception.

THE CEREMONY

Where will the ceremony take place?

In the main *gurdwara*.

When should guests arrive and where should they sit?

Arrive shortly before the time for which the ceremony has been called, although some *gurdwaras* with primarily Eastern Indian congregants begin weddings much later than what is indicated on an invitation, so it's best to inquire of your host beforehand when the ceremony will actually start.

As with all *gurdwara* services, everyone sits facing the *Siri Guru Granth Sahib*, sometimes with the men on the left and women on the right.

If arriving late, are there times when a guest should *not* enter the ceremony?

A guest may enter at any time during the service, except during the *ardas* (community prayer), which is the point during the service when everyone is standing. One should wait at the entrance to the main worship room until these prayers have ended.

Are there times when a guest should *not* leave the ceremony?

It is advised not to leave during the *ardas* (prayer), *hukam* (the reading from the *Siri Guru Granth Sahib*) or the "wedding rounds," which are special verses from the *Siri Guru Granth Sahib* recited by the couple in Gurmukhi and then in English (or the primary language of the *sangat*, the congregation).

Guests may wish to sit near the door if they plan on leaving the ceremony early.

Who are the major officiants, leaders or participants at the ceremony and what do they do?

- *The Granthi or Giani Ji*, the person reading the *hukam*, or portion, from the *Siri Guru Granth Sahib*. He or she also reads the four wedding rounds.
- *The minister*, the person who officiates at the wedding ceremony.

◾ *The bride and groom and their wedding party.*

◾ *Kirtanis,* musicians who lead the *sangat,* or congregation, in *kirtan* (songs of praise to God).

What books are used?

Booklets of sheets (containing transliteration and translation of the *kirtan* to be sung) may be available, depending on the *gurdwara*. These are often found at the front of the *gurdwara* and in front of the *Siri Guru Granth Sahib*. Effort should be made not to place these booklets on the floor. Since Sikhs respect the written word of God, anything containing it should not be stepped upon or marred in any way.

To indicate the order of the ceremony:

There may be a written program and/or the master of ceremonies may make periodic announcements.

Will a guest who is not a Sikh be expected to do anything other than sit?

A guest is expected to stand and sit at the same time as everyone else, but it is optional to sing or bow to the *Siri Guru Granth Sahib*. Family and close friends wishing to stand behind the *Siri Guru Granth Sahib* to offer support to the couple may do so at the time indicated by the minister.

Are there any parts of the ceremony in which a guest who is not a Sikh should *not* participate?

No.

If not disruptive to the ceremony, is it okay to:

◾ **Take pictures?** Yes, but only if intended solely for personal use.

◾ **Use a flash?** Yes, but only if intended solely for personal use.

◾ **Use a video camera?** Yes, but only if intended solely for personal use.

◾ **Use a tape recorder?** Yes, but only if intended solely for personal use.

Will contributions to the *gurdwara* be collected at the ceremony?

Money or flowers may be offered to the *Siri Guru Granth Sahib* if one chooses to bow to it, which is optional. Money may be placed in a box with a slot on it or on an offering plate. Either will be in front of the *Siri Guru Granth Sahib*. Other gifts may be placed in front of the *Siri Guru Granth Sahib*.

How much is customary to contribute?

The customary contribution is $1 to $5.

AFTER THE CEREMONY

Is there usually a reception after the ceremony?

Langar, or sacred food, may be served after (and sometimes during) the ceremony. *Langar* may be served inside or outside the *gurdwara* or in a special hall built for the purpose. An additional reception at another location may take place after the *langar* where a vegetarian meal is provided. This often consists of East Indian cuisine. Since alcoholic beverages are prohibited to Sikhs, it will not be served. It is not considered impolite if they decline the offered food for any reason. The reception may last anywhere from half an hour to several hours.

Would it be considered impolite to neither eat nor drink?

No.

Is there a grace or benediction before eating or drinking?

No.

Is there a grace or benediction after eating or drinking?

No.

Is there a traditional greeting for the family?

Just offer your congratulations.

Is there a traditional form of address for clergy who may be at the reception?

"Granthi" and then their first name, or *"Giani Ji."*

Is it okay to leave early?

Yes.

Funerals and Mourning

Sikhs believe in the cycle of reincarnation and that certain actions and attachments bind the soul to this cycle. The soul itself is not subject to death. Death is only the progression of the soul on its journey from God, through the created universe, and back to God again.

A Sikh tries to be constantly mindful of death so that he or she may be sufficiently prayerful, detached and righteous to break the cycle of birth and death and return to God. Because the soul never dies, there is no mourning at the death of a Sikh. All ceremonies commemorating a death include much prayer to help the soul be released from the bonds of reincarnation and to become one with God again.

After death, Sikhs prepare the body for the funeral with a yogurt bath while reciting prayers. Next the body is dressed in new clothes and the five symbols of a Sikh: *kesh,* or uncut hair; *kirpan,* the Sikh knife which represents compassion and one's task to defend the truth; *kara,* a stainless steel bracelet; *kachera,* special Sikh underwear; and *kanga,* a small comb.

A short ceremony takes place at the funeral home before the cremation. An *ardas,* or community prayer, is recited to begin the service. A minister may be present to offer prayers and say a few words, but this is optional. Two Sikh daily prayers, *Japji* and *Kirtan Sohila,* are recited, and the cremation begins. Although these prayers may be continuously recited throughout the cremation, the basic funeral service ends at this time, and guests may leave. This service usually lasts about 30 to 60 minutes.

Afterward, there may be another service at the *gurdwara,* but this is optional. Traditionally, the word "*akal,*" which means "undying," is chanted at this service to help release the soul to return to the Infinite. This second ceremony, which is a service unto itself, lasts about one hour.

BEFORE THE CEREMONY

How soon after the death does the funeral usually take place?

The body of a Sikh is always cremated. This usually occurs within three days after death.

What should a non-Sikh do upon hearing of the death of a member of that faith?

It is fine to call the family of the deceased to express your love and concern and offer help or support they may need. In calling or writing, it is best not to focus on loss or sadness, but rather to help the family and friends remember the joy of the soul returning to its true Home with God.

APPROPRIATE ATTIRE

Men: A jacket and tie or more casual, modest clothing. Any color is fine. Shoes may be worn inside a funeral home, but not in a *gurdwara* service. The head should be covered with a hat, cap or scarf.

Women: A modest dress, skirt and blouse, or pants suit. It is best if the legs are covered enough to sit comfortably cross-legged. Shoes may be worn inside a funeral home, but not at a *gurdwara* service. The head should be covered with a scarf, hat or veil. Open-toed shoes (which may be worn only in the funeral home, *not* in the *gurdwara*) and modest jewelry are permissible.

There are no rules regarding colors of clothing.

GIFTS

Is it appropriate to send flowers or make a contribution?

Flowers, food or contributions to a charity chosen by the family of the deceased may be given, but are not expected.

Is it appropriate to send food?

Yes, but do not send food that contains meat, fish, eggs or alcohol.

THE CEREMONY

Where will the ceremony take place?

The pre-cremation ceremony will take place at a funeral home. The optional, post-cremation ceremony will be at the *gurdwara*.

When should guests arrive and where should they sit?

It is best to arrive early enough to be seated before the funeral service begins. At a funeral home, one may sit wherever one wishes, but the family of the deceased will sit in the front. For *gurdwara* services, everyone sits on the floor facing the *Siri Guru Granth Sahib*, sometimes with the men on the left and women on the right.

If arriving late, are there times when a guest should *not* enter the ceremony?

One can enter the ceremony in the funeral home and quietly sit anywhere.

Wait at the entrance to the *gurdwara* until the *ardas*, or community prayer, ends and everyone has again been seated.

Will the bereaved family present at the funeral home before the ceremony?

Depending on the customs of a particular Sikh community, the body of the deceased may be displayed at a visitation before the funeral. If this is not the case, the family of the deceased will most likely arrive at the time of the ceremony and not before.

Is there a traditional greeting for the family?

Just offer your condolences.

Will there be an open casket?

Possibly, depending on the customs of a particular Sikh community.

Is a guest expected to view the body?

No.

What is appropriate behavior upon viewing the body?

Silently say a short prayer for the soul of the deceased as you pass by the casket.

Who are the major officiants at the ceremony and what do they do?

- *One person,* usually a close family member, officiates at the ceremony at the funeral home and leads the prayers recited there. Officiating at the service in the *gurdwara* are:

- *The Granthi or Giani Ji,* the person reading the *hukam* from the *Siri Guru Granth Sahib.* The *hukam,* which is a portion of the *Siri Guru Granth Sahib* chosen randomly by the reader, is first read in the original Gurmukhi language and then translated to English (or the main language of the congregation).

- *Attendants,* several people who sit behind the *Siri Guru Granth Sahib* and attend to it by frequently waving a long-handled brush made of long horse hair called a *chori sahib* above the *Siri Guru Granth Sahib* or who take out or put away the scriptures. The attendants also serve *prasad,* or sweet pudding, at the end of the service; read the *hukam* translation in English; and assist in the *gurdwara* in any way. Many people from the *sangat,* the congregation, participate in these functions.

- *Kirtanis,* musicians who lead the *sangat* in *kirtan,* songs of praise to God.

- *The master of ceremonies,* the person announcing guest speakers and the order of the service. This role is often fulfilled by the *gurdwara* secretary or *granthi.*

What books are used?

A *Nit Nem,* or daily prayer book of the Sikhs is used to recite the prayers before cremation. Since all prayers are read in Gurmukhi (the original language of the gurus), it is not expected for guests to also recite these. If desired, however, a *Nit Nam* with a transliteration may be available upon request.

To indicate the order of the ceremony:

In the funeral home, no one indicates the order of the ceremony that is held there. For the *gurdwara* service, there may be a written program and/or the Master of Ceremonies may make periodic announcements.

Will a guest who is not a Sikh be expected to do anything other than sit?

There are no expectations for guests attending the ceremony in the funeral home. Those guests attending the *gurdwara* ceremony will be expected to stand and sit at the same time as everyone else. It is entirely optional for guests to sing or bow to the *Siri Guru Granth Sahib*, although they are expected to accept *prasad* (sweet pudding), which is considered a blessing from the *Siri Guru Granth Sahib*. Customarily, one receives *prasad* with both hands together, palms up. One does not have to be a Sikh to eat the *prasad*.

Are there any parts of the ceremony in which a guest who is not a Sikh should *not* participate?

Guests may participate in all aspects of the ceremony in the funeral home. In the *gurdwara* ceremony, only Sikhs will be asked to serve *prasad*, read from the *Siri Guru Granth Sahib*, do the *ardas* (prayer) and to serve in any way needed. Other than this, guest may participate in every part of the *gurdwara* ceremony as desired.

If not disruptive to the ceremony, is it okay to:

- **Take pictures?** Only with prior permission of the family of the deceased and if intended solely for personal use.
- **Use a flash?** Only with prior permission of the family of the deceased and if intended solely for personal use.
- **Use a video camera?** Only with prior permission of the family of the deceased and if intended solely for personal use.
- **Use a tape recorder?** Only with prior permission of the family of the deceased and if intended solely for personal use.

Will contributions to the local Sikh temple be collected be collected at the service?

No contributions will be collected at a funeral home service. At *gurdwara* services, money or flowers may be offered to the *Siri Guru Granth*

Sahib at the time of bowing, but this is optional. Money may be placed in a box with a slot on it or on an offering plate. Either will be in front of the *Siri Guru Granth Sahib*. Other gifts may be placed in front of the *Siri Guru Granth Sahib*.

How much is customary to contribute?

The customary contribution is $1 to $5.

THE CREMATION

Should guests attend the cremation?

Usually only close family members remain for the cremation since it lasts several hours.

Whom should one ask for directions?

Friends or the family of the deceased.

What happens at the cremation?

An *ardas*, or community prayer, is recited to begin the service. A minister may offer prayers and say a few words, but this is optional. Two Sikh daily prayers, *Japji* and *Kirtan Sohila*, are recited, and the cremation begins.

Do guests who are not Sikhs participate at the cremation ceremony?

Not usually unless they are invited by the family to do so.

COMFORTING THE BEREAVED

Is it appropriate to visit the home of the bereaved after the funeral ceremony?

This is optional, though not really expected.

Will there be a religious service at the home of the bereaved?

Memorial services are often held at home, especially when the funeral ceremony has taken place in another city. Sometimes, the family of the deceased sponsors an *Akhand Path* (unbroken) or other reading of the *Siri Guru Granth Sahib* Siri. This may take place at their home, at the *gurdwara*, or elsewhere. During the *Akhand Path* service, the entire *Siri Guru Granth Sahib* is read in 48 hours in the Gurmukhi language or in 72 hours in English. People take turns reading the text.

Will food be served?

Possibly. Since Sikhs are prohibited from drinking alcoholic beverages, none will be offered.

How soon after the funeral will a mourner usually return to a normal work schedule?

Usually one returns to a normal work routine anywhere from a few days to a few weeks after the funeral. This is at the personal discretion of each individual.

How soon after the funeral will a mourner usually return to a normal social schedule?

Usually one returns to a normal social routine anywhere from a few days to a few weeks after the funeral. This is at the personal discretion of each individual.

Are there mourning customs to which a friend who is not a Sikh should be sensitive?

When visiting, it is best not to focus on loss or sadness, but rather to help the family and friends remember the joy of the soul returning to its true Home with God.

Are there rituals for observing the anniversary of the death?

No, although some Sikhs may choose to remember a deceased loved one in prayer during a *gurdwara* service on the anniversary of a death. Some Sikhs also choose to hold a special *gurdwara* and *langar* at the anniversary.

V · HOME CELEBRATIONS

The Home or Business Blessing

When does it occur?

Before occupying a new house or apartment or launching a new venture or business.

What is its significance?

To bless a new home or enterprise with success and happiness. Many Sikhs may hold a *gurdwara* service called an *Akhand Path*, during which the entire *Siri Guru Granth Sahib* is read in 48 hours in the Gurmukhi language or in 72 hours in English. People take turns reading the text.

Other Sikhs may choose to serve *langar*, or sacred food, in the new home or business location.

What is the proper greeting to the celebrants?
"Congratulations."

BEFORE THE CEREMONY

Are guests usually invited by a formal invitation?
Yes.

If not stated explicitly, should one assume children are invited?
Yes.

If one can't attend, what should one do?
Politely decline by note or a telephone call. A housewarming gift is appropriate for a new dwelling, but this is entirely optional.

APPROPRIATE ATTIRE

Men: A jacket and tie or more casual, modest clothing. Shoes are always removed before entering the *gurdwara*, and the head must always be covered while in the *gurdwara*. Guests may wear any hat, cap or scarf that covers the top of the head.

Women: A modest dress, skirt and blouse, or pants suit. It is best if the legs are covered enough so one can comfortably sit cross-legged. Shoes are always removed before entering the *gurdwara*, and the head must always be covered with a scarf, hat or veil which covers the top of the head while in the *gurdwara*. Modest jewelry is permissible.

There are no rules regarding colors of clothing.

GIFTS

Is a gift customarily expected?
No. This is optional.

If one decides to give a gift, is a certain type of gift appropriate?
Anything for a new home or business.

THE CEREMONY

If the hosts choose to have an *Akhand Path*, a 48- to 72-hour reading of the *Siri Guru Granth Sahib*, it is preceded by a one-hour *gurdwara* service at which the following officiate:

- *The Granthi or Giani Ji*, the person reading the *hukam* from the *Siri Guru Granth Sahib*.
- *Attendants*, several people who sit behind the *Siri Guru Granth Sahib* and attend to it by frequently waving a long-handled brush made of long horse hair called a *chori sahib* above the *Siri Guru Granth Sahib* or take out or put away the scriptures. The attendants also serve *prasad*, or sweet pudding, at the end of the service; read the *hukam* translation in English; and assist in the *gurdwara* in any way. Many people from the *sangat*, the congregation, participate in these functions.
- *Kirtanis*, musicians who lead those present in *kirtan*, songs of praise to God.

It is customary to arrive for the service at the time for which it has been called.

What are the major ritual objects of the ceremony?

If there is an *Akhand Path*, the following are used:

- *The manji sahib*, the "bed" or platform for the *Siri Guru Granth Sahib*. It is covered by ornate cloths called *"ramalas."*
- *The chandoa*, the canopy hanging over the *Siri Guru Granth Sahib*.
- *The adi shakti or khanda*, a symbol shaped like a circle surrounded by two swords and cut through by one double-edged sword. It symbolizes the primal, creative energy of the universe. The sword cutting through the circle represents the breaking of the cycle of birth and death.
- *The kirpan*, a special knife used to bless *langar* ("sacred food") and *prasad* (sweet pudding) during the *ardas* (community prayer).
- *The chori sahib*, a long-handled brush made of long horse hair. It is identical to brushes used in ancient India that were waved over royalty to show their state of sovereignty. It is waved over the *Siri Guru Granth Sahib* to symbolize its sovereignty, to purify the energy around it, and to show its status as a living guru.

What books are used?

Booklets of sheets (containing transliteration and translation of the *kirtan* (songs of praise to God) to be sung may be available. Efforts should be made not to put them on the floor. Since Sikhs respect the written word of God, anything containing it should not be stepped upon or marred in any way.

Will a guest who is not a Sikh be expected to do anything other than sit?

A guest will be expected to stand and sit at the same time as everyone else. It is entirely optional for the guest to sing or bow to the *Siri Guru Granth Sahib*. Guests are expected to accept *prasad* (sweet pudding) which is considered a blessing from the *Siri Guru Granth Sahib*.

Customarily, one receives *prasad* with both hands together, palms up. One does not have to be a Sikh to eat the *prasad*.

Are there any parts of the ceremony in which a guest who is not a Sikh should *not* participate?

Only Sikhs will be asked to serve *prasad*, read from the *Siri Guru Granth Sahib*, do the *ardas* (prayer) and to serve in any way needed. Other than this, a guest may participate in every part of the service as desired.

If not disruptive to the ceremony, is it okay to:

- **Take pictures?** Yes, but only if intended solely for personal use.
- **Use a flash?** Yes, but only if intended solely for personal use.
- **Use a video camera?** Yes, but only if intended solely for personal use.
- **Use a tape recorder?** Yes, but only if intended solely for personal use.

EATING AND DRINKING

Is a meal part of the celebration?

Possibly.

Will there be alcoholic beverages?

No.

Would it be considered impolite to neither eat nor drink?

No.

Is there a grace or benediction before eating or drinking?

No.

Is there a grace or benediction after eating or drinking?

No.

At the meal, will a guest be asked to say or do anything?

No.

Will there be:

◘ **Dancing?** No.

◘ **Music?** Only *kirtan*, songs of praise to God.

GENERAL GUIDELINES AND ADVICE

None provided.

Chapter 16 Contents

16

Unitarian Universalist

(also known as Unitarian or Universalist)

I · HISTORY AND BELIEFS

The Unitarian Universalist Association was created in 1961 when the American Unitarian Association and the Universalist Church of America merged. The purpose of the union was "to cherish and spread the universal truths taught by the great prophets and teachers of humanity in every age and tradition, immemorially summarized in the Judeo-Christian heritage as love to God and love to man."

The newly-formed Unitarian Universalist Association included both American and Canadian congregations. In the same year, 1961, the Canadian Unitarian Council was organized to provide services to Canadian congregations, which are members of both bodies.

Like its predecessors, the new denomination is committed to living in the tension between humanistic liberalism and Christianity, and prefers following reason, conscience and experience to following creeds. Unitarian Universalist churches make no official pronouncements on God, the Bible, Jesus, immortality or other theological questions that are often answered with finality by more traditional religions. Instead, Unitarian Universalism deems a religious way of life as being too important to be left to rigid creeds and dogmas, and there is frequent discussion among members and clergy about whether the faith has, indeed, grown beyond Judeo-Christianity and become something more universal. Unitarian Universalists reject the attitude that salvation is attainable only through the mediation of Jesus Christ and membership in a Christian Church. Thus, many believe that Unitarian Universalism is not a Christian faith today, although its historical and theological roots are undeniably Christian.

Unitarians trace their origins to a movement that began shortly after the death of Jesus Christ. According to present Unitarian teachings, many who personally knew Jesus rejected claims of his divinity. Instead, they focused on his humanity and his teachings, not on his alleged godliness. The movement was eventually named Arianism, after Arius, a priest from Alexandria who preached this belief. After the Council of Nicea adopted in 325 A.D. the concept of the Trinity—God, the Father; God, the Son; God, the Holy Ghost—those who embraced this idea denounced believers in God's unity as heretics.

Nevertheless, by the 16th century, Unitarian ideas had gained a foothold in Switzerland, Britain, Hungary and Italy. In 1683, the first Unitarian church to use that name was established in Transylvania. And by the first decade of the 19th century, 20 Unitarian churches had been established in England.

In the United States, Unitarianism got its impetus from the preaching and writings of William Ellery Channing in the early 19th century. Strongly concerned with liberal social causes, such as abolitionism and educational reform, the faith also gave birth to the Transcendentalism associated with Ralph Waldo Emerson and Henry David Thoreau.

While Unitarianism most often attracted the highly educated and intellectual, especially in New England, Universalism was initially an evangelistic, working-class movement with an uneducated clergy. Their "universalism" rested on a belief that all souls would eventually attain salvation. As with Unitarianism, it dates from the early days of Christianity, most notably the writings of Origen, an early Church father.

In the United States, circuit-rider ministers helped spread the faith so well that by the 1850s there were about 800,000 Universalists. By the 1900s, Universalism was the sixth largest denomination in the United States. After that, membership steadily declined, although its theological development eventually so paralleled that of Unitarianism that the two denominations could eventually merge.

In 19th-century Canada, Unitarian congregations were established in Montreal and Toronto, with the assistance of British Unitarians. Universalism entered Canada from the United States, and was largely centered in the Maritimes and Southern Ontario. Many Icelandic Lutherans in Manitoba were attracted to the more liberal Unitarian faith and established a number of congregations there. Unitarianism in Canada remained a very small faith group until the end of World War II, when there was a strong movement away from more traditional faiths, and new congregations and lay-led fellowships were established in many parts of the country.

Each local Unitarian Universalist congregation, which may be called a church, society or fellowship, adopts its own bylaws, elects its own officers and approves its budget. Each local congregation is affiliated with one of the 23 districts of the Unitarian Universalist Association of Congregations.

U.S. churches: 1,033
U.S. membership: 213,342
(1999 data from the Unitarian Universalist Association of Congregations)

For more information, contact:
The Unitarian Universalist Association of Congregations
25 Beacon Street
Boston, MA 02108-2800
(617) 742-2100

Canadian churches: 44
Canadian membership: 5,038
(data from the Canadian Unitarian Council)
For more information, contact:
Canadian Unitarian Council
55 Eglinton Avenue, Suite 705
Toronto, ON M4P 1G8
(416) 489-4121

352 · *How to Be a Perfect Stranger*

II · THE BASIC SERVICE

Unitarian Universalism teaches that worship invites those present to focus on the transcendental, the intimate and the worthy. It helps us regain a sense of ourselves, and reminds us that we may challenge greed or violence which pollutes the human condition.

Local culture, inherited traditions, a particular minister or a lay worship team all contribute to the style of Unitarian Universalist worship. Some services are formal, and maintain a sense of decorum and a devotional atmosphere. Other services are marked by applause or a dialogue between congregants and whoever is speaking from the pulpit.

But whatever the style, the community remains the locus of the holy. Unitarian Universalists recognize the power of solitude and personal devotion, but they worship together for the strength gained from the presence and wisdom of others.

Usually, a service begins with an invocation and music. Some services also begin by lighting a candle or a flaming chalice, which is the symbol of the faith. The balance of the service may have scripture readings, poetry and other readings chosen from the spiritual heritage of many faiths. There may also be a sermon, periods of silence and announcements that share the joys and concerns of individual congregants with the entire community. Services usually end with closing words, benedictions and blessings.

Most congregations hold services on Sunday mornings, although smaller and, especially, relatively new congregations may hold services on Saturday or Sunday evenings. This is done not for theological reasons, but because of the availability of space where services are held. Services may last about 60 to 75 minutes.

APPROPRIATE ATTIRE

Men: A jacket and tie or more casual attire, such as slacks, a sport jacket and an open collar. No head covering is required.

Women: A dress or a skirt and blouse or a pants suit. Hems need not reach below the knees nor must clothing cover the arms. Open-toed shoes and modest jewelry are permissible. No head covering is required.

There are no rules regarding colors of clothing.

THE SANCTUARY

What are the major sections of the church?

Unitarian Universalists worship in a variety of settings—from a Gothic nave to a large living room, from a 19th-century meeting house to a rented school auditorium. The following applies to those services held in a church building:

- *The podium or dais,* which is used by speakers and includes the the lectern or pulpit.
- *The choir loft,* where the choir and/or the organist sit and perform.
- *The pews,* where congregants and guests sit.

THE SERVICE

When should guests arrive and where should they sit?

Arrive at the time for which the service has been called or shortly before that time. Ushers may be present to advise guests where to sit. If not, sit wherever you wish.

If arriving late, are there times when a guest should *not* enter the service?

Do not enter during a meditation or prayer.

Are there times when a guest should *not* leave the service?

Do not enter during a meditation or prayer.

Who are the major officiants, leaders or participants and what do they do?

- *The minister,* who officiates at the service.
- *The director of religious education,* who may preside during the children's portion of the service.
- *The parish chair or president,* who may welcome congregants and guests and may co-lead the service.
- *The choir and/or music director,* who presides over the musical elements of the service.

What are the major ritual objects of the service?

- *The flaming chalice:* This is the symbol of Unitarian Universalism. The chalice symbolizes sharing, generosity, sustenance and love. The flame symbolizes sacrifice, courage and spiritual illumination. The flaming chalice is usually located on the lectern or pulpit.

(A few churches may have a cross. Some have a range of symbols, such as a cross, a Star of David, a Buddhist wheel, a Tao circle and a Sufic winged heart.)

What books are used?

A Bible may be used during Unitarian Universalist worship. No particular translations of the Bible are used. Some congregations have compiled anthologies of contemporary writings to be used for readings during services. Used at almost every service are a Book of Common Prayer and a hymnal, *Singing the Living Tradition*, edited by the Hymnbook Resource Commission (Boston, Ma.: The Unitarian Universalist Association, 1993).

To indicate the order of the service:

A program will be distributed.

GUEST BEHAVIOR DURING THE SERVICE

Will a guest who is not a Unitarian Universalist be expected to do anything other than sit?

It is expected for guests to stand with congregants when they rise for songs. It is optional for guests to sing and read prayers aloud with congregants if this does not violate their own religious beliefs. There is no kneeling during a Unitarian Universalist service.

Are there any parts of the service in which a guest who is not a member of the Unitarian Universalist Church should *not* participate?

No.

If not disruptive to the service, is it okay to:

◘ **Take pictures?** Yes.
◘ **Use a flash?** No.
◘ **Use a video camera?** Yes.
◘ **Use a tape recorder?** Yes.

Will contributions to the church be collected at the service?

An offering plate will be passed throughout most congregations during the service. Some congregations prefer to encourage parishioners to contribute to the church community in other ways, such as teaching in the religious education program, working on church committees or hosting church-related meetings at one's home.

How much is customary to contribute?

It is entirely optional for guests to contribute. If they choose to do so, a contribution between $1 and $4 is appropriate.

AFTER THE SERVICE

Is there usually a reception after the service?

Yes. This is usually held in the reception area of the church and may consist of coffee, tea, cookies and fruit. There is no grace or benediction before or after eating or drinking. The reception may last about 30 to 60 minutes.

Is there a traditional form of address for clergy who may be at the reception?

"Mr.," "Ms.," "Dr.," "Reverend" or simply call the clergyperson by his or her first name.

Is it okay to leave early?

Yes.

GENERAL GUIDELINES AND ADVICE

Most Unitarian Universalist services are quite informal and non-traditional.

SPECIAL VOCABULARY

Key words or phrases which might be helpful for a visitor to know:

- *UU:* Shorthand for "Unitarian Universalist."
- *YRUU:* Shorthand for "Young Religious Unitarian Universalists," a youth group for Unitarian Universalists who are in junior and high school.
- *P&P:* Shorthand for "Principles and Purposes," which are those concepts on which Unitarian Universalism is based.

DOGMA AND IDEOLOGY

Unitarian Universalists believe:

- Personal experience, conscience and reason should be the final authorities in religion. Religious authority lies not in a book or a person or an institution, but in ourselves.

- One cannot be bound by a statement of belief. Unitarian Universalism does not ask anyone to subscribe to a creed.
- Religious wisdom is ever-changing, and human understanding of life and death, the world and its mysteries is never final, and revelation is continuous.
- All men and women have worth. Differences in opinion and lifestyle should be honored.
- One should act as a moral force in the world, and ethical living is the supreme witness of religion. The here and now and the affects that our actions will have on future generations are of great concern. Relations with each other, with other peoples, nations and races should be governed by justice, equity and compassion.

Some basic books and pamphlets to which a guest can refer to learn more about Unitarian Universalism:

Our Chosen Faith, by John A. Buehrens and F. Forrester Church (Boston, Ma.: Beacon Press, 1989).

Pocket Guide to Unitarian Universalism, edited by William F. Schulz (Boston, Ma.: Skinner House Books, 1993), which may be obtained from The Unitarian Universalist Bookstore, 25 Beacon Street, Boston, MA 02108, tel: (800) 215-9076.

III · HOLY DAYS AND FESTIVALS

- *Easter:* Always falls on the Sunday after the first full moon that occurs on or after the Spring equinox of March 21. Commemorates the renewal of life through a service which emphasizes light and rebirth. The traditional greeting is "Happy Easter."
- *Passover:* (Celebrated in some congregations.) Begins with the 15th day of the Hebrew month of Nisan, which is usually in late March or early to mid-April. The holiday celebrates the deliverance of the Jewish people from slavery in Egypt. The celebration may include a Passover *seder,* a festive ritualistic meal, on the Sunday closest to the first day of Passover. The seders are usually held at home; some are held in the church. The traditional greeting is "Happy Passover."
- *Thanksgiving:* Celebrated on the fourth Thursday of November. Celebrates harvest and home, usually with a church service which emphasizes thanksgiving and a traditional Thanksgiving dinner at home. The traditional greeting is "Happy Thanksgiving."

▪ *Chanukah:* (Celebrated in some congregations.) Observed for the eight days beginning with the 25th day of the Hebrew month of Kislev, which is usually in early to mid-December. The celebration may include an evening dinner either at home or in the church reception hall. It is often an intergenerational celebration with youths, parents and elders from the congregation present. The traditional greeting is "Happy Chanukah."

▪ *Christmas:* Always falls on December 25. Celebrates the promise of all children to be prophets in their own time. Churches usually have at least one Christmas Eve candle-lit ceremony as well as ceremonies on Christmas Day. The traditional greeting is "Merry Christmas."

▪ *Winter and Summer Solstice:* (Celebrated in some congregations.) The winter solstice occurs either on December 21 or 22; the summer solstice occurs either on June 20 or 21. The dates depend on the movement of the earth around the sun. Solstice ceremonies are often informal, and may include dancing and/or chanting. The holidays signify the cosmic cycle and movement from darkness to light and rebirth. The traditional greeting is "Happy Solstice."

IV · LIFE CYCLE EVENTS

Birth Ceremony

Depending on the specific congregation, this may be called a "christening," a "naming" or a "dedication." "Christening" means "to make Christian" and emphasizes the importance of a faith community to nurture and sustain individuals and families in times of joy and sorrow. "Naming" signifies that each child is a unique individual whose name is a powerful symbol of their individuality. "Dedication" may include these meanings, as well as underscore a covenant with God, the church and the family, in which parents dedicate themselves to lovingly raise their child in a home that will promote the fullest growth of the child's body, mind and spirit.

The ceremony may contain traditional elements, such as water from a baptismal font. Or the water may come from the sea, thus representing the source of all life. A rose may be presented to the child or the family to represent the beauty and fragility of life.

The ceremony is the same for males and females. It is often performed for an infant, although older children or even adults may desire such a ceremony to publicly experience such a dedication. The 15- to 30-minute long ceremony is usually part of a Sunday worship service.

BEFORE THE CEREMONY

Are guests usually invited by a formal invitation?

Sometimes.

If not stated explicitly, should one assume that children are invited?

Yes.

If one can't attend, what should one do?

RSVP with regrets.

APPROPRIATE ATTIRE

Men: A jacket and tie or more casual attire, such as slacks, a sport jacket and an open collar. No head covering is required.

Women: A dress or a skirt and blouse or a pants suit. Hems need not reach below the knees nor must clothing cover the arms. Open-toed shoes and modest jewelry are permissible. No head covering is required.

There are no rules regarding colors of clothing.

GIFTS

Is a gift customarily expected?

No.

Should gifts be brought to the ceremony?

See above.

THE CEREMONY

Where will the ceremony take place?

In the main sanctuary of the parents' church.

When should guests arrive and where should they sit?

Arrive at the time for which the ceremony has been called or shortly before that time. Ushers may be present to advise guests where to sit. If not, sit wherever you wish.

If arriving late, are there times when a guest should *not* enter the ceremony?

Do not enter during meditation or prayer or the dedication itself.

Are there times when a guest should *not* leave the ceremony?

Do not enter during meditation or prayer or the dedication itself.

Who are the major officiants, leaders or participants at the ceremony and what do they do?

- *The minister,* who officiates at the ceremony.
- *The director of religious education,* who may preside during the child's portion of the ceremony.
- *The infant and his or her parents and godparents.*

What books are used?

The dedication ceremony will probably be printed in the program for the ceremony.

To indicate the order of the ceremony:

A program will be distributed.

Will a guest who is not a Unitarian Universalist be expected to do anything other than sit?

It is expected for guests to stand with congregants when they rise for songs and to participate in parts of the ceremony that require the congregants to respond to the minister or to the family of the child whose dedication is being observed. It is optional for guests to sing and read prayers aloud with congregants if this does not violate their own religious beliefs. There is no kneeling during a Unitarian Universalist ceremony.

Are there any parts of the ceremony in which a guest who is not a Unitarian Universalist should *not* participate?

No.

If not disruptive to the ceremony, is it okay to:

- **Take pictures?** Yes.
- **Use a flash?** No.
- **Use a video camera?** Yes.
- **Use a tape recorder?** Yes.

Will contributions to the church be collected at the ceremony?

An offering plate will be passed throughout most congregations during the service. Some congregations prefer to encourage parishioners to contribute to the church community in other ways, such as teaching in the religious education program, working on church committees or hosting church-related meetings at one's home.

How much is customary to contribute?

It is entirely optional for guests to contribute. If they choose to do so, a contribution between $1 and $4 is appropriate.

AFTER THE CEREMONY

Is there usually a reception after the ceremony?

Possibly. If so, it may be a small, low-keyed, casual reception in the reception hall of the church or in the home of the parents whose child was dedicated. There may be light food, possibly alcoholic beverages, and neither singing nor dancing. The reception may last about 30 to 60 minutes.

Would it be considered impolite to neither eat nor drink?

No.

Is there a grace or benediction before eating or drinking?

Sometimes.

Is there a grace or benediction after eating or drinking?

Sometimes.

Is there a traditional greeting for the family?

Just offer your congratulations.

Is there a traditional form of address for clergy who may be at the reception?

"Mr.," "Ms.," "Dr.," "Reverend" or simply call the clergyperson by his or her first name.

Is it okay to leave early?

Yes, whenever one wishes.

Initiation Ceremony

Teens between 14 and 16 years are eligible for what is called a "coming of age" ceremony, which is comparable to confirmation in other faiths and acknowledges the onset of young adulthood. The ceremony varies from congregation to congregation, with each congregation choosing whether to even have one. Usually, the ceremony is the same for males and females and is performed for an entire class of teens, not for individuals.

The ceremony may be a service unto itself or part of a regular Sunday worship service. The ceremony lasts slightly more than one hour.

BEFORE THE CEREMONY

Are guests usually invited by a formal invitation?

No.

If not stated explicitly, should one assume that children are invited?

Yes.

If one can't attend, what should one do?

RSVP with regrets.

APPROPRIATE ATTIRE

Men: A jacket and tie or more casual attire, such as slacks, a sport jacket and an open collar. No head covering is required.

Women: A dress or a skirt and blouse or a pants suit. Hems need not reach below the knees nor must clothing cover the arms. Open-toed shoes and modest jewelry are permissible. No head covering is required.

There are no rules regarding colors of clothing.

GIFTS

Is a gift customarily expected?

No, although a gift is not inappropriate. If one chooses to give a gift, appropriate items are cash in the range of $25 to $50 or personal or spiritual items, such as books or pins with a flaming chalice motif.

Should gifts be brought to the ceremony?

Yes.

THE CEREMONY

Where will the ceremony take place?

In the main sanctuary of the church.

When should guests arrive and where should they sit?

Arrive at the time for which the ceremony has been called or shortly before that time. Ushers may be present to advise guests where to sit. If not, sit wherever you wish.

If arriving late, are there times when a guest should *not* enter the ceremony?

Do not enter during meditation or prayer or the coming of age ceremony itself.

Are there times when a guest should *not* leave the ceremony?

Do not enter during meditation or prayer or the coming of age ceremony itself.

Who are the major officiants, leaders or participants at the ceremony and what do they do?

- *The participating teens.*
- *The minister,* who officiates at the ceremony.
- *The director of religious education,* who may preside during part of the ceremony.
- *A youth group leader.*
- *The youths' teacher or mentor.*

What books are used?

A hymnal, *Singing the Living Tradition*, edited by the Hymnbook Resource Commission (Boston, Ma.: The Unitarian Universalist Association, 1993).

To indicate the order of the ceremony:

A program will be distributed.

Will a guest who is not a Unitarian Universalist be expected to do anything other than sit?

It is expected for guests to stand with congregants when they rise for songs. It is optional for guests to sing and read prayers aloud with congregants if this does not violate their own religious beliefs. There is no kneeling during a Unitarian Universalist ceremony.

Are there any parts of the ceremony in which a guest who is not a Unitarian Universalist should *not* participate?

No.

If not disruptive to the ceremony, is it okay to:

▪ **Take pictures?** Yes.
▪ **Use a flash?** No.
▪ **Use a video camera?** Yes.
▪ **Use a tape recorder?** Yes.

Will contributions to the church be collected at the ceremony?

An offering plate will be passed throughout most congregations during the service. Some congregations prefer to encourage parishioners to contribute to the church community in other ways, such as teaching in the religious education program, working on church committees or hosting church-related meetings at one's home.

How much is customary to contribute?

If guests choose to contribute, a contribution between $1 and $4 is appropriate.

AFTER THE CEREMONY

Is there usually a reception after the ceremony?

No.

Is there a traditional greeting for the family?

Just offer your congratulations.

Is there a traditional form of address for clergy whom a guest may meet?

"Mr.," "Ms.," "Dr.," "Reverend" or simply call the clergyperson by his or her first name.

Marriage Ceremony

Marriage is the committed joining of two lives as witnessed by the community. Unitarian Universalism does not necessarily consider marriage to be a union that will last for the entirety of one's life. It also supports same-sex marriages, a stance that reflects the faith's long-time call for lesbians and gays to be fully included in the religious community and in society at large.

The wedding ceremony is a ceremony unto itself. It may last about 30 to 60 minutes.

BEFORE THE CEREMONY

Are guests usually invited by a formal invitation?

Yes.

If not stated explicitly, should one assume that children are invited?

No.

If one can't attend, what should one do?

Send a written RSVP and a gift.

APPROPRIATE ATTIRE

Men: A jacket and tie. No head covering is required.

Women: A dress. Hems need not reach below the knees nor must clothing cover the arms. Open-toed shoes and modest jewelry are permissible. No head covering is required.

There are no rules regarding colors of clothing.

GIFTS

Is a gift customarily expected?

Yes. Small household items such as sheets, small appliances or kitchenware or cash in the amount of $25 to $100 are appropriate.

Should gifts be brought to the ceremony?

Gifts may be sent to the home of the newlyweds.

THE CEREMONY

Where will the ceremony take place?

In the main sanctuary of the church, in a special area elsewhere in the church or in a home.

When should guests arrive and where should they sit?

Arrive shortly before the time for which the ceremony has been called. Ushers will advise guests where to sit. Often, relatives and friends of the bride and of the groom sit on different sides of the aisle.

If arriving late, are there times when a guest should *not* enter the ceremony?

Do not enter during the processional of the wedding party.

Are there times when a guest should *not* leave the ceremony?

Do not leave during the recessional of the wedding party.

Who are the major officiants, leaders or participants at the ceremony and what do they do?

The minister, who officiates at the ceremony and witnesses the vows of the bride and groom.

The bride and groom and members of their wedding party.

Friends of the bride and groom, who may lead those present in a meditation or read aloud a text chosen by the couple.

What books are used?

A hymnal, *Singing the Living Tradition*, edited by the Hymnbook Resource Commission (Boston, Ma.: The Unitarian Universalist Association, 1993).

To indicate the order of the ceremony:

A program may be distributed.

Will a guest who is not a Unitarian Universalist be expected to do anything other than sit?

No.

Are there any parts of the ceremony in which a guest who is not a Unitarian Universalist should *not* participate?

Yes. Do not participate in the affirmation or the welcoming of the couple from members of the congregation.

If not disruptive to the ceremony, is it okay to:

- **Take pictures?** No.
- **Use a flash?** No.
- **Use a video camera?** No.
- **Use a tape recorder?** Yes.

Will contributions to the church be collected at the ceremony?

No.

AFTER THE CEREMONY

Is there usually a reception after the ceremony?

A reception is usually held in the church reception hall, in a catering hall or at a home. Food served may be hors d'oeuvres, a complete meal, coffee, cake and alcoholic beverages. There will probably be music and dancing. The reception may last for two hours.

Would it be considered impolite to neither eat nor drink?
Yes.

Is there a grace or benediction before eating or drinking?
Yes.

Is there a grace or benediction after eating or drinking?
Sometimes.

Is there a traditional greeting for the family?
Just offer your congratulations.

Is there a traditional form of address for clergy who may be at the reception?
"Mr.," "Ms.," "Dr.," "Reverend" or simply call the clergyperson by his or her first name.

Is it okay to leave early?
Yes, but after the wedding cake has been cut and served.

Funerals and Mourning

There is no specific Unitarian Universalist doctrine about afterlife. Some Unitarian Universalists believe in an afterlife; some doubt that there is one.

The Unitarian Universalist ritual that marks one's death is called a "memorial service," not a funeral.

The memorial service is a ceremony unto itself and may last about 30 to 60 minutes. Some memorial services may last more than one hour.

BEFORE THE CEREMONY

How soon after the death does the memorial service usually take place?

Usually within one week; sometimes up to one month after the death. The length of time between the death and the memorial service is determined solely at the discretion of the family.

What should someone who is not a Unitarian Universalist do upon hearing of the death of a member of that faith?

Telephone or visit the bereaved to express your condolences and share your memories of the deceased. Such comments as "I am so very sorry for your loss" are appropriate. Such comments as "Now he/she is with God" or "It was God's will" are not appropriate.

APPROPRIATE ATTIRE

Men: A jacket and tie. No head covering is required.

Women: A dress. Hems need not reach below the knees nor must clothing cover the arms. Open-toed shoes and modest jewelry are permissible. No head covering is required.

Somber colors are recommended for clothing.

GIFTS

Is it appropriate to send flowers or make a contribution?

Flowers may be delivered to the home of the bereaved before the memorial service. Also, contributions ranging from $10 to $200 may be made to a fund or charity designated by the family or the deceased.

Is it appropriate to send food?

Yes. This may be sent to the home of the bereaved upon hearing of the death or after the memorial service.

THE CEREMONY

Where will the ceremony take place?

Usually in a funeral home; sometimes in a church.

When should guests arrive and where should they sit?

Arrive shortly before the time for which the memorial service has been called. Sit wherever you wish, except for the first two or three rows, which are usually reserved for the close family of the deceased.

If arriving late, are there times when a guest should *not* enter the ceremony?

No.

Will the bereaved family be present at the funeral home or church before the ceremony?

Sometimes.

Is there a traditional greeting for the family?

Express your condolences. Such comments as "I am so very sorry for your loss" are appropriate.

Will there be an open casket?

Rarely.

Is a guest expected to view the body?

Guests are not expected or obligated to view the body.

What is appropriate behavior upon viewing the body?

If one chooses to view the body, walk slowly and reverently past the casket.

Who are the major officiants at the ceremony and what do they do?

- *The minister,* who delivers a sermon and meditation and commits the body to the grave.
- *The eulogist,* who is chosen by the family of the deceased and delivers a eulogy in honor of the deceased.
- *The music director and organist,* who provide music.

What books are used?

A hymnal, *Singing the Living Tradition,* edited by the Hymnbook Resource Commission (Boston, Ma.: The Unitarian Universalist Association, 1993).

To indicate the order of the ceremony:

Usually either a program will be provided or a display near the front of the room where the memorial service is held will indicate the order.

Will a guest who is not a Unitarian Universalist be expected to do anything other than sit?

It is expected for guests to stand with congregants when they rise for songs or prayer. It is optional for guests to sing and read prayers aloud with congregants if this does not violate their own religious beliefs. There is no kneeling during a Unitarian Universalist memorial service.

Are there any parts of the ceremony in which a guest who is not a Unitarian Universalist should *not* participate?

No.

If not disruptive to the ceremony, is it okay to:

- **Take pictures?** No.
- **Use a flash?** No.
- **Use a video camera?** No.
- **Use a tape recorder?** Only with prior approval of the family of the deceased.

Will contributions to the church be collected at the ceremony?

No.

THE INTERMENT

Should guests attend the interment?

This is entirely optional.

Whom should one ask for directions?

The funeral director.

What happens at the graveside?

Prayers are recited and the body is committed to the ground.

Do guests who are not Unitarian Universalists participate at the graveside ceremony?

No. They are simply present.

COMFORTING THE BEREAVED

Is it appropriate to visit the home of the bereaved after the memorial service?

Yes. The length of the visit depends on one's relationship with the bereaved and with the deceased. When visiting, express your sympathy to the bereaved and offer specific help to them. Fond memories of the deceased are especially appreciated.

Will there be a religious service at the home of the bereaved?

No.

Will food be served?

Yes, possibly including alcoholic beverages.

How soon after the memorial service will a mourner usually return to a normal work schedule?

This is left to the discretion of the mourner, but is usually a few days to a few weeks.

How soon after the memorial service will a mourner usually return to a normal social schedule?

This is left to the discretion of the mourner, but is usually a few days to a few weeks.

Are there mourning customs to which a friend who is not a Unitarian Universalist should be sensitive?

No.

Are there rituals for observing the anniversary of the death?

No.

V · HOME CELEBRATIONS

Not applicable to Unitarian Universalism.

Chapter 17 Contents

17

Wesleyan

I · HISTORY AND BELIEFS

The Wesleyan movement, which began in the early 18th century, centers around the scriptural truth concerning the doctrine and experience of holiness, which declares that the atonement of Christ for the sins of humanity provides not only for the regeneration of sinners, but also for the entire sanctification of believers. "Regeneration" is often referred to as "The New Birth." Members of the Wesleyan Church believe that when a person repents of his or her sin and believes in Jesus Christ, then that person is also adopted into the family of God and assured of his or her salvation through the witness of the Holy Spirit. "Sanctification" is considered to be the work of the Holy Spirit through which one is separated from sin and is enabled to love God. John Wesley, whose preaching began the faith in England, referred to this teaching and experience as "perfect love."

Wesley, an Anglican priest, was a prodigious evangelical preacher, writer and organizer. While a student at Oxford University, he and his brother, Charles, led the Holy Club of devout students, whom scoffers called the "Methodists."

Wesley's teachings affirmed the freedom of human will as promoted by grace. He saw each person's depth of sin matched by the height of sanctification to which the Holy Spirit, the empowering spirit of God, can lead persons of faith.

Although Wesley remained an Anglican and disavowed attempts

to form a new church, the "societies" he founded eventually became another church body known as Methodism. During a conference in Baltimore, Maryland, in 1784, the Methodist Episcopal Church was founded as an ecclesiastical organization.

John Wesley, as well as the early Methodist leaders in the United States, had uncompromisingly denounced slavery. But many ministers and members of the Methodist Episcopal Church eventually owned slaves because of the economic advantages of doing so. When some Methodist ministers in the North began to agitate for abolition, others tried to silence them. By 1843, enough churches had withdrawn from the Church to form their own denomination, which they called the Wesleyan Methodist Connection. After the Civil War, some churches in the Connection rejoined the larger Methodist body. Others were convinced that the effects of slavery had not yet been eradicated and that their stand against liquor and secret societies could best be maintained by being independent.

The church's name changed three times: In 1891, to the Wesleyan Methodist Connection (or Church) of America; in 1947, to the Wesleyan Methodist Church of America; and in 1968, to the Wesleyan Church when it merged with the Pilgrim Holiness Church. The Wesleyan Church of Canada, which consists of the Atlantic and Central districts, is the Canadian portion of the Wesleyan Church. The roots of the Central district extend back to 1889 and the former Wesleyan Methodist Church of America, while those of the Atlantic district reach back to 1888 and the Reformed Baptist Church.

Building on its abolitionist heritage, the Wesleyan Church takes strong social stands. These include opposing discrimination against interracial marriage or against age discrimination. The Church also invokes biblical principles against homosexuality and abortion, and lends moral support to any member who claims exemption from military combat as a conscientious objector and asks to service the nation as a noncombatant.

Each local church membership convenes in a local church conference at least once a year to address the business of the local church to elect the local board of administration that is chaired by the senior pastor. Members vote for the pastor of their choice and renew this at a vote taken at intervals of approximately every four years. The pastoral contract is subject to a ratifying vote by the district conference to which the local church belongs.

A quadrennial General Conference elects three General Superintendents who serve as the Church's titular, administrative and spiritual leaders. The General Conference, which is composed of equal numbers of laypersons and clergy, also elects five ministry directors and a General Secretary who serve the denomination on a full-time basis.

U.S. churches: 1,580
U.S. membership: 118,021
(*data from the* 1998 Yearbook of American and Canadian Churches)

For more information, contact:
The Wesleyan Church
P.O. Box 50434
Indianapolis, IN 46250-0434
(317) 570-5154

Canadian churches: 87
Canadian membership: 7,500
(*data from the Wesleyan Church of Canada, Central District*)

For more information, contact:
The Wesleyan Church of Canada
Atlantic District
P.O. Box 20
41 Summit Ave.
Sussex, NB E0E 1P0
(506) 433-1007

The Wesleyan Church of Canada
Central District
3 Applewood Drive, Suite 101
Belleville, ON K8P 4E3
(613) 966-7527

II · THE BASIC SERVICE

The worship service is a gathering to proclaim and celebrate the ultimate overthrow of evil and the present transformation of those individuals who experience God's redeeming grace.

376 · How to Be a Perfect Stranger

Some local churches may believe that worship is primarily accomplished through teaching and focus on the sermon at the service. Others perceive worship to provide a prime opportunity for evangelism and will coordinate the hymn selection and the content of the sermon to move toward a closing invitation for those previously uncommitted to Christ to become a disciple of Him. Still other congregations view worship as a time to praise God. These churches worship primarily through songs that praise God for His transcendence and holiness. Most Wesleyan congregations blend all these elements of worship. Services are held on Sunday morning and last about one hour.

APPROPRIATE ATTIRE

Men: A jacket and tie. More casual attire is also appropriate if modest. No headcovering is required.

Women: A dress or a skirt and blouse or a pants suit. More casual attire is also appropriate if modest. Hems need not reach below the knees nor must clothing cover the arms. Open-toed shoes and modest jewelry are permissible. No headcovering is required.

There are no rules regarding colors of clothing.

THE SANCTUARY

What are the major sections of the church?

- *The chancel,* which includes the pulpit, the communion altar, the altar. Many Wesleyan pastors invite those with special burdens or notable expressions of thanks to kneel at the altar during the pastoral prayer. This is entirely voluntary and guests are welcome to participate along with members. Occasionally, at the close of a sermon, the pastor may invite anyone present who is ready to accept Christ as his or her Savior to come forward to the altar and stand or kneel for the benediction and for private words of counsel or encouragement.
- *The narthex or foyer,* where congregants and guests are greeted by the head usher, a hostess and/or a member of the pastoral staff.
- *The auditorium,* where worshippers are seated.

THE SERVICE

When should guests arrive and where should they sit?

Arrive at the time for which the service has been called or shortly before that time. Ushers will advise guests where to sit.

If arriving late, are there times when a guest should *not* enter the service?

Do not enter while prayers are being recited or while Scripture is being read.

Are there times when a guest should *not* leave the service?

If possible, do not leave unless there is an emergency. Generally, all congregants and guests remain in the auditorium until the final benediction at the end of the service.

Who are the major officiants, leaders or participants and what do they do?

▪ *The minister,* who recites pastoral prayers and delivers a sermon.
▪ *The staff pastor or lay person,* who directs the worship.
▪ *The music minister,* who directs the choir and congregational hymns.

What are the major ritual objects of the service?

None.

What books are used?

A variety of translations of the Bible are used. The most common are the New International Version and the New King James Bible. Several hymnals are also used, including *Praise and Worship* (Kansas City, Mo.: Lillenas Publishing Co., 1993).

To indicate the order of the service:

A program will be distributed.

GUEST BEHAVIOR DURING THE SERVICE

Will a guest who is not a member of the Wesleyan Church be expected to do anything other than sit?

It is expected for guests to stand and sing with the congregation. It is entirely optional for guests to kneel and read prayers aloud with congregants if this does not violate their own religious beliefs. Guests may remain seated while congregants are kneeling.

Are there any parts of the service in which a guest who is not a member of the Wesleyan Church should *not* participate?

Guests who are not Christians should not participate in communion since this is available only to Church members or to those who belong to other Christian denominations.

If not disruptive to the service, is it okay to:

◼ **Take pictures?** No.

◼ **Use a flash?** No.

◼ **Use a video camera?** No.

◼ **Use a tape recorder?** Yes.

Will contributions to the church be collected at the service?

Yes. The offering plate will be passed through the congregation during the service. The passing of the plate may vary from one-fourth to one-half to three-quarters of the way through the service.

How much is customary to contribute?

It is entirely optional for guests to contribute. If they choose to do so, a contribution between $1 and $5 is appropriate.

AFTER THE SERVICE

Is there usually a reception after the service?

No.

Is there a traditional form of address for clergy whom a guest may meet?

"Pastor."

GENERAL GUIDELINES AND ADVICE

Members of the Wesleyan Church welcome the opportunity to informally and individually welcome visitors.

SPECIAL VOCABULARY

Key words or phrases which might be helpful for a visitor to know:

◼ *Introit:* Literally means "to go into" or "to enter." A specific type of arrangement at the beginning of a service in which the minister, choir and congregants participate either in unison or in response. This may be music or a Scripture verse; a choral response sung at the beginning of a service; or a psalm, anthem or hymn.

◼ *Offertory:* The portion of the service set apart for the collection and presentation of the congregation. Also, a musical composition played or sung during an offertory.

- *Pastoral prayer:* Prayer offered in public worship by the pastor in which he endeavors to pray on behalf of the entire congregation.
- *Call to Worship:* An invitation addressed to the congregation to enter united into the worship of God. It is never addressed to God, but to those congregants present.

DOGMA AND IDEOLOGY

Members of the Wesleyan Church believe:

- God, the Father, is the source of all that exists, be it matter or spirit. With the Son (Jesus Christ) and the Holy Spirit, God made man in His image, to whom He forever declares his good will.
- Jesus Christ was conceived by the Holy Spirit and born of the Virgin Mary. His death on the cross and subsequent burial were intended to be a sacrifice for original sin and for the transgressions of humanity. Christ rose bodily from the dead and ascended into heaven, where He will intercede for all humanity until He judges all humanity when He returns at the end of time.
- The Holy Spirit is the administrator of grace to all humanity. The Holy Spirit is ever present, and assures, preserves, guides and enables the believer.
- The Old and New Testaments comprise the Holy Scriptures and are the inspired and infallibly written Word of God. In both Testaments, life is offered to humanity through Christ, who is the only mediator between God and man.
- The creation of each person in the image of God included having the ability to choose between right and wrong. Thus, each person is morally responsible for his or her own choices. But since the fall of Adam, individuals do not have the strength to do what is right. This is due to the corruption of the nature of every person, and is reproduced in each of Adam's descendants. Because of this, each individual's nature is continually inclined to evil and he or she cannot, by him or herself, call upon God or exercise faith for salvation. But through Christ, the grace of God makes possible what individuals cannot do by themselves.
- Christ's offering of Himself on the cross provides sufficient atonement for every individual. But it is effective for the salvation of those who reach the age of accountability only when they repent and exercise faith in Christ.

◼ One should dress modestly, abstain from all forms of gambling and from using or trafficking in substances that are deleterious to one's physical and mental health, such as alcohol, tobacco and drugs taken for other than medical purposes.

◼ "Speaking in tongues" is not necessarily evidence of the presence of the Holy Spirit and can be controversial and divisive.

Some basic books and pamphlets to which a guest can refer to learn more about the Wesleyan Church:

How to Be Born Again by Billy Graham (Waco, Tex.: Word Books, 1977).

The Person and Work of the Holy Spirit: A Wesleyan Perspective by Dr. Charles Carter (Grand Rapids, Mich.: Baker Book House, 1974).

Holiness for Ordinary People by Dr. Keith Drury (Indianapolis, Ind.: Wesley Press, 1994).

"This We Believe: The Articles of Religion, Membership Commitments, Elementary Principles and Special Directions of the Wesleyan Church" (Indianapolis, Ind.: Wesley Press, 1993), which may be obtained from The Office of the General Secretary, The Wesleyan Church, P.O. Box 50434, Indianapolis, IN 46250-0434.

III · HOLY DAYS AND FESTIVALS

◼ *Advent.* Begins with the Sunday nearest November 30 and includes the four Sundays prior to Christmas. The holiday emphasizes preparing for Christ's coming with His birth at Christmas. There is no traditional greeting for this holiday.

◼ *Christmas.* Always falls on December 25. Celebrates the birth of Christ. The traditional greeting is "Merry Christmas."

◼ *Chrismastide.* This consists of the one or two Sundays between Christmas and Epiphany. "Celebration" on the second Sunday usually has an emphasis on the New Year. There is no traditional greeting for this holiday.

◼ *Epiphany.* Begins on the Sunday following January 6 (which is the Day of Epiphany, which is variously celebrated as the time of the visit of the Wise Men to the Baby Jesus, and as the date of Jesus' baptism). Continues for four to nine Sundays, depending on the date of Easter; Epiphany continues until the last two Sundays immediately before Easter. The Sunday immediately preceding Easter is celebrated as Palm Sunday, and marks Christ's entry into Jerusalem the

Sunday before His crucifixion. The word "Epiphany" means "appear-ance" or "manifestation" and the holiday emphasizes Christ's mani-festation of Himself to the world. There is no traditional greeting for this holiday.

■ *Lent*. Begins with Ash Wednesday (which falls exactly 46 days before Easter) and includes five Sundays, plus Palm Sunday, which marks Jesus' entry into Jerusalem five days before His crucifixion. Lent concludes with Holy and its Maundy Thursday, Good Friday (when Christ was crucified) and the Saturday before Easter; it ends with Easter Sunday. ("Maundy," which refers to "commandment," was applied to this day because of the ancient custom of washing the feet of the poor on this day in fulfillment of Christ's commandment to love one another.) Lent emphasizes fasting, prayer, self-examination, self-denial, Christian discipline and complete commitment to Christ. There is no traditional greeting for this holiday.

■ *Easter*. Always falls on the Sunday after the first full moon that occurs on or after March 21. Commemorates the death and resurrection of Christ. The traditional greeting is "Happy Easter" or "He is risen." A guest may respond with "He is risen, indeed," or simply with a hand-shake.

■ *Eastertide*. Begins with Easter Sunday and continues through Ascen-sion Day, which is the fortieth day after Easter. The holiday empha-sizes Christian hope and triumph as demonstrated in Christ's resurrection. There is no traditional greeting for this holiday.

■ *Whitsuntide*. Begins with Pentecost, which is the seventh Sunday after Easter and continues through the next to the last Sunday in August. The holiday emphasizes the continuing ministry of the Holy Spirit and the fellowship and mission of the Church. There is no tra-ditional greeting for this holiday.

■ *Kingdomtide*. Begins with the last Sunday in August and continues through the Sunday nearest November 23. The holiday emphasizes the "kingship" of Christ, which celebrates the preeminent Lordship of Christ over earth and its inhabitants. There is no traditional greet-ing for this holiday.

IV · LIFE CYCLE EVENTS

Birth Ceremony

This is called a baptism. The Wesleyan Church holds that God's grace atones for all infants until they reach an age of accountability, which varies with each individual. Accordingly, the ceremony of infant baptism constitutes an act of dedication by the child's parents to provide him or her with Christian training and examples. The baptism, during which the child is sprinkled with water, may occur any time from infancy until around age two. The five- to seven-minute baptismal ceremony is part of a regularly scheduled Sunday worship service.

BEFORE THE CEREMONY

Are guests usually invited by a formal invitation?

No. Guests who do not belong to the parent's congregation are invited orally either on the telephone or in person.

If not stated explicitly, should one assume that children are invited?

Yes.

If one can't attend, what should one do?

Visit the parents and the child at a later date after the baptism.

APPROPRIATE ATTIRE

Men: A jacket and tie. More casual attire is also appropriate if modest. No headcovering is required.

Women: A dress or a skirt and blouse or a pants suit. More casual attire is also appropriate if modest. Hems need not reach below the knees nor must clothing cover the arms. Open-toed shoes and modest jewelry are permissible. No headcovering is required.

There are no rules regarding colors of clothing.

GIFTS

Is a gift customarily expected?

No.

Should gifts be brought to the ceremony?

See above.

THE CEREMONY

Where will the ceremony take place?

In the main auditorium of the parents' church.

When should guests arrive and where should they sit?

Arrive at the time for which the ceremony has been called or shortly before that time. Ushers will advise guests where to sit.

If arriving late, are there times when a guest should *not* enter the ceremony?

Do not enter while prayers are being recited or while Scripture is being read.

Are there times when a guest should *not* leave the ceremony?

If possible, do not leave unless there is an emergency. Generally, all congregants and guests remain in the auditorium until the final benediction at the end of the worship service.

Who are the major officiants, leaders or participants at the ceremony and what do they do?

- *The minister,* who conducts the actual ceremony of the dedication and baptism.
- *The parents and the child.*

What books are used?

The Church does not provide a particular litany for the baptismal ceremony. For the rest of the worship service, congregants and guests use a Bible and hymnal. A variety of translations of the Bible are used. The most common are the New International Version and the New King James Bible. Several hymnals are also used, including *Praise and Worship* (Kansas City, Mo.: Lillenas Publishing Co., 1993).

To indicate the order of the ceremony:

A program will be distributed.

Will a guest who is not a member of the Wesleyan Church be expected to do anything other than sit?

No.

Are there any parts of the ceremony in which a guest who is not a member of the Wesleyan Church should *not* participate?

Guests who are not Christians should not participate in communion since this is available only to Church members or to those who belong to other Christian denominations.

If not disruptive to the ceremony, is it okay to:

◙ **Take pictures?** Yes.
◙ **Use a flash?** Yes.
◙ **Use a video camera?** Yes.
◙ **Use a tape recorder?** Yes.

Will contributions to the church be collected at the ceremony?

Yes. The offering plate will be passed through the congregation during the service. The passing of the plate may vary from one-fourth to one-half to three-quarters of the way through the service.

How much is customary to contribute?

It is entirely optional for guests to contribute. If they choose to do so, a contribution between $1 and $5 is appropriate.

AFTER THE CEREMONY

Is there usually a reception after the ceremony?
No.

Is there a traditional greeting for the family?
Just offer your congratulations.

Is there a traditional form of address for clergy whom a guest may meet?
"Pastor."

Initiation Ceremony

The Wesleyan Church utilizes a variety of catechistic tools when training and educating children. These do not include a ceremony for formal initiation.

Marriage Ceremony

The Wesleyan Church teaches that man and women are both created in the image of God, and that human sexuality reflects that image in terms of intimate love, communication, fellowship, subordination of the self to the larger whole and fulfillment. The marriage relationship is a metaphor for God's relationship with His covenant people and for revealing the truth that relationship is between one God with His people. Therefore, God's plan for human sexuality is that it be expressed only in a monogamous life-long relationship between a man and a woman within the framework of marriage. This is the only relationship designed for the birth and the rearing of children.

The only biblical grounds for even considering divorce is the sexual sin of the spouse. This includes adultery, homosexuality, bestiality or incest.

The wedding ceremony is a ceremony unto itself. It may last about 15 to 30 minutes.

BEFORE THE CEREMONY

Are guests usually invited by a formal invitation?
Yes.

If not stated explicitly, should one assume that children are invited?
Yes.

If one can't attend, what should one do?
RSVP with regrets and send a gift.

APPROPRIATE ATTIRE

Men: A jacket and tie. No headcovering is required.

Women: A dress or a skirt and blouse. Hems need not reach below the knees nor must clothing cover the arms. Open-toed shoes and modest jewelry are permissible. No headcovering is required.

There are no rules regarding colors of clothing.

GIFTS

Is a gift customarily expected?
Yes. Small household items such as sheets, small appliances or kitchenware or cash or bonds in the amount of $15 to $100 are appropriate.

Should gifts be brought to the ceremony?
Gifts may either be brought to the ceremony or sent to the home of the newlyweds.

THE CEREMONY

Where will the ceremony take place?

In the main auditorium of the church.

When should guests arrive and where should they sit?

Arrive shortly before the time for which the ceremony has been called. Ushers will advise guests where to sit.

If arriving late, are there times when a guest should *not* enter the ceremony?

Do not enter during the processional of the wedding party.

Are there times when a guest should *not* leave the ceremony?

Do not leave during the recessional of the wedding party.

Who are the major officiants, leaders or participants at the ceremony and what do they do?

- *The minister,* who officiates at the ceremony and witnesses the vows of the bride and groom.
- *The bride and groom and their wedding party.*

What books are used?

No books are used by guests and participants.

To indicate the order of the ceremony:

A program will be distributed.

Will a guest who is not a member of the Wesleyan Church be expected to do anything other than sit?

It is expected for each guest to stand with the other guests.

Are there any parts of the ceremony in which a guest who is not a member of the Wesleyan Church should *not* participate?

No.

If not disruptive to the ceremony, is it okay to:

- **Take pictures?** No.
- **Use a flash?** No.
- **Use a video camera?** No.
- **Use a tape recorder?** Yes.

Will contributions to the church be collected at the ceremony?

No.

AFTER THE CEREMONY

Is there usually a reception after the ceremony?

A reception is held in the church reception hall, in a catering hall or at a home. Food served may be hors d'oeuvres, finger foods, punch, coffee and cake. There will be no alcoholic beverages. There may be music, especially classical, contemporary or religious, but no dancing. The reception may last for one and a half to two hours.

Would it be considered impolite to neither eat nor drink?

No.

Is there a grace or benediction before eating or drinking?

Yes.

Is there a grace or benediction after eating or drinking?

No.

Is there a traditional greeting for the family?

Just offer your congratulations.

Is there a traditional form of address for clergy who may be at the reception?

"Pastor."

Is it okay to leave early?

Yes.

Funerals and Mourning

The Wesleyan Church teaches that, upon the second resurrection of Christ, the just will be resurrected to eternal life. At a later date, the wicked will be resurrected into eternal damnation. (The Church maintains that a distinction in time for these two resurrections is indicated by Jesus in Luke 20:35, 36 and by St. John in Revelation 20:5, 6.) The body of the resurrected body will be whole and identifiable.

The funeral ceremony is a ceremony unto itself and may last about 30 to 60 minutes.

BEFORE THE CEREMONY

How soon after the death does the funeral usually take place?

Two to three days.

What should someone who is not a member of the Wesleyan Church do upon hearing of the death of a member of that faith?

Telephone or visit the bereaved to express your condolences.

APPROPRIATE ATTIRE:

Men: A jacket and tie. More casual attire is also appropriate if modest. No headcovering is required.

Women: A dress or a skirt and blouse or a pants suit. More casual attire is also appropriate if modest. Hems need not reach below the knees nor must clothing cover the arms. Open-toed shoes and modest jewelry are permissible. No headcovering is required.

Somber colors are recommended for clothing.

GIFTS

Is it appropriate to send flowers or make a contribution?

Flowers may be sent to the home of the bereaved before or after the funeral or to the funeral itself. In lieu of flowers, contributions may be made to a fund or charity designated by the family or the deceased.

Is it appropriate to send food?

Yes. This may be sent to the home of the bereaved upon hearing of the death or after the funeral.

THE CEREMONY

Where will the ceremony take place?

In a church or a funeral home or at the site of the grave itself.

When should guests arrive and where should they sit?

Arrive early. Ushers will advise guests where to sit.

If arriving late, are there times when a guest should *not* enter the ceremony?

No.

Will the bereaved family be present at the funeral site before the ceremony?

No.

Is there a traditional greeting for the family?

Just express your sympathy for the bereaved and your appreciation for the deceased.

Will there be an open casket?

Usually.

Is a guest expected to view the body?

Yes.

What is appropriate behavior upon viewing the body?

Be quiet and respectful. Gaze silently at the deceased for a brief moment.

Who are the major officiants at the ceremony and what do they do?

- *The minister,* who delivers a sermon and meditation and commits the body to the grave.
- *Musicians,* who provide music at the beginning and end of the funeral ceremony.

What books are used?

A variety of translations of the Bible are used. The most common are the New International Version and the New King James Bible.

To indicate the order of the ceremony:

The minister may make periodic announcements.

Will a guest who is not a member of the Wesleyan Church be expected to do anything other than sit?

No.

Are there any parts of the ceremony in which a guest who is not a member of the Wesleyan Church should *not* participate?

No.

If not disruptive to the ceremony, is it okay to:

- **Take pictures?** No.
- **Use a flash?** No.
- **Use a video camera?** No.
- **Use a tape recorder?** Yes.

390 · How to Be a Perfect Stranger

Will contributions to the church be collected at the ceremony?

No.

THE INTERMENT

Should guests attend the interment?

This is entirely optional.

Whom should one ask for directions?

The funeral director or another member of the staff of the funeral home.

What happens at the graveside?

There is a Scripture reading, prayers are recited and the body is committed to the ground. Hymns may be sung.

Do guests who are not members of the Wesleyan Church participate at the graveside ceremony?

No. They are simply present.

COMFORTING THE BEREAVED

Is it appropriate to visit the home of the bereaved after the funeral?

Yes. The length of the visit depends on one's relationship with the bereaved and with the deceased. When visiting, express your sympathy to the bereaved and offer specific help to them. You may possibly offer a brief prayer for the deceased and reflect upon the life of the deceased.

Will there be a religious service at the home of the bereaved?

No.

Will food be served?

No.

How soon after the funeral will a mourner usually return to a normal work schedule?

Within one to two weeks.

How soon after the funeral will a mourner usually return to a normal social schedule?

Within four to five weeks.

Are there mourning customs to which a friend who is not a member of the Wesleyan Church should be sensitive?

No.

Are there rituals for observing the anniversary of the death?

No.

V · HOME CELEBRATIONS

Not applicable to the Wesleyan Church.

Glossary

Abdu'l-Baha ("Ab-DOOL-bah-HAH"): [Arabic] The son of Baha'u'l-lah, the founder of the Baha'i faith. His name means "Servant of Baha."

Age of Accountability: Usually the age at which one can tell right from wrong and at which, in many Christian faiths, one is baptized. The age of accountability may begin in early adolescence, although some youths have been baptized as young as seven or eight years of age.

Allah'u'Abha ("Ah-lah-oo-ab-HAH"): [Arabic] A Baha'i phrase that means "God is most glorious."

Anointing: An ancient Christian practice in which the sick are anointed with oil in the name of the Lord. Prayers are also recited for the sick to be healed. This practice is observed in Pentecostal churches, the Church of the Brethren and other Christian denominations. In the Church of the Brethren, anointing is most often done at home or in small group settings, although some congregations have anointings in public worship.

Ardas ("AHR-das"): [Gurmukhi] Community prayer led by one person in a Sikh *gurdwara* service. Blessings for special occasions or events may be requested during the *ardas*.

Ayyam-i-ha ("Ah-yah-mee-HAH"): [Arabic] "Days of Ha," which Baha'is celebrate from February 26 through March 1. The holiday is devoted to hospitality, charity and gift-giving and to spiritually preparing one's self for the annual fast that lasts for all 19 days of the last month in the Baha'i calendar.

The Bab ("Bob"): [Arabic] Literally means "gate" or "door" and is used in the Baha'i faith to refer to Mirza Ali Muhammed, a direct descendent of the Prophet Muhammed, who announced in mid-19th century Persia that he was the forerunner of the Universal Messenger of God.

Baha'i ("Ba-HIGH"): [Arabic] A follower of Baha'u'llah.

Baha'u'llah ("Bah-HAH-oo-LAH"): [Arabic] The founder of the Baha'i faith, whose name means "Glory of God."

Blessingway Ceremony: A ceremonial chant that recounts the Navajo Creation story and which is usually recited over two nights. It is performed to maintain a positive or healthy environment and to prevent imbalance or disharmony.

Conversation: Considered to be at the heart of what it means to be a member of the Church of the Brethren, whose members expect to receive new revelations as they discuss the Bible and try to remain open to fresh interpretations of it.

Dedication: The term in Pentecostal Churches for a ceremony for infants or young children during which the child's parents publicly commit themselves to raise the child in the teachings of Jesus.

Divine Healing: Supernatural healing.

Dynamis ("THEE-nah-mees"): [Greek] Used in the Orthodox Churches; means "with greater power."

Feast: The centerpiece of the Baha'i community is the Nineteen Day Feast, which is held every 19 days and is the local community's regular worship gathering—and more. The feast day is held on the first day of each of the 19 months in the Baha'i calendar and helps sustain the unity of the local Baha'i community. A Baha'i feast always contains spiritual devotion, administrative consultation and fellowship. "Feast" does not imply that a large meal will be served, but that a "spiritual feast"—worship, companionship and unity—will be available.

Festival of Ridvan ("RIZ-von"): [Arabic] A 12-day Baha'i holiday celebrated from April 21 through May 2; it commemorates the 12 days in 1863, when Baha'u'llah, the prophet-founder of the Baha'i faith, publicly proclaimed in a garden in Baghdad his mission as God's messenger for this age.

Foot Washing: Commemorates Christ's washing of His disciples' feet at the Last Supper. In some Pentecostal Churches, men and women are in separate rooms and each gender washes the feet of other members of the same gender. Depending on their church's tradition, they may wash the feet of just one individual or of all those present. Individual churches in each faith determine the form and the frequency with which they will practice foot washing.

Foursquare: A biblical term used in the Book of Exodus to refer to the tabernacle, in the Book of Ezekiel to refer to the Temple of the Lord, and in the Book of Revelations to refer to Heaven. Adopted in 1922 to refer to the new Pentecostal church founded by Aimee Semple McPherson, the International Church of the Foursquare Gospel.

Holy Communion: Also called the "Lord's Supper." A rite through which Christians believe they receive either the symbolic or the real body and blood of Christ as assurance that God has forgiven their sins.

Langar ("LAHN-gahr"): [Gurmukhi] The vegetarian meal prepared in a prayerful environment and served as an offering after or throughout a Sikh worship service to the *sangat,* or community of worshippers.

Lessons: Readings from the Bible (or "Scripture"), including the Old Testament (the Hebrew scriptures, written before the birth of Jesus); the Epistles (generally from one of the letters of St. Paul or another New Testament writer); and the Gospel (a reading from Matthew, Mark, Luke or John, the "biographers" of Jesus).

Lifting Up of Hands: Holding up one's hands during prayer and praise in anticipation of receiving the presence and power of the Holy Spirit. Often occurs during Pentecostal worship.

Love Feast: Also called an "agape meal" (pronounced: "ah-GAH-pay"). Held at least once a year in each congregation of the Church of the Brethren. This ceremony includes a mutual footwashing between two congregants, who then embrace and give each other a "holy kiss." This is followed by a simple meal and communion. The ritual echoes Jesus' washing of the feet of His disciples at the Last Supper, where He sought to draw them closer into the fold of His love and to demonstrate the love and regard they have for one another.

Naw-Ruz ("Naw-ROOZ"): [Arabic] The Baha'i New Year's Day which occurs on March 21. The day is astronomically fixed so the new year commences on the first day of spring.

Offertory: The portion of a Christian service set apart for the collection from congregants.

Potlatch Ceremony: A diverse, complex series of ceremonies practiced by the Native Peoples of the northwest coast of North America. Their central function is to maintain balance and harmony among one's community. It generally consists of a community feast during which the host, typically a family, presents gifts to guests and also reenacts their family's oral history from mythic times to the present.

Prasad ("prah-SAHD"): [Gurmukhi] The sweet pudding served toward the end of a Sikh service that consists of water, honey, wheat flour, and clarified butter. Prasad is considered to be a blessing from the *Siri Guru Granth Sahib* that everyone can eat.

Prokimenon ("Proh-KEE-min-non"): [Greek] Used in the Orthodox churches; means "offertory."

Proskomen ("PROS-koh-men"): [Greek] Used in the Orthodox churches; means "Let us attend."

The Rapture: The "catching away" of believers by the Lord upon the return of Jesus Christ.

Regeneration: Also known as "Born Again." Occurs when a person has fully accepted Jesus Christ as their Savior.

Sacred Circle: A symbolic representation of many Native peoples' conception of the world and life. It captures ecological cycles of life and death and represents one's journey along the path of life.

Sacred Sites: Sites that Native Peoples recognize as being imbued with a specific or special aspect of the sacred.

Sanctification: Pentecostal doctrine in which holiness is considered to be a progressive work of God's grace beginning with regeneration.

Salvation: Also known as Saved and Born Again: Different terms for accepting Christ as one's Savior and His teachings as guiding principles.

Sangat ("SAHN-gaht"): [Gurmukhi] The congregation of Sikhs and guests who come together for a Sikh worship service.

Sat Nam ("SAHT NAHM"): [Gurmukhi] A common phrase and greeting among Sikhs that means "True Name" and acknowledges the God in all.

Shoghi Effendi ("SHOW-gey Eh-FEN-dee"): The grandson of Abdu'l-Baha, who was the founder of the Baha'i faith. Shoghi Effendi was also called the "Guardian."

Shunning: The Amish practice of avoiding a fellow Amish who has transgressed.

Siri Guru Granth Sahib ("SEE-ree GOO-roo GRANTH-SAH-HEEB"): [Gurmukhi] Scriptures compiled by the fifth Sikh guru, Arjan Dev, which contain sacred writings by several Sikh gurus and Hindu and Moslem saints. Since then, Sikhs have bowed before the Siri Guru Granth Sahib, consulted it as their only guru, and treated it with reverence.

Speaking in Tongues: Speaking in a language unknown to those speaking it, a phenomenon associated with the coming of the Holy Spirit (the empowering quality of God) and common to Pentecostal faiths.

Stomp Dances: A common style of dance with Native tribes that are originally from the Southeastern United States. The primary rhythm is provided by singing, the use of gourds rattled by men and turtle shells that are filled with pebbles and tied to women's legs.

Sun Dance Ceremony: The most important annual religious ceremony for about thirty Plains tribes. Its meaning varies somewhat from tribe to tribe, but it is basically a test of courage and a demonstration of personal sacrifice. During the three-day ceremony, men undergo "piercing," or being suspended from a sacred pole by skewers of wood inserted into their chests.

Sweat Lodge Ceremony: A ceremony common to many Native religions. Its functions vary from tribe to tribe, but it is generally intended to provide purification and healing and to restore balance in one's life.

Theotokos ("The-oh-TOH-kohs"): [Greek] Used in the Orthodox churches; means "Mother of God."

Wisdom Keepers: Also known as Elders. Living repositories of Native Americans' traditional wisdom, ceremonial practices and customs. The title does not necessarily imply old age, for the title is earned through extensive training and practice.

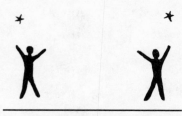

Calendar of
Religious Holidays and Festivals

The list below presents the dates, on the Gregorian calendar, of major religious holidays and festivals.

O: Orthodox Churches (Christian)
W: Western Churches (Christian)

Religious Holiday/Festival	1999	2000	2001
New Year's Day	Jan. 1	Jan. 1	Jan. 1
Christmastide	Jan. 3	Jan. 2	Dec. 3
Birth of Guru Gobind Singh	Jan. 5	Jan. 5	Jan. 5
Epiphany	Jan. 6	Jan. 6	Jan. 6
Christmas (O-Armenian)	Jan. 6	Jan. 6	Jan. 6
World Religion Day	Jan. 17	Jan. 16	Jan. 21
Birth of Guru Har Rai	Jan. 31	Jan. 31	Jan. 31
Ayyam-i-ha/Days of Ha	Feb. 26	Feb. 26	Feb. 26
Ash Wednesday	Feb. 17	Mar. 8	Feb. 28
Lent begins (O)	Feb. 22	Mar. 13	Feb. 26
First Day of Eastertide	Apr. 4	Apr. 23	Apr. 15
Naw-Ruz	Mar. 21	Mar. 21	Mar. 21
Palm Sunday (W)	Mar. 28	Apr. 16	Apr. 8
Annunciation	Mar. 25	Mar. 25	Mar. 25
Palm Sunday (O)	Apr. 4	Apr. 23	Apr. 8
Holy (Maundy) Thursday	Apr. 1	Apr. 20	Apr. 12
Good Friday (W)	Apr. 2	Apr. 21	Apr. 13

Religious Holiday/Festival	1999	2000	2001
Holy (Good) Friday (O)	Apr. 9	Apr. 28	Apr. 13
First Day of Festival of Ridvan	Apr. 21	Apr. 21	Apr. 21
First Day of Passover	Apr. 1	Apr. 20	Apr. 8
Easter (W)	Apr. 4	Apr. 23	Apr. 15
Easter (Pascha) (O)	Apr. 11	Apr. 30	Apr. 15
Birth of Guru Teg Bahadur	Apr. 18	Apr. 18	Apr. 18
Birth of Guru Angad	Apr. 18	Apr. 18	Apr. 18
Ascension Day	May 20	June 8	May 25
Pentecost (W)	May 23	June 11	June 3
Pentecost (O)	May 30	June 18	June 3
First Day of Whitsuntide	May 23	June 11	June 3
Birth of Guru Arjan	May 2	May 2	May 2
Declaration of the Bab	May 23	May 23	May 23
Birth of Guru Amar Das	May 23	May 23	May 23
Race Unity Day	June 13	June 11	June 10
Summer Solstice	June 21	June 21	June 21
Birth of Guru Hargobind	July 5	July 5	July 5
Martyrdom of the Bab	July 9	July 9	July 9
Birth of Guru Har Krishnan	July 23	July 23	July 23
First Day of Kingdomtide	Aug. 29	Aug. 27	Aug. 26
Elevation of the Cross	Sept. 14	Sept. 14	Sept. 14
World Communion Sunday (W)	Oct. 3	Oct. 1	Oct. 7
Birth of Guru Ram Das	Oct. 9	Oct. 9	Oct. 9
Birth of the Bab	Oct. 20	Oct. 20	Oct. 20
Birth of Baha'u'llah	Nov. 12	Nov. 12	Nov. 12
Thanksgiving	Nov. 25	Nov. 24	Nov. 22
Birth of Guru Nanak	Nov. 23	Nov. 23	Nov. 23
The Day of the Covenant	Nov. 26	Nov. 26	Nov. 26
First Sunday of Advent (O, W)	Nov. 28	Dec. 3	Dec. 2
Winter Solstice	Dec. 22	Dec. 21	Dec. 21
First Day of Chanukah	Dec. 4	Dec. 22	Dec. 10
Christmas Eve (W)	Dec. 24	Dec. 24	Dec. 24
Christmas (O, except Armenian, W)	Dec. 25	Dec. 25	Dec. 25

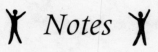 Notes

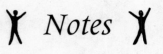

Notes

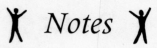 Notes

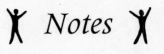 Notes

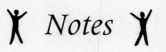

Notes

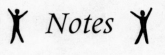 Notes

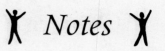

Notes

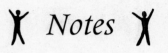 Notes

About SKYLIGHT PATHS Publishing

Through spirituality, our religious beliefs are increasingly becoming *a part of* our lives, rather than *apart from* our lives. Nevertheless, while many people are more interested than ever in spiritual growth, they are less firmly planted in *traditional* religion. To deepen their relationship to the sacred, people want to learn from their own and other faith traditions, in new ways.

SkyLight Paths sees both believers and seekers as a community that increasingly transcends traditional boundaries of religion and denomination. Many people want to learn from each other, *walking together, finding the way.*

The SkyLight Paths staff is made up of people of many faiths. We are a small, highly committed group of people, a reflection of the religious diversity that now exists in most neighborhoods, most families. We will succeed only if our books make a difference in your life.

We at SkyLight Paths take great care to produce beautiful books that present meaningful spiritual content in a form that reflects the art of making high quality books. Therefore, we want to acknowledge those who contributed to the production of this book.

PRODUCTION
Bridgett Taylor & David Wall

EDITORIAL & PROOFREADING
Jennifer Goneau & Martha McKinney

COVER DESIGN
Chelsea Dippel

PRINTING AND BINDING
Lake Book, Melrose Park, Illinois

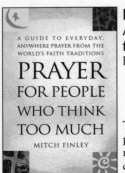

Other Interesting Books—Spirituality

VOICES FROM GENESIS
Guiding Us Through the Stages of Life
by *Norman J. Cohen*

A brilliant blending of modern midrash and the life stages of Erik Erikson's developmental psychology. Shows how the pathways of our lives are quite similar to those of the leading figures of Genesis who speak directly to us, telling of their spiritual and emotional journeys.

6" x 9", 192 pp. HC, ISBN 1-879045-75-3 **$21.95**

SELF, STRUGGLE & CHANGE
Family Conflict Stories in Genesis
and Their Healing Insights for Our Lives
by *Norman J. Cohen*

The people described by the biblical writers of Genesis were in situations and relationships very much like our own. We identify with them. Their stories still speak to us because they are about the same problems we deal with every day. Here a modern master of biblical interpretation brings us greater understanding of the ancient text and of ourselves in this intriguing re-telling of conflict between husband and wife, father and son, brothers, and sisters.

6" x 9", 224 pp. Quality Paperback, ISBN 1-879045-66-4 **$16.95**
HC, ISBN -19-2 **$21.95**

FINDING JOY
A Practical Spiritual Guide to Happiness
by *Dannel I. Schwartz* with *Mark Hass*

Searching for happiness in our modern world of stress and struggle is common; *finding* it is more unusual. This guide explores and explains how to find joy through a time-honored, creative—and surprisingly practical—approach based on the teachings of Jewish mysticism and *Kabbalah*.

"Lovely, simple introduction to Kabbalah....
A singular contribution."
—*American Library Association's* Booklist

•AWARD WINNER•

6" x 9", 192 pp. Quality PB, ISBN 1-58023-009-1 **$14.95**
HC, ISBN 1-879045-53-2 **$19.95**

MOSES—THE PRINCE, THE PROPHET
His Life, Legend & Message for Our Lives
by *Rabbi Levi Meier, Ph.D.*

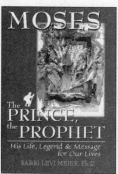

How can the struggles of a great biblical figure teach us to cope with our own lives today? A fascinating portrait of the struggles, failures, and triumphs of Moses, a central figure in Jewish, Christian, and Islamic tradition. Drawing upon stories from *Exodus, midrash* (finding contemporary meaning from ancient Jewish texts), the teachings of Jewish mystics, modern texts, and psychotherapy, Meier offers new ways to create our own path to self-knowledge and self-fulfillment—and face life's difficulties head-on.

6" x 9", 224 pp. HC, ISBN 1-58023-013-X **$23.95**

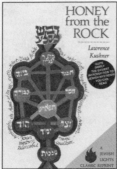
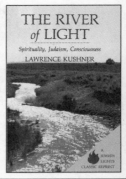

Spiritual Inspiration . . .
The Kushner Series

INVISIBLE LINES OF CONNECTION
Sacred Stories of the Ordinary
by *Lawrence Kushner*

Through his everyday encounters with family, friends, colleagues and strangers, Kushner takes us deeply into our lives, finding flashes of spiritual insight in the process. This is a book where literature meets spirituality, where the sacred meets the ordinary, and, above all, where people of all faiths, all backgrounds can meet one another and themselves. Kushner ties together the stories of our lives into a roadmap showing how everything "ordinary" is supercharged with meaning—*if* we can just see it.

6" x 9", 160 pp. Quality Paperback, ISBN 1-879045-98-2 **$15.95**
HC, ISBN -52-4 **$21.95**

THE BOOK OF WORDS
Talking Spiritual Life, Living Spiritual Talk
by *Lawrence Kushner*

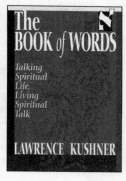

Kushner lifts up and shakes the dust off primary religious words we use to describe the spiritual dimension of life. The *Words* take on renewed spiritual significance, adding power and focus to the lives we live every day. For each word Kushner offers us a startling, moving and insightful explication, and pointed readings from classical Jewish sources that further illuminate the concept. He concludes with a short exercise that helps unite the spirit of the word with our actions in the world.

6" x 9", 160 pp. Beautiful two-color text.
Quality Paperback, ISBN 1-58023-020-2 **$16.95**
HC, ISBN 1-879045-35-4 **$21.95**

THE BOOK OF LETTERS
A Mystical Hebrew Alphabet
by *Lawrence Kushner*

In calligraphy by the author. Folktales about and exploration of the mystical meanings of the Hebrew Alphabet. Open the old prayerbook-like pages of *The Book of Letters* and you will enter a special world of sacred tradition and religious feeling. More than just symbols, all twenty-two letters of the Hebrew alphabet overflow with meanings and personalities of their own.

Rabbi Kushner draws from ancient Judaic sources, weaving talmudic commentary, Hasidic folktales, and kabbalistic mysteries around the letters.

"A book which is in love with Jewish letters."
—*Isaac Bashevis Singer* (לז)

• **Popular Hardcover Edition** •
6" x 9", 80 pp. Hardcover, two colors, inspiring new Foreword
ISBN 1-879045-00-1 **$24.95**

• **Also available in a Deluxe Gift Edition** (*$79.95*) **and Collector's Limited Edition** (*$349.00*) •
Call 1-800-962-4544 for more information.

Children's Spirituality

BUT GOD REMEMBERED
Stories of Women from
Creation to the Promised Land

For ages 8 and up

by *Sandy Eisenberg Sasso*
Full-color illustrations by *Bethanne Andersen*

NONDENOMINATIONAL, NONSECTARIAN

A fascinating collection of four different stories of women only briefly mentioned in biblical tradition and religious texts, but never before explored. Award-winning author Sasso brings to life the intriguing stories of Lilith, Serach, Bityah, and the Daughters of Z, courageous and strong women from ancient tradition. All teach important values through their faith and actions.

9" x 12", 32 pp. HC, Full-color illus., ISBN 1-879045-43-5 **$16.95**

IN GOD'S NAME

For ages 4 and up

by *Sandy Eisenberg Sasso*
Full-color illustrations by *Phoebe Stone*

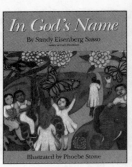

Selected by Parent Council, Ltd.™

MULTICULTURAL, NONDENOMINATIONAL, NONSECTARIAN

Like an ancient myth in its poetic text and vibrant illustrations, this modern fable about the search for God's name celebrates the diversity and, at the same time, the unity of all the people of the world. Each seeker claims he or she alone knows the answer. Finally, they come together and learn what God's name really is, sharing the ultimate harmony of belief in one God by people of all faiths, all backgrounds.

9" x 12", 32 pp. HC, Full color illus., ISBN 1-879045-26-5 **$16.95**

GOD IN BETWEEN

For ages 4 and up

by *Sandy Eisenberg Sasso*
Full-color illustrations by *Sally Sweetland*

NONDENOMINATIONAL, NONSECTARIAN, MULTICULTURAL

If you wanted to find God, where would you look?
A magical, mythical tale that teaches that God can be found where we are: within all of us and the relationships between us.

9" x 12", 32 pp. HC, Full-color illus., ISBN 1-879045-86-9 **$16.95**

For ages 4 and up

GOD'S PAINTBRUSH
by *Sandy Eisenberg Sasso*
Full-color illustrations by *Annette Compton*

MULTICULTURAL, NONDENOMINATIONAL,
NONSECTARIAN

Invites children of all faiths and backgrounds to encounter God openly in their own lives. Wonderfully interactive, provides questions adult and child can explore together at the end of each episode.

11" x 8½", 32 pp. HC, Full-color illus., ISBN 1-879045-22-2 **$16.95**

Children's Spirituality

A PRAYER FOR THE EARTH
The Story of Naamah, Noah's Wife
by *Sandy Eisenberg Sasso*
For ages 4 and up
Full-color illustrations by *Bethanne Andersen*

NONDENOMINATIONAL, NONSECTARIAN

This new story, based on an ancient text, opens readers' religious imaginations to new ideas about the well-known story of the Flood. When God tells Noah to bring the animals of the world onto the ark, God *also* calls on Naamah, Noah's wife, to save each plant on Earth.

9" x 12", 32 pp. HC, Full-color illus., ISBN 1-879045-60-5 **$16.95**

THE 11TH COMMANDMENT
Wisdom from Our Children
For all ages
by *The Children of America*

MULTICULTURAL, NONDENOMINATIONAL, NONSECTARIAN

"If there were an Eleventh Commandment, what would it be?"
Children of many religious denominations across America answer this question—in their own drawings and words—in *The 11th Commandment*.

8" x 10", 48 pp. HC, Full-color illus., ISBN 1-879045-46-X **$16.95**

IN OUR IMAGE
God's First Creatures
by *Nancy Sohn Swartz*
For ages 4 and up
Full-color illustrations by *Melanie Hall*

NONDENOMINATIONAL, NONSECTARIAN

A playful new twist to the Creation story. Celebrates the interconnectedness of nature and the harmony of all living things.

9" x 12", 32 pp. HC, Full-color illus., ISBN 1-879045-99-0 **$16.95**

PARENTING AS A SPIRITUAL JOURNEY
Deepening Ordinary & Extraordinary Events into Sacred Occasions
by *Rabbi Nancy Fuchs-Kreimer*

A perfect gift for the new parent, and a helpful guidebook for those seeking to re-envision family life.

Draws on experiences of the author and over 100 parents of many faiths, revealing the transformative spiritual adventure that parents can experience while bringing up their children. Rituals, prayers, and passages from sacred Jewish texts—as well as from other religious traditions—are woven throughout the book.

"This is really relevant spirituality. I love her book."
—*Sylvia Boorstein, author of*
It's Easier Than You Think
and mother of four

6" x 9", 224 pp. Quality Paperback, ISBN 1-58023-016-4 **$16.95**

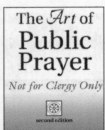